RY

ALLEN LANE

David J. Breeze and Brian Dobson

HADRIAN'S WALL

Copyright © David J. Breeze and Brian Dobson, 1976
First published 1976

Allen Lane
Penguin Books Ltd
17 Grosvenor Gardens
London SW1W 0BD

ISBN 0 7139 0523 9

Printed in Great Britain by
Western Printing Services Ltd
Bristol

Set in Linotype Times

Contents

List of Plates

List of Plates

The authors and publishers would like to thank the following for supplying photographs for use in this volume: Mr P. Connolly, Plates 11–14; Department of the Environment, England, Plates 3, 6, 7, 17, 18, 22, 24, 25, 26, 29; Department of the Environment, Scotland, Plate 10; Dr V. A. Maxfield, Plates 15, 16, 28; Newcastle-upon-Tyne Museum of Antiquities, Plates 4, 5, 9, 19, 21, 23, 27; Turners Ltd, Newcastle-upon-Tyne, Plates 1, 2, 8, 20. Crown copyright is reserved on Plates 3, 6, 7, 10, 17, 18, 22, 24, 25, 26, 29.

List of Text Figures and Maps

List of Text Figures and Maps

Figures 1, 16 and 45 have been drawn by Mr Tom Borthwick. They illustrate Hadrian's Wall, the Antonine Wall and North Britain in the Roman period, and provide names for the sites discussed in the text. All the other line drawings have been prepared by D. J. Breeze. They have been produced at uniform scales for comparative purposes. North usually lies at, or towards, the top of the page. As far as possible stone has been reproduced as a solid line, while turf is hatched. The forts on the distribution maps are not named as the maps are only intended to give an impression of the occupation of North Britain in each period; total accuracy cannot be attained either now or in the future.

List of Tables

To Pamela and Anne

Preface

The number of books on Hadrian's Wall has multiplied disconcertingly of late. Nevertheless there still seems a place for a book concerned above all with the history of the Wall. This book therefore is not a guide to the Wall nor is it a description in detail of the actual physical remains. It is an attempt to review the evidence for this the best-known and best-preserved of all Rome's artificial frontiers in order to explain why it was built at a particular time on a particular line across Britain, and to follow its history till the end of Roman control in Britain.

The book starts therefore with a condensed history of Roman Britain and the Empire up to the decision to build Hadrian's Wall, concentrating on Roman thought about frontiers in general and Rome's aims and objectives in Britain in particular. Next the building of the Wall is examined in detail, using a variety of evidence which allows some reconstruction of the planning and timetabling of the project. The following chapter deals with the abandonment of Hadrian's Wall, still in process of modification, for a new Wall in Scotland. This, the Antonine Wall, is examined in depth to see the differences and similarities between the two Walls. In the next chapter the later history of these Walls till the final abandonment of the Antonine Wall and the return to Hadrian's Wall is discussed and the new arrangements for controlling the northern frontier considered.

There is a natural pause at this point in the story. In the third century the northern frontier saw an era of peace broken by the first appearance of the Picts (under that name at least) and the Scots at the end of the century. These new dangers of the fourth century lead to a completely different situation from that of the first and second centuries. The fourth century also sees a complete reorganization, civil and military, of the administration of the empire, and a complete change in the organization of the army. The tranquil interlude of the third century and the turbulent fourth century are therefore discussed after two general chapters on the organization of the army and life in the forts, which apply to the first, second and third centuries A.D., and to some extent to the fourth.

These two chapters are divided rather arbitrarily, but the first, 'The Army of the Wall', is intended to give the basic organization of the units in the Roman army and the lay-out of the Roman fort. It also acts as a glossary for some of the discussion in the historical chapters which involves unit organization and the internal buildings in forts, such as the suggested garrisons for the Wall forts. The second of these chapters, 'Life on the Wall', is an attempt to show what life on Hadrian's Wall was like, concentrating on the soldiers but not ignoring their dependants who created the *vici*, the villages outside the forts where soldiers' families and traders lived. Some notes on the later developments in the army are appended here.

There follows a chapter on the third and fourth centuries, and a conclusion. Some matters have been relegated to appendices. A list of emperors and governors is given, for reference purposes, which supplements chronological tables in the text. The units which at one time or another were stationed in the forts of the Wall, its outposts and its Cumberland coast flank, are listed by names of unit and by fort. There is a rather longer treatment of the gods worshipped on the Wall than would be possible in the main text without over-extending the chapter on 'Life on the Wall'. Finally the places on the Wall are singled out where some of the features referred to in the text, details of construction or types of buildings in forts, may be most clearly seen.

It has already been said that this book is not a guide nor a gazetteer, nor can it be an exhaustive account of every aspect of the Wall. The purpose is to show how the Wall came to be, what it was and how it developed, how it influenced and was influenced by its alternative, the Antonine Wall, and what happened during its later history. Life on the Wall for the soldiers garrisoned there, and as far as the evidence allows, for their dependants, is described in the light of evidence from the Wall and elsewhere. The bias is military, for the Wall was built and garrisoned by soldiers, though paradoxically its own purpose was bureaucratic rather than military, the establishment of a tidy method of controlling movement into and out of the Empire. The full effects of the Wall on the native peoples north and south of it, the full story of the civil settlements under its shadow, still remain to be discovered and recorded. Till these are known the story must be incomplete.

The views here presented are of course personal ones, and there can be no pretence that they represent the final solution or even the 'official' agreed one. For convenience the writing of this book has been divided between us, David Breeze taking the chapters on 'The Building of the Wall', 'The Antonine Wall', 'The Two Walls', and 'The Third and Fourth Centuries', Brian Dobson the Preface, Conclusion and those on 'The Concept of a Frontier'. 'The Army of the Wall' and 'Life on the Wall'. The appendices are mostly Brian Dobson's work, apart from that on 'The Evidence on the Ground'. But the separation is purely one of convenience; the book is in every way a joint product.

The citation of evidence has presented a problem. This has been met by giving references rather than full texts for the evidence, citing where possible Dr J. C. Mann's valuable collection of relevant literary, epigraphic and numismatic evidence in addition to standard works. A running bibliography has been preferred to footnotes. There is no attempt to provide a bibliography for the Wall. Attention is drawn simply to the major books or articles bearing on the points under discussion.

Our views are personal ones, but many of them have been formed in active discussion with other scholars, from whom we have learnt much. We should like to mention with special gratitude Eric Birley, who introduced us both to Wall studies, and who has done so much to make Hadrian's Wall more intelligible, and John Gillam, whose deep knowledge of Hadrian's Wall has been a continual source of stimulation. We are grateful also to the many others whose names appear in the following pages. We owe a particular debt of gratitude to Dr John Mann and Dr Valerie Maxfield, who were kind enough to read through our typescript and make constructive comments and criticism, and to Mr H. Russell Robinson, who looked through the section on

Preface

armour and equipment. We have learned much from all of these, but the responsibility for the views here put forward remains our own.

Finally we should like to thank our wives, who have perhaps suffered most throughout this partnership, in this volume and in others, for their long patience and forbearance with us over our Wall fever. We dedicate this book to them.

Edinburgh and Durham   August 1974

One

The Concept of a Frontier

(*Hadrianus*) *murumque per octoginta milia passuum primus duxit, qui bar-baros Romanosque divideret.*

(Hadrian) was the first to build a wall, eighty miles long, to separate the Romans from the barbarians.

(*Scriptores Historiae Augustae, Vita Hadriani*, 11 2)

Such is the sole surviving Roman comment on the reason for the building of Hadrian's Wall. Why, almost eighty years after the invasion of Britain under the emperor Claudius in A.D. 43, should his ninth successor as emperor, Hadrian, decide in A.D. 122 that the Empire should be given artificial boundaries where no natural ones existed; and that in Britain the boundary should take the form of a wall, effectively to divide the inhabitants, willing or unwilling, of the Empire, from the barbarians outside? To understand why, the history of the province must be examined in the wider context of the Roman Empire.

The Early Empire

Rome in A.D. 43 already had eight centuries of history behind her. Archaeology and literary tradition now agree reasonably well that there had been a settled community at Rome from about the middle of the eighth century B.C. During that time defeat in war had been virtually unknown to her since the sack of the city by the Gauls in 390 B.C. She had not even lost the war against Hannibal of Carthage, the second Punic War, and since her victory in that war at Zama in 202 B.C. no power had been capable

5

1 Hadrian's Wall (land over 600 ft stippled)

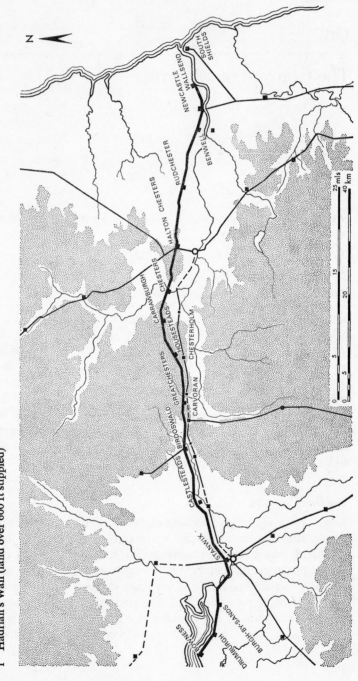

of challenging her. This run of success, unparalleled in world history, was founded on an army which was unbeatable on its chosen battle ground, the open field. This single fact meant that even when Rome was reluctant to assume the role of supreme power after the victory over Hannibal the role was hers. As Dr J. C. Mann has said, 'Roman history is essentially the virtually unique story of a nation trying to catch up with the situations produced by the incredible success of its army.' The idea of a more or less permanent boundary between Roman and barbarian was unthinkable, for it would set a limit to Rome's ability to conquer.

Rome saw her ability in terms of government and war. The remaining arts could be left to others:

Tu regere imperio populos, Romane, memento
(Hae tibi erunt artes) pacisque imponere morem
Parcere subiectis et debellare superbos

'Do you, O Roman, be mindful to rule the nations at your command (these will be your skills) and impose the law of peace; show mercy to those who have submitted and crush the proud in war'
(*Aeneid* VI 851–3)

So wrote Vergil, court poet to Augustus, the first emperor. Peace was to be achieved by force. Those who submitted would certainly receive merciful terms, that was true, but the *superbi*, those who resisted, must be crushed; then would the *pax Romana* be world-wide.

World conquest did not seem so remote a possibility. The world was not a big place to the Roman of the first century A.D.; according to the best theories, it was perhaps 10,000 miles east–west by 4000 miles north–south. Augustus already claimed its conquest in his account of his achievements, the great monument known as the *Res Gestae divi Augusti*; that it was not quite complete was a matter of detail. His trusted lieutenant, Agrippa, kept a map of the world in his portico; he presumably thought on similar lines.

Such concepts could not embrace the idea of frontiers as permanent boundaries, still less armies strung out along frontier lines in forts and fortresses. The Roman army operated in groups of legions, under the command of the emperor, his lieutenants, or

7

the governors of provinces. Their essential task was to seek out the enemy forces and destroy them in battle, to inflict so crushing a defeat that the enemy would sue for peace. Occupation of ground was unimportant, so that Roman wars often take on the aspect of wrestling bouts, to be settled by falls or submissions, with a number of rounds separated by regular retirement to winter quarters in friendly territory – rather than a succession of lines on a map, representing territory gained in each year's campaign.

The dispositions of the legions were related to these aims. In the first century A.D. great army groups lay around Cologne and Mainz, ready to strike into Germany, or if need be intervene in already-conquered Gaul. In the east three or four legions were concentrated at Antioch, astride the main east–west route from Parthia. Elsewhere internal problems bulked larger than the enemy beyond the limit of Roman territory; in Spain, Dalmatia, Judaea, Egypt, the threat to security arose from within the province. Even the great river 'frontiers', the Rhine and Danube, on closer inspection prove to have been convenient stopping-places before another leap forward (which in the event never came in quite the form expected) and useful clear boundaries for the control of unauthorized movement; militarily they had little value. In fact rivers are rarely if ever cultural boundaries dividing one people from another; they are routes along which people, goods and ideas flow, affecting both banks. They only become important as frontiers because they provide clearly visible lines for bureaucracies wishing to invent frontiers and control movement across them.

The military dispositions of the first great period with which we have to deal, up to the late 80s A.D., consisted then of legions in bases chosen with an eye to swift assembly of mobile striking forces. The auxiliary forces, infantry and cavalry support troops gradually acquiring stature and importance, were often grouped around the legions. When they were not, their forts were for the most part winter quarters, placed with an eye to their convenience when assembling the summer task force, and for ease of winter provisioning. They could well be situated also with an eye to controlling and protecting newly-conquered tribes, so in some areas the Roman dispositions might take the form of a network of forts, linked by strategic all-weather roads. In such a network there would be an outer strand of Roman troops posted nearest to the border of Roman territory, but there would be no special emphasis on it. More important still, only a small minority of forts would be garrisoned when the army was on campaign. The verdict was sought on the field of battle, with only the minimum number of troops on the lines of communication.

What attention was paid to the frontier, then, and what reality had it? Rome had found early that, after an enemy had been defeated in war, occupation of at least some of his territory became necessary. So the overseas empire had been reluctantly born after the first war against Carthage. Rome took over the boundaries of the state that had submitted to her, voluntarily or after defeat, and the responsibility for the defence of that state's territory. But she saw no military advantage in stringing her forces along those boundaries, nor any advantage in emphasizing their position by erecting barriers. Boundaries would set limits to her own expansion, without warding off encroachment or infiltration from without.

This situation obtained from the accession to sole power of the first Roman emperor, Augustus, in 31 B.C., to the 80s A.D. It was inherited from the late Republic, but there was one important difference. Under the Republic expansion was largely the work of individual generals and governors, who sought in conquest military glory in the form of triumphs or ovations, and the booty to recoup the money spent on past elections to magistracies and to fill their purses for the next ones, with little restraint from the Senate. Under the Empire, even though the emperor inherited the destiny of Rome to conquer the world, and could take on necessary but unattractive tasks like the subduing of the Alpine tribes and the extension of Dalmatia, even the full conquest of Spain, he could not and would not authorize a general advance. If the emperor was to control he had to limit the scope of his governors. Only the most trusted general could be allowed military success. Thus only the most secure of emperors with good and trustworthy lieutenants would conduct advances on more than one front at a time; worse still, the caution or weariness of an emperor might bring all expansion to a premature halt. Thus the shock the aged Augustus received from the loss of three

legions in Germany in A.D. 9 seems to have inspired his advice to
his successor Tiberius to keep the Empire within its limits –
advice which he had never followed himself till the reverses of
the revolt in Illyricum, beginning in A.D. 6, were followed by the
disaster of A.D. 9. His successor, Tiberius, was already old, tired
and disillusioned, and the advice was found acceptable and acted
upon. For nearly thirty years there was no expansion.

Julius Caesar in Britain

The invasion of Britain by Julius Caesar in 55 B.C. is typical
of the way Rome expanded under the late Republic. From his
base in Gallia Narbonensis (Provence) Caesar had already
conquered the rest of Gaul (France and Belgium) with the necessary protestations that he was safeguarding his province and the
interests of Rome. The reality of the dangers he claimed to be
eliminating need not be discussed here, but it is abundantly clear
that Caesar would have sought glory and booty whatever the
situation, as part of the normal career of an ambitious nobleman
in the late Republic. His initial success was so great that he was
in danger, so it seemed, of running out of tribes to conquer, and
so risking recall. The invasion of Britain justified the retention of
his command for a further five years; he needed this justification
so much that in 55 he took tremendous risks, invading too late in
the campaigning season to make more than a reconnaissance in
force, and nearly met with complete disaster. The glamour of
crossing the ocean to an island that till then Romans had hardly
believed to exist was sufficient to gain him a record number of
days of public thanksgiving in Rome, exceeding what he had
been given for the conquest of Gaul.

Caesar returned in 54 B.C., and won the formal submission of
the British tribes opposed to him, but he did not winter there,
although that seems to have been his original intention. Un-
certainty about the security of the so-recently-conquered Gaul
and about the political situation in Rome may have persuaded
him not to risk being isolated beyond the Channel. Seneca asserts
that he heard while still in Britain of the death of Julia, his
daughter and Pompey's wife; if this was so it would be sufficient
to bring Caesar back to Gaul to see its effects on his alliance with

Pompey. Events in Gaul, which proved not to have been finally subdued, kept him from returning to Britain before the outbreak of civil war; significantly when he was sole master of the Roman world and seeking new worlds to conquer he did not think of Britain. For the governor of Gaul it had been the best place to conquer, a far easier one than Germany. For the master of Rome it was of peripheral interest; the east was the place to win military glory, now that his choice was unrestricted. The point is worth making, as it has a great influence on the history of Roman Britain, and of the Wall; Britain was never a number one priority. Also, whatever Caesar had written in his commentaries in order to justify the invasion, Gaul could be held down without conquering Britain.

For nearly a hundred years after Caesar no Roman military action was initiated against Britain. Although Britain in one sense was embarrassingly unfinished business (it should have been created a province after its submission to Caesar) and there are odd references to Augustus' intention to do something about it, he found much more important things to do; Tiberius' acceptance of Augustus' advice meant the shelving of the British venture for another quarter of a century. As was the way of Rome, diplomatic relations with the rising British kingdoms continued, and the successor to Tiberius, the young Caligula, had thoughts of invading Britain, with the usual fugitive princeling to hand to supply a pretext, just as he had thoughts of invading Germany. It was a natural return to expansion after the unnatural check imposed by the aged Augustus and Tiberius. Both enterprises were abandoned, probably because of the uncertain loyalty of Caligula's commanders on the Rhine, and his insecurity in Rome.

The Invasion of Britain

Caligula's successor, Claudius, dragged from behind a curtain after the murder of his nephew to be made emperor because of the troops' loyalty to his dynasty, was also insecure. Created emperor in 41, he faced a serious rebellion in 42, only thwarted by the continuing loyalty of the troops. His situation was precarious; he lacked the glory of military success, the imperial

11

virtue. A triumph must be obtained, the easiest place to win one, Britain. It was not so much the glory of defeating the dominant tribe in southern England, the Catuvellauni, led by Togodumnus and Caratacus, the sons of the great king Cunobelinus, lately dead, that mattered. It was once more the glory of crossing Ocean, the feat that had so impressed Caesar's contemporaries. This done, and the neighbouring tribes to the Catuvellauni defeated or made allies of Rome, Claudius could leave Britain after his stage-managed victory, telling his governor to conquer 'the rest'. Britain still retained the interest of Claudius while Caratacus was at liberty; his capture was an appropriate occasion to bore everybody with reminders of Claudius' one great success. The capture also marked a change of tempo in Britain – as the emperor loses interest the pace of conquest slows. Claudius ordered one of the leading generals of the day, Domitius Corbulo, to withdraw across the Rhine when he had crossed it on a punitive expedition. Corbulo wryly commented on the greater good fortune of those who had been generals under the Republic. Now only the emperor could initiate expansion.

A new and youthful emperor, Nero, marked a change of tempo once more. Rid of his mentors, he launched out at both ends of the Empire. Scapula, the captor of Caratacus, had died in office and been replaced as governor of Britain by Didius Gallus, who had kept things quiet. His successors were two specialists in mountain warfare, Quintus Veranius and Suetonius Paulinus. Their activities were directed towards the conquest of the tribes of the Welsh hills, the north being temporarily tranquillized under a client (dependant) queen supported by Roman arms. It was again characteristic of Roman priorities that the governor Paulinus was away campaigning when another client kingdom, that of Prasutagus, king of the Iceni of East Anglia, was being absorbed into the Roman province. The rebellion led by the widow of Prasutagus, Boudicca, showed how casual the approach to pacification had been. Plans for advance were shelved, and as civil war broke out in the Empire only seven years later there was reason enough for governors during those years to keep things cool. Vettius Bolanus, the last of these governors, could not keep the client kingdom of Brigantia, covering the greater part of northern England, under Roman domination. Queen

Cartimandua, who had strengthened her claim on Roman support by delivering Caratacus to them, quarrelled with her consort Venutius. Venutius won, the queen was rescued by Roman troops, and with a civil war raging no more could be done. Clearly, however, Brigantia could not be left in the hands of the fiercely anti-Roman Venutius.

When the civil war was over the new emperor, Vespasian, was one of the relatively few senators who knew Britain, where he had served during the invasion and first campaigns. The governors he sent in succession were faithful adherents and great generals, two of whom, Petillius Cerealis and Gnaeus Iulius Agricola, also had previous experience in Britain. The conquest of the Welsh peninsula, northern England and southern Scotland in a decade suggests strongly that the real hindrance to earlier conquest had been the lack of personal involvement on the part of the emperor; Nero's enthusiasm had been quenched by the Boudiccan rebellion.

Did this conquest of the north reflect a change of policy, forced on Rome by the collapse of the northern client kingdom? Many have thought so, and some have even suggested that lowland England, largely won in the first hectic years after 43, was the original limit of Rome's objectives. Naturally there is no way of demonstrating whether this view is correct. There seems, however, no need to interpret the military dispositions in the early period as representing successive frontier lines. They suggest rather an overall distribution of troops in winter quarters, and perhaps the holding of certain key points to hold down the conquered, protect the provincials against raids, and pass the winter quietly before the summer campaign took them into enemy territory. They contrast markedly with the forts strung out along linear earthworks and rivers of the Empire in the second and succeeding centuries. The Fosse Way, the great road that runs from Lincoln to Exeter, both legionary bases in the early years, is not a frontier line. Roads were not to be used in this way for another forty years. The other 'evidence' for a linear frontier in these years, Ostorius Scapula's intention to control everything 'this side' (south) of Trent and Severn (if that is really what Tacitus said originally), seems rather to indicate the area of the province which in Scapula's view should be regarded as pacified. To make pacification effective disarmament was necessary (provincials were not allowed to carry arms except on journeys or for hunting); the first to object were the Iceni, a client kingdom well within the province. This consolidation before advance, characteristic of Scapula, as Tacitus remarks, does not justify any conclusion that he was establishing a permanent frontier. There is no convenient stopping line, like the Rhine or Danube, in Britain south of the Forth–Clyde isthmus, and no evidence that the Romans thought that they had reached one. The frontier at any time would be the boundaries of the tribes allied to or subject to Rome, with perhaps a few forts pushed forward to hold important river-crossings or passes.

There is no way of demonstrating that the client kingdom of Brigantia was to be a permanent arrangement; the history of other client kingdoms makes this seem highly unlikely. The agreement reached with Cartimandua, like that with Prasutagus of the Iceni, could have been part of the diplomatic offensive at the time of the invasion in 43, with the immediate objective of isolating the Catuvellauni. Alternatively it may have been part of the arrangements made by Claudius or his governor to control the largest of the British tribes on the vulnerable northern flank of the new province. It would lapse at her death, unless Rome chose to renew it. If she had died when Prasutagus did her kingdom would presumably also have been absorbed into the province. In the event the success of Venutius and the eviction of Rome's nominee Cartimandua meant that Rome had a war on her hands.

From Agricola to Trajan

By A.D. 81 then, not yet forty years from the invasion, the Roman governor Agricola had carried Roman arms to the Forth–Clyde isthmus. How far his predecessor Petillius Cerealis had come in his operations against the Brigantes and consequently how far Agricola's advance was into new territory does not matter for our purposes. What does is that at this point his son-in-law and biographer, the great Roman historian Tacitus, puts in an interesting thought: 'If the courage of our army and the glory of the name of Rome would have allowed it, a halting-place could have been found inside Britain', i.e. an alternative was conceivable to the straightforward advance till the northernmost coast was reached. The year, as determined by the dating of Agricola's governorship accepted here, would, significantly, be 81; Titus, Vespasian's son, after only two years in power had died and his brother Domitian had become emperor. It was time to halt and await the new emperor's orders. Agricola had already served a term as long as the average for a governor; he might well be replaced. It would seem that Agricola toyed with putting forward a scheme for the conquest of Ireland if further advance in Britain was deemed unnecessary. The Forth–Clyde isthmus is in fact the most sensible *terminus* within Britain, as it offers the shortest line and the country beyond is so difficult.

The word that eventually came from Rome was, it would appear, 'Forward' (the emperor determined what the valour of the army and the glory of the Roman name allowed): Agricola marched north and duly brought the enemy to battle in the classic Roman style at Mons Graupius.

This victory seemed decisive, to Agricola at least, but it was not pursued. Agricola himself was recalled but he had already served twice the average term of a governor. Forts were built at the mouths of the glens; a legionary fortress was begun at Inchtuthil. Whether these forts represented an earnest attempt to contain the Highlanders rather than to conquer them must remain uncertain; they could have been merely a pause for breath. In the 140s Lollius Urbicus did not reoccupy these advanced positions though he did reoccupy sites to their rear, on the road running up Strathmore, which suggests that the glen forts were more than purely defensive in intent. The legionary fortress at Inchtuthil also seems a springboard for further advance, in the tradition of Gloucester, York, Caerleon and Chester, rather than a legionary base in the front line of a purely defensive system, for which there would be no good precedent.

Decisive in the abandonment of further conquest seems to have been the withdrawal of one of the four legions of Britain, II Adiutrix, in order to meet a crisis on the Danube. The legion intended for Inchtuthil, presumably XX Valeria Victrix, had to go to the new fortress at Chester to replace II Adiutrix. Auxiliaries may also have gone with II Adiutrix to the Danube;

in any event it was not thought practicable to maintain auxiliary garrisons north of the Forth–Clyde isthmus. It must be remembered that in the previous fifteen years all of Wales, northern England and southern Scotland had been brought into the province. A network of auxiliary forts extended over this area to hold it down, with new legionary fortresses at York, Caerleon and Chester. Holding more without a fourth legion would have courted disaster, and the fourth legion was needed urgently on the Danube. Nevertheless its withdrawal marked the end of total conquest as a possible way of making Britain secure until Severus attempted to revive it over a century later.

The evacuation of all north of the Forth–Clyde isthmus seems to have been in 87 or not long after; the Romans remained in southern Scotland for almost a generation, but it would seem that somewhere about the turn of the first and second centuries A.D. they withdrew to the Tyne–Solway line.

The years from the recall of Agricola in 84 or 85 to the completion of the withdrawal from Scotland at the beginning of the second century, and from then up to the beginning of the building of the Wall in A.D. 122, are amongst the most obscure in the history of Roman Britain. Tacitus in his biography of his father-in-law Agricola had summarized the achievements of all the previous governors, and given a more detailed account of Agricola's campaigns; this information is supplemented by other literary sources, for Caratacus and Boudicca by Tacitus' own accounts in the *Annals*.

The pattern is reasonably clear. An attack on Britain, lying on the edge of the Roman world and across Ocean, had a certain glamour that had commended itself at critical stages to Caesar, Caligula and Claudius. The initial impetus from Claudius died away after the capture of Caratacus; the renewed efforts of the young Nero foundered on the Boudicca rebellion. Vespasian, with his personal interest, initiated the renewed drive that almost conquered the whole island, a policy continued by his two sons.

The rule of his younger son, Domitian, was a turning-point in the history not only of Roman Britain but of the Empire as a whole. He began with advance, in Britain, in Germany, and on the Danube. But defeat on the Danube stopped the advance in Britain, and rebellion on the Rhine compromised recovery on the Danube. In Germany the advance simply stopped, and the stop-lines became frontiers. The same seems to have happened in Britain, for Tacitus in the *Agricola* does not mention an abandonment of the idea of conquest; indeed there is no evidence that the recall of Agricola in itself vitally affected Roman policy in Britain. As events were to turn out the halt was fatal, as Tacitus saw when he was writing the *Histories* in, as far as can be estimated, about 105. If this reconstruction of events is correct all north of the Forth–Clyde isthmus was given up shortly after 87, as a result of the transfer of II Adiutrix to the Danube. The final withdrawal to the Tyne–Solway isthmus seems to have been the work not of Domitian, murdered in 96, or his successor Nerva who died in 98, but the great warrior-emperor Trajan.

Trajan

What were Trajan's intentions as far as Britain was concerned? It may seem wrong to put this question before considering the evidence for what he did do, but the interpretation of the evidence in fact depends on a general appraisal of Trajan's intentions. He was of course ambitious for military glory, like a true Roman, and despite the favourable picture given by our sources there is little clear evidence that his great wars of conquest against Dacia and particularly against Parthia were motivated solely, if at all, by considerations of the needs of the Empire. There is nothing to suggest that he had any interest in Britain, except perhaps as a source of reinforcements for the wars elsewhere. He was not personally committed to conquest in Britain, and might accept a withdrawal from some territory to gain stability in Britain while he was engaged personally elsewhere.

By some such speculation must be found a reason why Trajan authorized the final withdrawal to the Tyne–Solway line, in what seems to have been an orderly evacuation of sites, with timber structures fired by the retreating Roman army. The scale of the occupation of the Lowlands had already been drastically reduced under Domitian; the further withdrawal may have allowed units to be transferred from Britain to the Dacian wars. There is no need to postulate disaster – that would have to be avenged – and a Roman decision is more likely. This policy of reduced commitments to produce stability is reflected in the rebuilding in stone of the new legionary fortresses at York, Caerleon and Chester; the old fortress sites had been handed over, to colonies of veteran legionaries at Gloucester and Lincoln, and to the *civitas Cornoviorum* at Wroxeter. Rebuilding in stone implies that the legionary bases were not to be moved in the foreseeable future, and that the fourth legion, withdrawn under Domitian, was not to return and make total conquest possible. The abandonment of conquest did raise the problem of frontier control in a new form, for it was beginning to be clear that there would be a more-or-less permanent frontier.

Before turning to the Stanegate system, which is interpreted as the solution offered by Trajan or his governors to this problem, it must be pointed out that Trajan's objectives – if correctly interpreted – were not entirely achieved. A unit, the *cohors I Cugernorum*, won the military distinction of the emperor's names, *Ulpia Traiana*, and a grant of citizenship to all its non-citizen soldiers concerned in a particular exploit in Britain between 103 and 122. An officer commanding the *cohors II Asturum*, in Germany in 89 but in Britain by 105, was decorated in a British war before becoming tribune of a legion, III Cyrenaica, in Egypt, a province that the legion had left by 128. In 117, when Hadrian succeeded Trajan, we are told that the Britons could not be kept under Roman control. A further complication is the possibility that Trajan had reduced the garrison of Britain to two legions by transferring the legion IX Hispana to the legionary base at Nijmegen in Holland in compensation for legions transferred from the Rhine to wars further east. It is not surprising however that there should be fighting in Britain when Trajan was perhaps attempting to make the military situation there stable and permanent. There was periodic serious fighting in Britain till the early third century.

But did Trajan have a frontier system in Britain? Thought had been changing since the dreams of world conquest of the age of Augustus. The world was now bigger than had been thought. The terrain beyond the Mediterranean world was increasingly alien and unattractive. Domitian's conquests in Germany had been real enough, but advance had frozen on the Taunus ridge and in the Wetterau. The frontier line there has no special logic; it is simply where the advance happened to stop. Positions were linked under Domitian by a series of watchtowers on a road. About the same time, perhaps, a similar series of watchtowers along a road was erected along the Gask ridge in Scotland, in the short period between the move north of the Forth–Clyde isthmus in 83 and the evacuation of the land north of the isthmus by 90 at latest. It seems that the 'stop-lines' were being given some permanence; it was worth-while supplementing normal patrolling with static observation towers. It reflects the possibility of a final frontier between Rome and Barbary. Significantly it was under Domitian that the army groups which had waited so long on the Rhine to conquer Germany had their base areas made into provinces, Upper and Lower Germany. That was the only Germany they would ever conquer, although still in 98 Tacitus was hoping for that final conquest of free Germany: *'tam diu Germania vincitur'* ('the conquest of Germany is taking such a long time'). Domitian knew better – the legions on the Rhine were reduced from eight to six; soon there would be only four. Professor H. Schönberger sees the years 89–90 as 'a historical turning-point and the final abandonment of the offensive against free Germany'.

Watchtowers appear on the south bank of the Danube on Trajan's Column in Rome, the great pillar adorned with a frieze showing scenes from his Dacian wars which Trajan set up in Rome. It is likely that frontier control, the observation of movement into and out of the empire, had started early on these great rivers of Rhine and Danube, so convenient as boundaries. As early as 70 a German tribe, the Tencteri, had complained that they only had access to the *colonia Agrippina* (Cologne) if they were unarmed and practically naked, under guard and after paying a fee. In 98 Tacitus describes how the Hermunduri, on the upper Danube, had the privilege, unique to them among the German tribes, of trading not on the bank of the Danube but deep in the province and even inside a Roman colony; they could enter and leave without guards. To enforce rigid controls the rivers must be watched; the towers on the Taunus and Wetterau represented the first extension of such controls to frontiers without rivers.

Significantly it is also under Trajan that there is evidence for the stationing of *numeri* in Upper Germany. These contingents of troops retained the characteristics of irregulars, unlike the normal auxiliary cavalry (*alae*) and infantry (*cohortes*) regular units, standardized in organization and to some extent in equipment, with a fixed term of service. *Numeri* were to see much employment on frontier lines, particularly those with no great river barrier. Finally under Trajan appear small forts in Upper Germany, similar to those of the Stanegate system.

The Stanegate System (see Fig. 15a)

If, then, Trajan meant to stabilize the situation in Britain, and accept that in Britain as on the Taunus and in the Wetterau installations on the furthest line of foreseeable advance were necessary to control movement, these were the devices to his hand: watch-towers; *numeri*; small forts; and a road in default of a major river as a convenient boundary to the empire. The Forth–Clyde isthmus had been abandoned; the next obvious, indeed only possible line, was the Tyne–Solway. There was a road already here, built under Agricola or his successors. It linked two forts which guarded important river crossings on routes into Scotland, Corbridge on the east and Carlisle on the west. It is probably best to reserve the term 'Stanegate' for the road between these two sites, and exclude extensions which may be postulated but are not proven. The Stanegate ran through a natural gap formed by the valleys of the Tyne and Irthing. It has been assumed for some time that Trajan did in fact base a frontier system on this road, the Stanegate, but the evidence is inadequate. It seems that at some point during his reign withdrawal to this line had taken place. On pottery evidence forts at Corbridge, Chesterholm, Nether Denton and Carlisle had been in existence since the Flavian period. Carvoran is generally assumed to be of similar date, though evidence is lacking, and Old Church Brampton is thought to have had a short occupation of about the time of Trajan. Newbrough has yielded pottery of the fourth century alone, but an earlier fort on this site is generally postulated as it fits a regular spacing of forts along the Stanegate. Finally Haltwhistle Burn and Throp have yielded pottery now thought to be Trajanic. Various schemes for the Stanegate have been put forward, generally tied to alternating large and small forts. What follows is one more attempt to reconstruct the development of this frontier, relying on logic and parallels from elsewhere in the Empire rather than the inadequate evidence from the sites themselves.

Probably in the first phase of the Stanegate forts were provided at one-day marching intervals to protect the movement of troops and convoys of supplies, who thus could always sleep under a fort's walls. These forts should be Chesterholm and Nether Denton, and the dating given to the Samian pottery from these sites is consonant with their construction as forts on this strategic road under Agricola's successors. So far these forts were only part of the network of roads and forts which was the norm for the disposition of units. The next stage in development, if correctly interpreted, would mark the transformation of an ordinary military road into a frontier road by the building of forts in the gaps between the existing forts; forts would then be at a half-day's marching interval – the spacing on Hadrian's Wall when forts were built on its line.

Unfortunately the three forts at the heart of the discussion regarding the Stanegate – Newbrough, Carvoran and Old Church Brampton – are of very uncertain date. A Trajanic Newbrough is inferred purely on spacing grounds, as only a small fort apparently associated with fourth-century pottery has been found; the fort at Carvoran is uninvestigated; excavation of Old Church Brampton suggested a short occupation at about this time, corresponding to that at Throp and Haltwhistle Burn. This evidence, for what it is worth, supports the idea that the 'half-day forts' belonged to the Trajanic conversion of a road into a frontier. Until a frontier is established there is no need for more than the normal-spaced forts of Chesterholm and Nether Denton on the road. Carvoran is a possible exception as it is related to another road, the Maiden Way coming over from Kirkby Thore; it may have been built near the road junction before the Stanegate became a frontier road.

The placing of forts at a half-day's interval on the strand of the network nearest the enemy was a military measure, to bring more troops into the crucial area. Stationing troops in more forts rather than in larger forts provided local patrolling and a closer military presence to any point on the road.

Table 1   The spacing of forts on the Stanegate

	Distance	Distance
Carlisle		
Old Church Brampton		7½
Nether Denton	13½	6
Carvoran		4½ (or road junction)
Chesterholm	11	6½
Newbrough		6
Corbridge	13½	7½

The first column shows the distance in miles between the original forts, the second the distances when the 'half-day' forts were added.

The next element to be examined has little to do with military problems but a lot to do with control of movement across a frontier: the building of small forts between the normal-sized forts. This has still to be proven as a consistent feature along the Stanegate, for only two sites seem certain though another four have been suggested. The certain forts are at Haltwhistle Burn and Throp, 210 by 170 feet and 200 by 195 feet respectively, with areas of rather under one acre overall. Haltwhistle Burn, with its stone internal buildings, has a curious plan. There seems to be one barrack, a possible granary, and other buildings that may be for administration. The most likely interpretation is that the fort is the base for a unit, most of which was out-stationed. If the unit was organized like the *numerus* at Hesselbach in Upper Germany three out of the four centuries may have been detached in this way. This is to go well beyond the evidence, of course; all that can be said with certainty is that this small fort is

Trajanic, that it could not accommodate a regular *ala* or cohort, and that unlike the Trajanic small forts in Germany or the Hadrianic milecastles it is not mainly taken up by accommodation.

2 The small fort at Haltwhistle Burn on the Stanegate.
   Scale 1 in. = 60 ft (1:720)

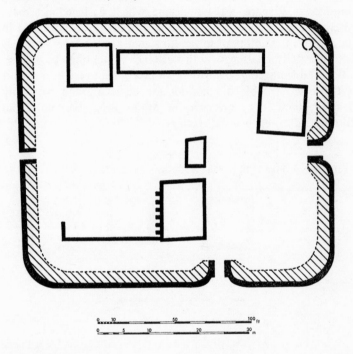

Whether small forts similar to Haltwhistle Burn and Throp existed between all the forts spaced at half-a-day's marching intervals on Trajan's new frontier is uncertain. Only excavation can confirm the likely sites that have been suggested. Small forts may have been built only where local conditions justified them; presumably they are related to control by patrol and observation of the passage of natives across the frontier. The out-stationed troops from Haltwhistle Burn must have been accommodated somewhere, and the most likely place may be the observation towers that have been linked with the Stanegate system. Dating evidence is lacking, as it is for some of the forts and all but two of the suggested small forts. The tower on Walltown Crags, later incorporated into the Wall as turret 45a, and the one on Pike Hill, incorporated into the Wall as an extra tower, must be accepted on structural grounds – they clearly precede the Wall and were built without reference to it. Both occupy commanding positions in advance of the Stanegate, which, designed as a road, rarely offered a good view to the north. Stress has been laid in the past on the ability of towers to signal to each other, but it is not clear that signalling over this distance would often be practicable or advantageous, compared with recourse to the nearest fort if there was trouble too hot for the observing and patrolling frontier guards. The evidence for Mains Rigg, Barcombe and Birdoswald towers is unsatisfactory.

3   Towers. a. Pike Hill; b. 45a (Walltown). Scale 1 in. = 36 ft (1:432)

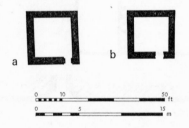

What happened west of Carlisle and east of Corbridge? There is no warrant to extend the Stanegate from sea to sea. West of Carlisle the Solway was a visible though not uncrossable boundary, better than the Stanegate road. Forts in this area were part of the network covering the military zone. Kirkbride may have played an important part, but the nature of the site at this time is uncertain. In the east the Tyne, unbridged below Corbridge, provided a convenient visible boundary. The fort at Washing Well, on the south bank of the Tyne, may have been part of the network in the east; it is still uninvestigated. The fort at South

Shields was not yet built, on the known site at least. The area south of the Tyne and east of the Pennines has few fort sites, sufficient, it seems, only to provide shelter a day's march apart on the great Dere Street route. In contrast forts west of the Pennines and on Stainmore are often less than a day's march apart.

Clearly much is uncertain about Trajan's 'frontier' in Britain. It is too easy to postulate without real evidence forts, small forts, towers, even an extension of a fort and small fort system west of Carlisle and east of Corbridge. A few suggestions only may be made. Rebuilding the legionary fortresses in stone, in itself perhaps no more than was necessary some thirty years after their construction in timber, may have been the occasion for a decision that Britain, like Germany, was to stay as it was, without significant expansion. Such stability made necessary some system of border control. Observation towers had already come into use under Domitian and existed on the Danube under Trajan. Fortlets of milecastle size appeared on the German frontier under Trajan; small forts, containing *numeri* four centuries strong, may also have appeared under him. In the light of these the Stanegate towers and small forts almost as big as those in Germany, based like them on a lateral road, may indicate the extension of the German type of frontier control to Britain. At the same time strengthening the numbers of fighting troops on what now became the frontier road by stationing them at half-day instead of day intervals gave it a special military importance and made possible more intensive patrolling.

The military control of north Britannia was still a network, but the outer strand had been thickened. At the same time the military forces, mobile units designed to fight the enemy in the field, begin to be drawn into the paralysing role of frontier guards. But this development is still in its infancy. The situation is still extremely fluid – between 85 and 122 at least four structural phases have been identified at Corbridge and Chesterholm.

Can the process be dated? The legionary fortresses were being rebuilt from early in the reign, Caerleon in 99–100, Chester perhaps after 102, York in 107–8. On the Stanegate the forts at half-day intervals, the small forts and towers must belong to a period after the evacuation of southern Scotland, as they presuppose that the Stanegate is now the frontier, or, to be more precise, the point at which frontier control is exercised. It was no more a tribal or cultural boundary than the later Hadrian's Wall, and some area to the north remained Rome's responsibility. That evacuation is now dated to 105 at latest, and though the only good evidence is that the second fort at Corbridge was built in 103 or later a date in the early years of the second century seems very likely.

Trajan thus acted in much the same way in Britain and Upper Germany: he recognized, like Domitian when he turned from expansion after the Saturninus rebellion of 89, that Rome would not expand on these two frontiers. In Britain and in Upper Germany there was no river to act as a convenient administrative boundary. In both similar expedients seem to have been used, though the details of the system in Britain will be unknown until further excavation takes place. More obscure is the reason for ceding land in Britain; for some reason the Forth–Clyde isthmus could not become the frontier. The garrisons in the Lowlands had already been drastically thinned; perhaps occupying the isthmus in force and holding some forts to the north of it (as was necessary in the 140s) was more than was feasible or desirable, if it meant drawing troops away from Trajan's own wars.

Stabilization of frontiers in Upper Germany and Britain, even retreat from territory occupied in Britain: how are these to be reconciled with Trajan the conqueror? The different roles played by the personality of the emperor and the inexorable underlying trends of imperial history must be recognized. Trajan desired military glory; he may or may not have been mistaken in identifying his search for glory with the true interests of Rome. He was not the last emperor to do so or to seek expansion. But the logic of the realization that Rome was not going to conquer the world was working itself out. Even if Rome promptly concluded that the rest of the world was not worth conquering she would need frontiers, clear boundaries, as a fluid situation became static. As has been seen, this was already happening where a river formed the boundary, even before hopes of advance were given up.

The new system of frontier control required a visible boundary, such as was provided by a river. The concept of a permanent artificial barrier to supply this boundary seems to be the work of Hadrian, and to him and his work we must now turn. But despite his different personality Hadrian did not set the empire on a new path. He merely provided the logical culmination to the process of developing a frontier that had begun with Domitian.

Two

The Building of Hadrian's Wall

Hadrian's Wall is the concept of Hadrian much more than the Stanegate system is of Trajan; it is an accurate reflection of the man and his policies. Hadrian had gone through the normal career of a Roman senator, as Trajan had done. He had served with distinction as a legionary tribune, as a legionary commander, as a provincial governor. He had served Trajan faithfully, and probably had always been intended to be his successor (despite the doubts surrounding the adoption and the inevitable tensions between 'king' and 'heir-presumptive'); yet Hadrian and Trajan were far apart in thought. Hadrian intended to give the Empire permanent frontiers. His first act was to abandon the untenable conquests of Trajan in the East. Thereafter in two great journeys he visited all the armies of the Empire, inspecting them rigorously to ensure that they were kept in training and good discipline while winning their favour by his interest in their welfare and abolition of abuses. His policy was clear and decided: peace, stable, controlled frontiers, a well-trained and disciplined army, all under the vigilant eye of an itinerant emperor.

It has already been mentioned that when Hadrian came to power in 117 he found trouble in Britain. His biographer states simply that 'the Britons could not be kept under Roman control'. There is a coin showing BRITANNIA issued in 119 which is usually taken to imply a victory in Britain. This could mean either trouble within the province or attack from outside. Cornelius Fronto writing in 162 to his former pupil, the emperor Marcus Aurelius, refers to a large number of soldiers killed under

Hadrian by the Jews and by the Britons. The Jewish war was in the 130s but the British war, or wars, could have been at any time in the reign. The losses were clearly serious and may have been occasioned by the disorders at the beginning of the reign. It is however clear that the Ninth Legion was not destroyed in Britain at this time, as used to be thought. The legion was certainly in existence in the 130s and recent theories suggest that it was transferred to Lower Germany from Britain by Trajan or Hadrian and moved thence to one of the Eastern provinces, possibly being destroyed in Armenia by the Parthians in 161.

It was presumably in response to the disorders at the beginning of his reign that Hadrian decided to deal effectively with the northern frontier in Britain. His inclinations were to conserve rather than expand, and so he chose to improve the existing frontier on the Tyne–Solway line rather than conquer the whole of the island of Britain or move forward to the much shorter Forth–Clyde isthmus. Hadrian visited Britain himself in 122 and, among other matters, concerned himself with the problem of the frontier. The other frontiers of the empire were usually formed by natural boundaries: a sea, or a great river such as the Rhine or Danube, or a desert as in North Africa. In North Britain there was no such clear demarcation line and therefore Hadrian decided to create an effective frontier by the construction of a wall from sea to sea, a wall which would, as his biographer put it, divide the Romans from the barbarians.

The Position of the Wall

The construction of this Wall clearly demonstrated that the Stanegate system of frontier control, consisting of forts, small forts and watchtowers, but no running barrier, in operation perhaps for the previous twenty years, was insufficient. The only really effective method of control was a running barrier, a wall, which would allow the army to supervise small-scale movement of people, prevent petty raiding, hinder large-scale attacks and so encourage the peaceful exploitation of the province right up to the frontier line (see Figs. 15a and b).

The Wall was, however, planned with the existing system of frontier forts in mind. Its very position proclaimed that, for it was placed a mile or so in advance of these forts on the north rim of the Tyne Gap. The Wall was planned to be 76 Roman miles (just over 70 English miles) long from Newcastle upon Tyne, where a new bridge was constructed and named Pons Aelius in honour of the Emperor, to Bowness-on-Solway. It was to be a stone wall, 10 Roman feet wide, for the eastern 45 miles from Newcastle to the River Irthing, and a turf wall, 20 Roman feet wide at base, for the western 31 miles from the Irthing to the Solway.

In the centre the Wall made use of the Whin Sill, a volcanic outcrop forming a line of north-facing crags. This, the best-known and most-photographed section of the Wall, forms only a part of the central sector which lies between the rivers North Tyne and Irthing (it stretches from Wall mile 33b to mile 46). East and west of the crags the Wall passes through very different terrain. In the east the Wall runs on the north side of the Tyne valley, usually with a reasonable outlook to the north, until it negotiates the crossing of the North Tyne by a bridge at Choller-ford opposite Chesters (the North and South Tyne unite just above Hexham). From here the Wall climbs steadily until it reaches its most northerly point at Limestone Corner, where a splendid view to the north is achieved, and then runs on until the true crags are reached at Sewingshields. West of the crags the Wall runs towards the river Irthing. For some distance after crossing it at Willowford it perches rather uncomfortably on the north side of the Irthing gorge looking out towards the wastes of Spadeadam. With the change from limestone to sandstone at the Red Rock Fault the landscape softens, but the really dramatic change occurs after the crossing of the Eden at Stanwix, when the marshes of the Solway are reached at Burgh-by-Sands. From here the Wall lies just above the high-water mark till it runs down to the sea just beyond Bowness.

The Wall and Ditch (Fig. 18)

In front of the wall ran a ditch, except where the terrain rendered it superfluous, as on the Whin Sill – though here the ditch always reappears in the dips between the crags – or where, as at Limestone Corner, the effort to dig it through solid rock

30

was unjustified. The ditch was separated from the wall by an open flat space or berm. This berm was usually 20 feet wide on the stone wall because of the pressure on the south lip of the ditch from the weight of the wall. On the turf wall it was only 6 feet wide (the collapse of a turret on the turf wall into the ditch later demonstrated that 6 feet was insufficient). The width of the ditch varied from 26 feet to 40 feet, usually about 27 feet, the depth was 9 to 10 feet, and the profile was V-shaped with a square-cut drainage or cleaning-out channel at the bottom. The material dug out of the ditch was thrown on to the north side and smoothed out so as to heighten the outer scarp of the ditch. In certain places small irregular mounds can be seen on the north side of the ditch. These may be the original spoil dumps which the ditch-diggers did not spread out, or they may have resulted from later cleaning-out of the ditch. Certainly the ditch was not always completed. This is vividly seen at Limestone Corner, where large blocks of whinstone lie tumbled out on the north side of the ditch while a huge block still remains in the ditch with wedge-holes visible on its upper side. A little to the east the overburden appears to have been removed but no effort has been made to dig out the rock. Elsewhere, on Cockmount Hill and at Allolee, the ditch was only partially completed or not even started.

The stone wall consisted of two outer faces of dressed stones with a core of rubble usually bonded with mortar though occasionally with clay. It seems that one or two courses of facing stones were laid then the rubble and mortar core poured in, then a couple more courses, more core, and so on. Where water was likely to collect behind the wall drains were laid through the foundation. At first insufficient drains appear to have been provided, for drains were regularly placed at about 20-foot intervals when the turf wall was later rebuilt in stone. The stone used in the construction of the wall was quarried locally. Today some of these quarries can be recognized from the inscriptions, usually mere doodles, that the Roman masons left on the rock face.

It is impossible to be certain how high the wall was, or indeed how it was finished off at the top. Several considerations suggest that the wall was about 15 feet high. The remains of the flight of steps at milecastle 48 (Poltross Burn) if projected upwards give a height of about 14 feet for the wall top, while a height of 15 to 16 feet would be necessary for a soldier on the wall top to have seen into the bottom of the ditch. It is possible that when the wall was later narrowed from 10 Roman feet wide to 6 to 8 feet the height of the wall was also lowered, but there is really no evidence or necessity for this.

4   Roman quarries near Hadrian's Wall, not all necessarily of Hadrianic date

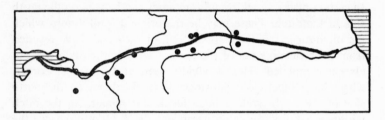

The turf wall was constructed of laid turves, each cut to regulation military size, 18 by 12 by 6 inches. The dark lines caused by the grass of the turves can still be seen when a section is cut through the turf wall. What little survives suggests that the front of the wall had a steep batter, while the back, at first vertical, continued at a more gentle slope. The most recent discussion of the turf wall by R. L. Bellhouse suggests that it was about 14 feet high, similar in height to the stone wall. It is difficult to answer the question why Hadrian's Wall was partly constructed in turf and not completed throughout in stone. The later rebuilding of the turf wall in stone demonstrates that this was not impossible, and if it was possible why was the whole wall not originally built in stone? Indeed this is closely linked to a second question, why was the stone wall so wide? It did not have to be 10 feet wide, for the later parts of the wall were built 6 feet wide. The massive nature of the stone wall has even led to the suggestion that Hadrian may have been influenced by travellers' accounts of the Great Wall of China, built some two hundred years before.

The purpose of the building in stone, apparently to excessive width and height, might be the erection of an enduring monument to Hadrian, very necessary to an emperor who had eschewed military glory. Hadrian's biographer was duly impressed. But if so, constructing part of the Wall in turf is even more inexplicable. It may be that building in stone west of the Red Rock Fault, where limestone for mortar ran out, would take longer, and so the turf wall was a temporary expedient, but clearer evidence is needed. Certainly it cannot be argued, as has been done, that there is no good building stone in Cumberland; this was manifestly disproved when the turf wall was rebuilt in stone. It also seems unlikely that the turf wall was constructed in a hurry as protection from a threat from the north; such a threat, if it existed, would have been dealt with by the army independently of the Wall. The provision of three outpost forts just to the north of the western end of the Wall has been taken to indicate a threat to the Wall from the south-west of Scotland, but it seems better to consider these forts as protection for a part of the province, possibly Brigantian tribal territory, isolated by the construction of the Wall.

Milecastles and Turrets

This Wall, be it of stone or turf, was not a closed frontier. Regularly spaced along it at intervals of one Roman mile were fortified gateways, conventionally called milecastles, though the term is misleading, for the milecastle was simply an adaptation of the normal fortlet constructed throughout Britain by the army since the earliest days of the conquest. The milecastles provided a way through the Wall with double gates at front and rear. Most of the earlier stone wall milecastles seem to measure about 60 by 50 Roman feet with a wall often the same width as the curtain wall itself, while many of the turf wall milecastles appear to have been about 70 by 60 feet internally. The milecastle walls were of stone on the stone wall and turf on the turf wall. One or two are known to have been surrounded by a ditch, but this seems to be unusual. Each milecastle contained one or two small buildings, presumably barrack-blocks for the soldiers, though at one milecastle a rather less substantial building was interpreted as a

5 Milecastles. a. 48 (Poltross Burn); b. 50 TW (High House).
Scale 1 in. = 36 ft (1:432)

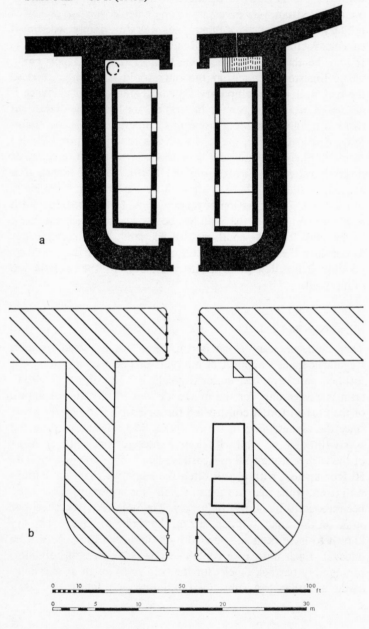

storehouse. These buildings were either stone or timber on the stone wall but were always of timber on the turf wall. They seem to come in two sizes – 20 to 32 feet by 12, and 52 feet by 12. The smaller building, divided into two rooms, is always found singly but the larger buildings, which are divided into four rooms, are in pairs in the two known examples. The milecastle also contained an oven, usually in the north-west corner, and in the opposite north corner a staircase to allow access to the wall top, and a tower over the north gate. The existence of this tower is normally assumed since it would complete the chain of regularly spaced observation towers along the Wall. The plan of milecastle 50 on the turf wall has been taken as corroborative evidence for this; there the north gate was constructed of ten upright timbers, the south gate of six, suggesting a more substantial structure over the north gate. Mr C. M. Daniels, however, has recently pointed out that supports for a tower require six timbers only and the other four probably served another purpose, possibly in connection with the revetting on the side walls of the gate passage.

6 Turrets. a. 18a (Wallhouses East); b. 52a (Banks East).
   Scale 1 in. = 36 ft (1:432)

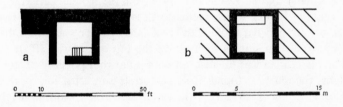

He emphasizes that, apart from this feature found only at one milecastle, the plans of the north and south gates of the milecastles were the same and he therefore suggests that both gates were surmounted by a tower.

The mile-long gap between fortlets was broken by two observation towers usually called turrets. The turrets were therefore one-third of a Roman mile apart, but unlike the milecastles they were of stone whether on the stone or the turf wall. They were about 20 feet square and recessed about 6 feet into the thickness of the stone wall. The turret was entered by a door in the south wall and to one side of this door, in the stone-wall turret, is usually found a stone platform. Four or five steps, where they survive, led on to the platform, which presumably formed the base or support for a means of access to the first floor, and the wall top. It was long considered that access was by a timber ladder, but in the most recent discussion of the problem Mr R. L. Bellhouse suggests a timber stair. In the turf-wall turrets no precisely comparable platforms have been found but most of these turrets contain a low stone dais, similar to the platforms but without any steps, beside the north wall. It has been suggested that this served as a raised bench where the soldier could eat his food and unroll his bedding clear of the filth which seems to have covered the floors of most turrets. In these towers Mr Bellhouse argues that access to the wall top was gained by a ladder propped up against the back of the turf wall. This seems unlikely: if a ladder was used on the turf wall why not also on the stone wall? It is more probable that access to the first floor was by similar means in both types of turrets. In one turf-wall turret, 51a, a rough stone base in the south-west corner probably served as a base for a stair or ladder to the upper floor, while in others this must have rested on the floor. The Rudge Cup and the Amiens Skillet, vessels in bronze from the Roman period with a running border which seems to depict the Wall, suggest that the towers had flat roofs with crenellated parapets and hint that they stood two storeys high above the top of the wall (Plate 9). The turret then was finished off with a flat roof possibly of stone slabs, though tiles found at some turrets suggest a low peaked roof. A height of 28 feet for the tower based on a width to height ratio of two to three has been suggested. Thus the elevated observation post would have been some 13 feet above the wall top. This seems very little gain in height for the extra effort of constructing a tower and, bearing in mind also the slight evidence from the 'souvenir' vessels, it may be considered that the turrets were somewhat higher than 28 feet. This would have caused no difficulty to Roman engineering skill and would not have placed an undue strain on the foundations.

The turrets, besides providing regular observation posts, furnished shelter for the soldiers manning the Wall. In some turrets special arrangements may have been made for sleeping, though in most cases the soldiers – if indeed they stayed overnight at the turrets – may have slept on the first floor. Nearly all turrets contain a hearth on the ground floor, where the soldiers would be able to cook their food and keep warm, and some a small water tank set into the ground. The turrets had one or more windows, their presence only recognized by the discovery of window glass at certain sites.

The Purpose of Hadrian's Wall

The milecastles and turrets provided the only accommodation for the soldiers on the Wall, for the original scheme included no forts on the line of the Wall. It must therefore be presumed that the forts already in existence behind the Wall on the Stanegate and on the south banks of the Tyne and Solway were to be kept in use. As mentioned earlier, the Wall was simply an adaptation of the system of frontier control based on those forts.

This plan for Hadrian's Wall provided for the separation of the barbarians from the Romans, spoken of by Hadrian's biographer, by creating a continuous barrier. Surveillance over the ground north of the Wall would be exercised from the turrets and milecastle towers, so that attempts at unauthorized crossing of the barrier by raiding parties and the like could be foreseen and prevented. More serious trouble would be dealt with by signalling, or sending a runner, back to summon aid from the forts on the line of the Stanegate up to two miles to the south. There was no point in signalling along the Wall since no milecastles had sufficient troops to deal with a major attack. The turrets therefore were watchtowers rather than signal-towers.

The purpose of the barrier was to control movement, not to prevent it, as the liberal provision of gateways demonstrates. Civilians, whether merchants, local farmers moving their cattle and sheep or simply local people visiting relatives on the other side of the Wall, would be allowed through the gateways, though only presumably when they had satisfied the guards of their peaceable intentions and on payment of customs dues. The regulations known for the Rhine frontier, already referred to, lay down that the frontier can only be crossed, unarmed, under guard and after paying a fee.

So many gates were provided that travellers had to walk no more than half a mile along the Wall to the nearest crossing point. But the gates were also provided to allow troops to move easily through the Wall to deal with an attack from the north as well as conduct the more humdrum day-to-day patrolling. Not least the lavish provision of gates must have facilitated the maintenance of the wall and ditch. Lavish is the word, for there is a clear overprovision of gates and there is something artificial about their regular, even over-regular, spacing which led to mile-castles and turrets being built in ludicrous positions on a steep hillside or with an almost precipitous drop immediately outside the north gate. This smacks of over-systematic planning, probably done at some distance, presumably by Hadrian himself, with little attention to local topography.

Each milecastle contained one or two barrack-blocks to accommodate the men who guarded the gateways, controlled the traffic and manned the north tower. It is difficult to be sure how many men might have been stationed at each milecastle. Only six milecastles have been completely excavated. Four contained a small two-roomed barrack-block and the two others two larger four-roomed buildings. The two-roomed unit is roughly equal in size to a normal *contubernium* or double-room (the old tent unit) for eight men in a full-sized barrack-block in a fort. Some mile-castles may therefore have been garrisoned by only eight men, but others by four times that number, thirty-two men. Each turret and milecastle tower would have required a minimum of six men to maintain a constant watch so the soldiers manning the turrets on either side of a milecastle with sleeping accommodation for only eight could not on present evidence have slept at the mile-castle. In fact the turret offered only slightly less space per man, if six be taken as the complement, than the milecastle barrack. Certainly the hearths associated with cooking-pots and animal bones in the turrets demonstrate that they cooked there. Even so eight men would hardly be sufficient to carry out all the necessary duties at a milecastle, including the guarding of the gate. There may have been as many as twelve if the men coming off duty simply took the sleeping places of the men relieving them. A parallel for this can be found in a marching camp, where only eight tents were pitched for the ten tent-parties, because two *contubernia* were on duty at any given time.

It is usually presumed that troops also patrolled the wall top; indeed this has been seen as the major activity of the soldiers and the primary means of observation. In fact there is no evidence for this type of patrolling on the Wall; it is not only unattested but appears impossible on other frontiers where there was no provision of an elevated sentry walk – such frontiers were either timber palisades or narrow stone walls. The most that can be said safely is that it is possible that the top of the wall was flat and could be patrolled, and that a parapet may have been supplied to protect such patrols. The Rudge Cup and the Amiens Skillet do not positively indicate that the Wall had a parapet. Some stones found at Cawfields have been interpreted as being from a crenellated parapet. Crenellation is the most convenient way of combining observation and protection, and was used by the Romans, as is shown by standing remains and by Trajan's Column. There is evidence for a parapet on the wall of the legionary fortress at York. On the turf wall the parapet was presumably of timber and, owing to the vast quantities of timber required, probably consisted of rough unseasoned posts and interwoven wattles. Patrolling of the wall top could usefully supplement observation from the towers, particularly in mist or at night, and help to deal with observed unauthorized attempts to cross the Wall.

R. G. Collingwood pointed out long ago that the wall top did not serve as a fighting platform but as this idea constantly re-emerges his arguments bear repeating. The wall top, allowing for a parapet about 2 feet wide, would vary in width from 8 to 4 Roman feet. There was scarcely room to pass behind a man fighting from the wall top, and the only access points to bring up reinforcements or remove wounded men were milecastles and turrets, some 540 yards apart. The Romans only fought from behind the shelter of walls as a last resort and developed no specialized weapons for fighting in this way until the changed conditions of the fourth century. There was no provision on the Wall for enfilading fire from projecting towers. Naturally there was no provision for artillery on the Wall, neither on the wall top itself nor at turrets. The Roman army was primarily intended to fight in the open and would if possible move out to engage the enemy long before the Wall was reached.

This army would, of course, come in the first instance from the forts immediately behind the Wall on the Stanegate; further support could be provided by the units stationed in the forts in the hinterland on the main roads which led to the Wall. The regular auxiliary units, infantry *cohortes* and cavalry *alae*, stationed at these forts might also have provided garrisons for the milecastles and turrets. If so they would have needed regular reliefs and the sending-out of men on such detached duties is regularly attested in Roman military documents, including some almost contemporary ones. A hundred years later soldiers from the unit garrisoning Dura on the Euphrates were sent out to garrison out-stations for three years and more. On the other hand the milecastle- and turret-men may have been members of a frontier militia specially raised for this purpose or drawn from the irregular units or *numeri* who may have garrisoned small forts on the Stanegate under Trajan. The finds from the mile-castles and turrets have been cited as evidence for and against the view that the men garrisoning them were of lower quality than the men of the *alae* and *cohortes*. No evidence has ever been found for the existence of a separate force, which supports the theory that these troops were drawn from the units behind the Wall.

The Cumberland Coast

Although the Wall itself ended at Bowness-on-Solway the system of control was extended westwards along the Cumberland coast. A chain of milefortlets (milecastles) and towers (turrets), very similar to those on the Wall itself, has been traced for 26 miles along the coast, and they may have continued for 40 miles in all to St Bees Head. There is no wall here; the sea is sufficient barrier in itself. The milefortlets, provided with only one entrance, do not act as gateways, but they do provide accommodation, though very little is known of this, and, with the towers, continue the look-out system. The milefortlets had ramparts of turf and were apparently about the same size as the milecastles with one exception, milefortlet 5, which measured 130 by 95 feet internally,

7 Cumberland coast structures. a. milefortlet 22 (Brownrigg); b. turret
15a (Bank Mill). Scale 1 in. = 36 ft (1:432)

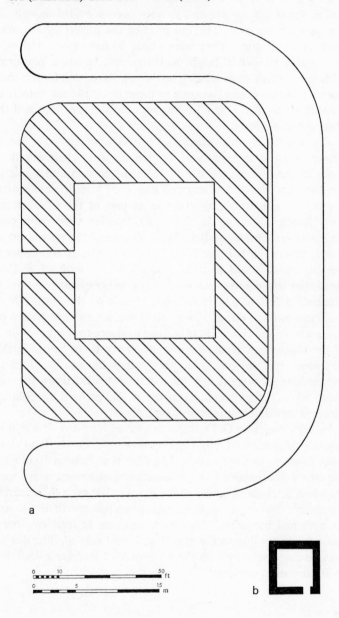

about three times the norm. The barracks were probably of timber and in some fortlets hearths have been discovered; a timber tower usually appears to have been provided though not always over the gate. The towers, like the turrets on the Wall itself, were of stone. They were about 20 feet square and were presumably similar in height to the turrets. In some, platforms with four or five steps leading to the top have been found; their purpose was no doubt the same as those in the turrets, namely to provide a base for a stair leading up onto the first floor and the observation platform.

This system of milefortlets and towers incorporated a fort at Maryport, itself apparently of Trajanic or early Hadrianic date, some 23 miles down the coast. The structures on either side of the fort were clearly laid out and measured from it, demonstrating the prior existence of the site as part of the Cumberland coast frontier defences. Evidently the frontier works were continued as far west as St Bees Head to control the movement of people across the Solway. What is in mind here is not seaborne assault, which could hardly be restricted to north of St Bees Head, but traffic across the estuary, probably of some antiquity. Similarly a fort was built at South Shields on the south side of the Tyne estuary, either now or shortly after, to keep an eye on the mouth of the river. There is some evidence too that the whole of the south bank of the Tyne from Newcastle to South Shields was supervised by one or more small posts, possibly fortlets, but nothing to suggest that the system extended down the east coast, where the geographical situation, and perhaps the political too, was very different from that on the west.

In 1975 Professor G. D. B. Jones located from the air a pair of parallel ditches apparently running down the Cumberland coast from Bowness to Cardurnock. The ditches were from 100 to 150 feet apart and enclosed the milefortlets and towers. They were less than 5 feet wide and 3 feet deep, smaller even than marching camp ditches, though in one place the north ditch was strengthened by stakes. They were recut on at least two occasions, probably due to the gravel and sand subsoil. The ditches may be contemporary with the first phase of Hadrian's Wall, but their purpose is unclear.

The Outpost Forts

The three outpost forts north of the Wall at Bewcastle, Netherby and Birrens were also apparently built at this time. Their purpose was not to give advance warning of an impending attack on the Wall – that could be done by scouts – but more likely to guard territory, presumably Brigantian, isolated from the rest of the province by the construction of the Wall. The discovery of a dedication to the goddess Brigantia, the personification of the tribe, at Birrens strongly suggests that this fort lay within, or on the very boundary of, the tribal territory. These forts had become necessary because the Wall would hinder assistance from units to the south. If this territory was not Brigantian the forts are difficult to account for unless Rome was directly interested in this area. It seems probable that they were built at this time, for a special road through the Wall was provided at milecastle 50 TW, presumably to Bewcastle. If the outpost forts were a later addition the road would have passed through the Wall at the neighbouring fort of Birdoswald.

The New Forts on the Wall

Before this simple plan for a wall from Newcastle upon Tyne to Bowness-on-Solway, a regular series of milecastles and turrets from Newcastle to St Bees Head and three outpost forts had been completed a major modification was made. This was the abandonment of the forts immediately behind the Wall and the construction of new forts on the Wall line. At the same time, or shortly after, it was also decided to construct an earthwork, known since the time of the Venerable Bede as the Vallum, behind the Wall all the way from Newcastle to Bowness.

When work was suspended the stone wall had been completed from Newcastle westwards for eighteen Roman miles to the Portgate, where Dere Street passed through the Wall, and work was proceeding between Portgate and the North Tyne and from the Irthing eastwards to turret 36b on the site of Housesteads. The turf wall had certainly been constructed in the Birdoswald area and, though evidence for the situation elsewhere is lacking, it may have been almost complete. Work was broken off so

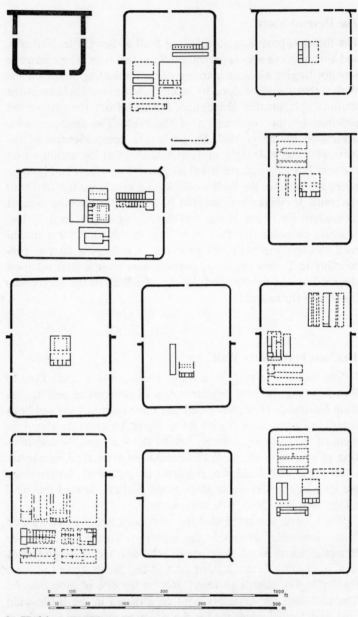

8 Hadrian's Wall forts, Hadrianic plans (later buildings are omitted).
From top left to bottom right: Drumburgh, Birdoswald, Great Chesters;
Housesteads, Carrawburgh; Chesters, Rudchester, Halton Chesters;
Benwell, Wallsend, South Shields. Scale 1 in. = 400 ft (1:4800)

abruptly that sections of wall were left standing to a variety of heights and the decision came so soon that two of the new forts were virtually complete under the governorship of A. Platorius Nepos, who began the original plan (see Fig. 15c).

The new forts varied in size from 3·35 to 9·32 acres and were all built for whole auxiliary units. The forts on the stone wall, together with Birdoswald, seem to have been constructed in stone, though undoubtedly many of the internal buildings would have been of timber on stone sill walls, and those on the turf wall of turf and timber.

The Wall forts, wherever local topography allowed, were positioned astride the Wall. This enabled three of the four main twin-portal gates to open north of the Wall. It seems clear that the main purpose of this change was to allow unrestricted access for major forces to the north. Hitherto the troops had to march a mile or two up to the Wall and then pass through a relatively narrow milecastle gateway before they could come to grips with the enemy the Wall got in the way of effective army manoeuvres. Each fort astride the Wall now had the equivalent of six milecastle gateways through the Wall. This decision was not undertaken lightly for it led to the infilling of stretches of ditch, the dismantling of already constructed wall, turrets and milecastles, the abandonment of at least nine existing forts and the construction of fourteen or fifteen new forts on the Wall and Cumberland Coast. It also reduced the usefulness of the milecastles and turrets already built and those completed or built later. The army clearly viewed with concern the disadvantage under which it suffered in the original plan.

The provision of forts astride the Wall was an experiment to meet an unprecedented situation. When most of the forts had been completed it was discovered that they did not need to project from the line of the Wall itself. The final forts to be built, Great Chesters and Carrawburgh, were simply attached to the rear of the Wall.

The defects of the original plan must have become most apparent in the east where the stone wall had been carried from Newcastle almost to the North Tyne before the decision was taken to put the forts on the Wall. The fort at Whickham, Washing Well, and any others which may have existed east of

Corbridge, were separated by the river Tyne from the Wall and by both from effective action further to the north. The forts on the Wall in this sector were built early, although they involved the biggest destruction of already constructed wall and ditch. In the central sector the Stanegate forts, with no river in the way and a curtain wall hardly begun, continued to function effectively and the building of new forts was delayed for some time.

The forts were relatively evenly spaced along the Wall with no special regard for strong or weak points. This emphasizes that they are only placed on the Wall for convenience; they are not an intimate part of the Wall complex nor the homes of frontier police. Rather they are the bases for an army force which could operate at short notice well up to the Forth–Clyde line (see Fig. 15d).

Table 2   The spacing of forts on Hadrian's Wall

Forts	Wall mile	Distance between forts
South Shields	–	
		c. $5\frac{1}{2}$
Wallsend	0	
		$6\frac{1}{3}$
Benwell	$6\frac{1}{3}$	
		7
Rudchester	$13\frac{1}{3}$	
		8
Halton Chesters	$21\frac{1}{3}$	
		6
Chesters	$27\frac{1}{3}$	
		$9\frac{1}{3}$
Housesteads	$36\frac{2}{3}$	
		$6\frac{1}{3}$
Great Chesters	43	
		$6\frac{1}{3}$
Birdoswald	$49\frac{1}{3}$	
		$7\frac{1}{3}$
Castlesteads	$56\frac{2}{3}$	
		9
Stanwix	$65\frac{2}{3}$	
		6
Burgh-by-Sands	$71\frac{2}{3}$	
		$8\frac{1}{3}$
Bowness-on-Solway	80	

It would seem that the original plan was for twelve forts equally spaced at intervals of $7\frac{1}{3}$ Roman miles. This was varied to allow for forts close to the river crossings on the line of the Wall at Chesters, Birdoswald and Stanwix. The spacing between

Wallsend and Chesters is reasonably regular, the large gap between Chesters and Housesteads (in its proper position) being plugged by a fort at Carrawburgh added after the construction of the Vallum. The space between Housesteads and the next river crossing, Birdoswald, was neatly halved by Great Chesters. Stanwix is almost at the position it should be if the forts were equally spaced. Castlesteads should have been situated halfway between Birdoswald and Stanwix but perhaps its position, a very odd one behind the Wall line, was dictated by a pre-existing fort. Finally Burgh-by-Sands is not quite halfway between Stanwix and Bowness, because, like Bowness itself and the later fort of Drumburgh, it avoids a marshland site.

The forts on the Cumberland coast followed a different pattern. Maryport already existed. Beckfoot and Moresby were then added to provide forts some twelve miles, about a day's march, apart. Burrow Walls, Mr Gillam has suggested, was not built till the fourth century.

It has been suggested that the forts which projected north of the Wall were cavalry forts, the infantry being content with only one twin-portal gate north of the Wall. However, it seems preferable to assume that all forts were intended to lie astride the Wall if possible. Examination of the size and ground plans of the forts, in conjunction with the slight epigraphic evidence, suggests that there were only two cavalry units on the Wall line (at Stanwix and possibly at Benwell), three infantry units (at Housesteads, Great Chesters and Birdoswald), while the other forts were garrisoned by mixed units of infantry and cavalry, *cohortes equitatae*. The three wholly infantry units were placed in the centre of the Wall furthest from the two main roads to the north, Dere Street passing through the Wall at the Portgate, and the road up Annandale crossing the Wall at Stanwix. The wholly cavalry and part-cavalry units were grouped round these two roads; it would appear that the cavalry could rapidly combine to form two forces of about 1000 men each in support of a substantial infantry force to deal with all but the most serious threat from the north. In peacetime the cavalry would presumably patrol at long distance while the infantry would be more concerned with the area immediately in front of the Wall. The largest cavalry unit and the most important fort on the whole Wall was placed at Stanwix

in the centre of the whole frontier complex including the
Cumberland coast. The commander of this unit would have been
the most senior on the Wall.

Nine, possibly more, of the sixteen new forts between South
Shields and Moresby replaced existing forts immediately behind
the Wall. However, the 'Stanegate' unit may not have moved
simply to the nearest fort, for Halton Chesters was not occupied

Table 3 The suggested garrisons of the Hadrian's Wall forts
(see Appendix 2)

Fort	Acreage	Garrison
South Shields	5	*ala Sabiniana* (?)
Wallsend	4	*cohors quingenaria equitata* (?)
Benwell	5·6	*ala quingenaria* (??)
Rudchester	4·5	*cohors quingenaria equitata*
Halton Chesters	4·3	*cohors quingenaria equitata*
Chesters	5·75	*cohors milliaria*
Carrawburgh	3·9	*cohors quingenaria equitata* (?)
Housesteads	5	*cohors milliaria peditata*
Great Chesters	3·36	*cohors VI Nerviorum quingenaria peditata*
Carvoran	3·6	*cohors I Hamiorum quingenaria peditata*
Birdoswald	5·33	*cohors I Tungrorum milliaria peditata* (?)
Castlesteads	3·75 (?)	*cohors quingenaria peditata* (??)
Stanwix	9·32	*ala Petriana milliaria*
Burgh-by-Sands	4·9	*cohors quingenaria peditata* or *milliaria peditata* (?)
Drumburgh	2	(??)
Bowness-on-Solway	7	*cohors milliaria equitata* (?)
Beckfoot	2·55	*cohors quingenaria peditata*
Maryport	5·8	*cohors I Hispanorum quingenaria equitata*
Moresby	3·6	*cohors quingenaria equitata* (?)

Total garrison of Hadrian's Wall:
Primary forts on Wall: 8800 men.
Primary forts on Wall and Cumberland Coast: 10,500 men.
All forts: 11,600 men.

by the *cohors milliaria equitata* which abandoned Corbridge. The 'fort decision' probably led to a reappraisal of the tactical position of many army units in the Wall area. Moreover, new units would have to be found for the seven additional forts. Presumably these would be withdrawn from stations in the Pennines and Wales, where several forts were abandoned about this time.

9   North England in the Hadrianic period (about 130). The open squares indicate that occupation at this time is not certain

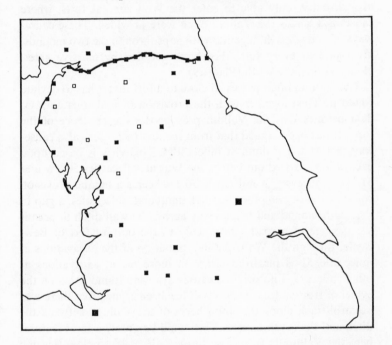

The Vallum

The decision to construct the Vallum was contemporary with or immediately post-dated the decision to move the forts up onto the Wall line. It cannot have been taken earlier as it would have reduced army movements to absurdity, while the relationship of the wall and the Vallum in certain places suggests that they were almost contemporary. The Vallum consists of a flat-bottomed ditch 20 feet wide and 10 deep with two mounds, 20 feet wide, one on either side, set back 30 feet from the lip of the ditch (Plate 1). Thus a cleared area 120 feet across was provided along the rear of the Wall which could not be crossed unwittingly or unobserved.

The Vallum was evidently a device to ensure the security of the Wall from the rear. The milecastles and turrets had been particularly vulnerable but now the population of the province, previously allowed to approach the Wall unhindered, were kept at a distance, only able to enter the Wall zone at forts, where causeways across the Vallum ditch were provided. These causeways of undug earth, together with gaps through the two mounds, are found at every fort; they were guarded by massive gates, closed against the south (Plate 29).

The Vallum often passes so close to a fort that it has to deviate round it. This, together with the provision of undug causeways, demonstrates that the Vallum presupposes the existence of the forts. It has been argued that from the first there were also causeways across the Vallum at milecastles. This view is based upon excavations carried out before the War at milecastles 50 TW and 51. The causeway at milecastle 50 TW seems a unique provision combined with two other features unique at milecastles, a gap in the south mound and a causeway across the wall ditch to permit the passage of a road, presumably to the outpost fort of Bewcastle, through the Wall; the interpretation of the excavations at milecastle 51 is far from clear. In more recent excavations at other milecastles no original causeways were found. Also on the evidence from milecastle 50 TW it has been argued that there was a patrol-track along the south berm of the Vallum, between the ditch and the south mound. This could be purely a local feature; here the Vallum is very close to the milecastle, so close that the north mound of the Vallum is omitted to the east of the milecastle, all the upcast being placed on the south mound. It seems unlikely that the track was normally on the south berm, particularly as there are no original causeways at milecastles 23, 30 and 42. More probably the fort causeways with their great guarded gateways were intended as the only access from the south to a track along the north berm, with the ditch as protection. Patrols and convoys on a south berm track would be separated by the Vallum ditch from troops on the Wall. Unbarred milecastle causeways make little sense alongside the gateways on the fort causeways, as the forts themselves needed no special protection. The gateways did not protect the forts but controlled access to the area between the Vallum ditch and the Wall, including the track along the north berm.

The track along the north berm would not only be used by army patrols, if these were considered necessary, but also by civilians. It seems unlikely that they would be allowed through the forts themselves, especially if they were driving their flocks, but after crossing the Vallum at the fort causeway they would be directed along the track on the north berm to a milecastle where they could pass through the Wall itself. Supplies for the milecastle garrisons would come by the same route; it is interesting that the road later provided along the Wall frequently ran along the north mound of the Vallum.

The Vallum reduced the number of crossing points through the Wall from an original seventy-eight or so to about fifteen, thereby greatly increasing the army's control over the movement of people. The Vallum also presupposes that resentment of the Wall and danger to it were coming from the south. Some incident may have made this obvious. The movement of the forts up on to the Wall line may suggest that free action by major forces north of the Wall had become a necessity. Such a large amount of work is unlikely to have been taken on simply from a desire to be more prepared for trouble. It is unfortunate that there is no more evidence as to where this possible trouble was coming from and how it was caused. Clearly, however, the task of Hadrian's Wall was proving more complicated than had been first visualized.

Other Modifications

Both the fort and Vallum decisions had an effect on the milecastles. It has been suggested that they now were used as sallyports, to surround an enemy force and trap it against the Wall. But the idea of penning an enemy against an obstacle is contrary to Roman military thought and practice; indeed it is officially proscribed in two surviving military manuals, since the enemy with nowhere to flee would fight all the harder, while the enemy could even foresee this possibility and turn the plan against the Romans. It was after all presumably the inadequacies of the milecastle gateways that had led to the siting of forts on the Wall. It is moreover unlikely that much action would take place immediately in front of the Wall; the army would try to deal with an attack before it got that far. More likely the milecastles continued to provide accommodation for the troops manning the Wall, like the fortlets on the Cumberland coast. The milecastle towers and the turrets presumably continued to act as watchtowers, though with reduced importance, but they now reported their observations to the forts on the Wall; certainly the system of milecastles and turrets was completed without apparent modification.

Work on the milecastles and turrets seems to have continued while the forts were being constructed, but a further modification was made to the Wall. The stone wall had been designed 10 Roman feet wide. It was incomplete when the decision to build the forts was taken. When nearly all the milecastles and turrets were completed but before work on the curtain had recommenced it was decided to narrow the wall. The new gauge is often stated to be 8 Roman feet thick, but narrower gauges are also attested. It seems as if working parties were allowed to complete the wall between 6 and 8 feet thick. This decision presumably speeded up the work, put well behind schedule by the building of the forts. Its value now lies in the clue it gives as to which work was done before the decision to build the forts, which after.

A number of minor modifications to the Wall remain to be noted. First, there is the extension of the Wall from Newcastle to Wallsend in narrow gauge, with a fort at Wallsend, but no Vallum to the rear. Presumably the river was considered to serve the purpose of the Vallum. A new fort was also added to the Wall at Carrawburgh, to fill the extra-long gap between Chesters and Housesteads, while right at the end of Hadrian's reign the fort of Carvoran just behind the Wall was rebuilt in stone. Also part of the turf wall was replaced in stone, probably towards the end of the reign. A start was evidently made at the Irthing and the first five miles west, up to about 54a, were completed. It may be, as has recently been suggested, that work was brought to a halt by the death of Hadrian in 138 and the decision to reoccupy Scotland. For part of these five miles the Wall was rebuilt on a new alignment. From 49 to 51 the new stone wall diverges from its predecessor to abut the north wall of Birdoswald fort leaving the two main side gates, previously north of the turf wall, behind the line of the new stone wall. This realignment may have been to provide more space behind the Wall at Birdoswald, for the fort sits uncomfortably close to the steep valley of the river Irthing; it was made possible by the realization that forts need not project to the north once they were placed on the line of the Wall – neither of the late forts of Great Chesters or Carrawburgh projects.

Hadrian, Nepos and Britain

The general survey of the building of Hadrian's Wall is now complete but it is only half the story, for a combination of archaeological and documentary evidence allows its construction to be described in much greater detail. Before proceeding to examine this it is necessary to look at the evidence.

Some of the archaeological clues which help us to work out the sequence of the building of the Wall have been mentioned. They include the filling of ditches; dismantling of already-built wall, turrets and milecastles in order to build forts; the Vallum's divergences round forts and its causeways of undug earth; and the fact that the stone wall was started in broad gauge and completed in a narrower gauge. This provides a sequence of building but gives no actual dates or timing.

The crucial evidence is supplied by the governor who was Hadrian's friend and chosen by him, it seems, to build his Wall, Aulus Platorius Nepos. He came to Britain not long before 17 July 122, for an auxiliary soldier discharged by the previous governor of Britain, Pompeius Falco, received a certificate of privileges, a diploma, with that date; on it Nepos is named as governor. The lapse of time between discharge and the certifying of the copy would be a matter of months, no more. Nepos came from the governorship of Lower Germany and it was from Germany that Hadrian came to Britain, again probably in 122. A third important movement from Lower Germany to Britain took place about this time, the transfer of the legion VI Victrix. As it worked on the Wall in the first full season of building the voyage may also have taken place in 122 or perhaps 123. Voyage it certainly was, and the altars to Neptune and Ocean at Newcastle erected by the legion suggest that it was dispatched from Lower Germany directly to the Tyne estuary, not to the legionary fortress at York. It is certainly tempting to connect all three movements from Germany to Britain and place them in the same year.

Hadrian had come to Britain from Germany, where he appears to have initiated an artificial barrier, a timber palisade, apparently the first of its type in Roman history. There had been a frontier defensive system on the Taunus, Wetterau and Odenwald sections of the German frontier from the time of Domitian. This was most developed on the Taunus and Wetterau. Here the frontier system consisted of a road linking turf and timber forts. Also along the road were timber towers some 540 to 650 yards apart. This is not so dissimilar from the contemporary Gask Ridge system in Perthshire where the watch towers, often rather closer together than in Germany, lay along – and on either side of – the road leading north from Ardoch to Bertha. Under Trajan some new forts were built on the Taunus and Wetterau and fortlets were added to the frontier. The startling new development under Hadrian probably took place during the visit of the emperor to the area in 121–2. The reign of Hadrian saw the construction of such barriers not only in Upper Germany, Raetia and Britain but also perhaps in Africa, where the frontier complex known as the Fossatum Africae was possibly built at this time. Hadrian's Wall, however, is the best known, best preserved, and most explored of all the artificial barriers of Hadrian's reign or any other.

Most major modifications to the frontiers during Hadrian's reign seem to have followed, and presumably resulted from, the emperor's visit to the frontier region. Thus in 122 he came to Britain to solve the problem of the British frontier, perhaps even with the intention of building an artificial barrier. His friend Platorius Nepos was brought over from Lower Germany to share the task and the glory; he is the only governor to be named after Hadrian on inscriptions from the Wall. The summoning of the

Sixth Legion from Vetera, the nearest occupied legionary base to Britain, may have been specifically for the Wall project, though Britain may in any case have been under-garrisoned if the Ninth had already left, as seems most probable.

Mr C. E. Stevens has, however, suggested that the Wall was actually begun before Hadrian set foot in Britain. He considers that Nepos' predecessor, Pompeius Falco, had been instructed to put the Wall in hand. Hadrian, on arrival, saw the basic weakness of the plan, and modified it by insisting that the forts be placed astride the line of the Wall, not left to the south of it in their old positions on the Stanegate. Two things argue against this theory. First, the timetable of Wall building suggests that work did not start until 122, or even 123. Secondly, it seems unlikely that the emperor's presence was necessary to authorize the fort decision. The greater decision was surely that to build the Wall. There is much to be said for the convergence of emperor, governor and legion in 122 to take, or implement, that decision though it may be that the legion was only summoned when the Wall decision had been taken. Finally it makes better sense for the conception of Hadrian's Wall to follow that of the German palisade, each beginning under the eye of the emperor. Hadrian had never been to Britain and was unlikely to instigate so radical a plan without first-hand knowledge.

Nepos was still in Britain in 124, but his governorship is unlikely to have extended beyond 126. It seems probable that but for the fort decision the Wall could have been completed within the three-year term of a normal governorship. The name of Nepos appears on inscriptions from milecastles 37, 38 and 42 in the central sector of the Wall, on – by a reasonably probable restoration – a tiny fragment of a wooden inscription from milecastle 50 on the turf wall and on inscriptions at the forts on Benwell and Halton Chesters, thus demonstrating that the fort decision was made and implemented during Nepos' governorship.

The Nature of the Evidence

To date more precisely this decision and others a new element must be introduced, an allocation of parts of the Wall system to working-gangs from different legions. This allocation can only be done because nearly the whole of the Wall is known to have been built by the three legions of the army of Britain. These were II Augusta normally based at Caerleon in South Wales, XX Valeria Victrix from Chester and the new legion VI Victrix, which now occupied the old home of IX Hispana, York. A certain amount of work was done by a detachment of the British fleet, who apparently built fort granaries at Benwell, Halton Chesters and Rudchester, and by one or more auxiliary units, who helped dig the Vallum, but they only played a small part.

Most of the work was done by the legionaries themselves, not simply under their direction. The legions contained craftsmen skilled in building, architect-engineers, surveyors, masons, carpenters, glaziers and so on, while the soldiers themselves were practised in the construction of forts and other military installations, both temporary and permanent. In one area only perhaps did help come from native levies, and that is in the carting of materials, though this is far from certain, for the Roman army also carried on its books carters and muleteers. The whole exercise was carried out by the army from the surveying of the line of the Wall through the cutting and dressing of the stone to the actual building operations.

Each legion built under the direction of its own officers to its own plans and consequently milecastles, turrets and even curtain built by each legion differed slightly. These differences can be best seen on the stone wall. Milecastles here vary in two particulars, in shape, according to whether their north–south axis is longer than their east–west axis (long axis) or shorter (short axis), and in the form of their gateways. Some gateways have one pair of responds for arches, some two. The combination of these features gives three types of milecastles. Mr R. Hunneysett has recently pointed out to us that the milecastles also vary in the position of their setting-out lines. Two legions seem to have used the internal face of the milecastle walls as their setting-out line, while the other legion used the outer face. Fortunately the two legions building long-axis milecastles used different setting-out lines so if other indications are lacking an alternative is now available.

Turrets vary in the position of their doorways, either to east or west, and in the thickness of their side walls, 4 or 3 feet. Two

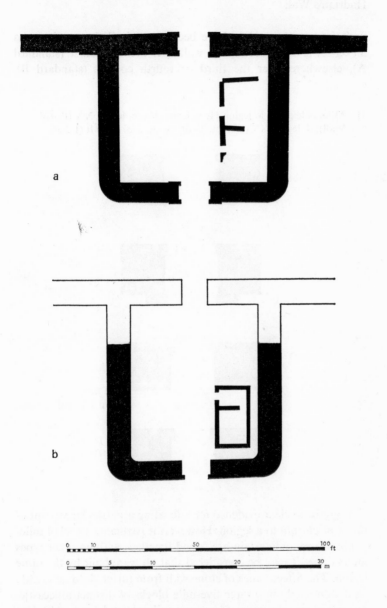

10 Milecastles. a. 37 (Housesteads) built by legion II; b. 9 (Chapel House) probably built by legion XX. For the presumed legion VI type milecastle see Fig. 5a. Scale 1 in. = 36 ft (1:432)

variations in the curtain have been recognized. In certain areas an off-set is introduced in the wall after the first course (standard A), elsewhere after the third or fourth courses (standard B).

11 Milecastle gates. a. legion II; b. legion VI; c. legion XX (Broad Wall); d. legion XX (Narrow Wall). Scale 1 in. = 20 ft (1:240)

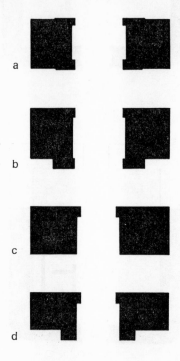

There is no clear evidence for allocating a particular variant of turret or curtain to a legion. However, if particular types of mile-castle, turret and curtain are found together, with no other types intervening, it may be considered that all were built by the same legion. The fifteen miles of stone wall from turret 7b to milecastle 22 divide neatly into three five-mile blocks of distinct milecastle, turret and curtain types. Short-axis milecastles (always with two pairs of responds) appear with broad wall turrets with east doors and standard A curtain. Long-axis milecastles with two pairs of

12 Stone Wall turrets. a. legion XX (7b); b. legion II (13a); c. legion VI
    (18a). Scale 1 in. = 36 ft (1:432)

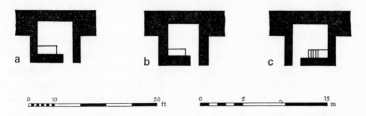

responds are found in association with narrow wall turrets with
west doors and standard B curtain, while long-axis milecastles
with one pair of responds are found together with narrow wall
turrets with east doors and standard A curtain. It seems easiest
to suppose that the legion responsible for the milecastles was
responsible for the whole five-mile stretch, building all structures
and the curtain.

13 Curtain. a. Standard A (legions II and XX); b. Standard B (legion
    VI); c. Standard C (later Hadrianic work). Scale 1 in. = 12 ft (1:156)

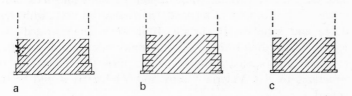

Inscriptions at certain milecastles allow the three types of
milecastles to be provisionally allocated to the three legions.
Four inscriptions from three milecastles, 37, 38 and 42, demonstrate unquestionably that the short-axis milecastle, whose gates
had two pairs of responds, was constructed by legion II Augusta.
There is an inscription of legion XX from milecastle 47. The
excavators of this milecastle considered it to be of the long-axis
type with one pair of responds and side walls of standard A construction, but their report does not eliminate the possibility of two
pairs of responds and walls of Standard B construction; in

plan the milecastle appears to be exactly the same as its neighbour milecastle 48 (Poltross Burn), which definitely has gates with two pairs of responds and walls of standard B construction (Fig. 5). An inscription from turret 33b, a narrow wall turret with an east door, records building by legion VI. If this inscription refers to the turret and belongs to the original building of the Wall this type of turret, long-axis milecastles with one pair of responds, and walls of standard A type – the supposed combination at milecastle 47 – were characteristic of legion VI. We must then assume that milecastle 47 did have two pairs of gate responds and standard B construction and that it and milecastle 48 were built by the same legion, the twentieth. This would reverse the normal allocation of milecastle types to legions VI and XX which is based on the excavators' interpretation of milecastle 47, certainly a XX Valeria Victrix milecastle. Until the status of milecastle 47 can be resolved a provisional allocation of one set of characteristics to legion VI and the other to XX must be made. The system adopted here was accepted in 1936, though the milecastle types were distinguished as long ago as 1911. According to this the twentieth legion built long-axis milecastles with one pair of responds, narrow wall turrets with east doors and standard A curtain, while legion VI built long-axis mile-castles with two pairs of responds, narrow wall turrets with west doors and standard B curtain. If it were demonstrated that legion VI did build turret 33b and milecastle 47 did have two responds and standard B side walls then the allocations of structures to XX Valeria Victrix and VI Victrix would be reversed.

14 Turf Wall turrets. a. legion XX(?) (52a); b. legion VI(?) (54a). Scale 1 in. = 36 ft (1:432)

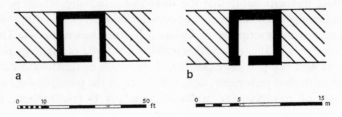

There is also some evidence for different milecastles and turrets on the turf wall. Both long-axis and short-axis milecastles are found, though lack of information prevents further analysis. Two types of turrets are also known. The variant with an east door has walls two and a half feet thick, while the other type has a west door and walls three and a half feet thick. Both types of turrets are found in conjunction with long-axis milecastles – no turret in association with a short-axis milecastle has yet been excavated. The legion which constructed long-axis milecastles and turrets with east doors and narrow walls on the stone wall, the twentieth legion, may have built similar structures on the turf wall, though no formal proof exists. If so the short-axis milecastle can be assigned to II Augusta and the turrets with broad walls and west doors to VI Victrix.

Mr R. L. Bellhouse has been able to adduce evidence for differences in the construction of milefortlets and towers on the Cumberland coast. All the known milefortlets are of the same size, if the anomalous milefortlet 5 (Cardurnock) is left to one side, and although most seem of long-axis type, a short-axis milefortlet has been inferred. Nearly all the milefortlets have entrances on the seaward side but some appear to have landward entrances. The towers vary in three ways: the footings for the walls (four types), the internal platform for the stair (three positions), and the siting of the door (either left or right, equivalent to west and east in the turrets). These differences suggest three basic tower types but much more work needs to be done before either these or the milefortlets can be allocated to legions.

It is possible to reconstruct the building programme on the stone wall, and to a lesser extent on the turf wall, by the allocation of the different types of milecastles, turrets and curtain to the three legions, and by the other evidence already cited. Before this is attempted, however, it is necessary to examine the order and method of construction of the length of wall assigned to each legion.

Construction Order and Methods

The primary task of each legion in its allotted length was to construct the milecastles and turrets, and there is some evidence

Table 4   The evidence for the allocation of work on Hadrian's Wall

Stone wall

Milecastles – 3 types
Turrets – 3 types
Curtain – 3 types

These types can be allocated as follows:

| Legion | Evidence from inscriptions | Structural evidence from: | | |
		Milecastles	Turrets	Curtain
II	Milecastles 37, 38, 42 Platorius Nepos	short axis 2 pairs responds	broad wall (4 feet) east door	A 1 course below off-set
XX (?)	Milecastle 47	long axis 1 pair responds	narrow wall (3 feet) east door	A
VI (?)		long axis 2 pairs responds	narrow wall (3 feet) west door	B 3 courses below off-set

Turf wall

Milecastles – 2 types known
Turrets – 2 types known

| Legion | Evidence from inscriptions | Structural evidence from: | |
		Milecastles	Turrets
XX	Milecastle 50 TW Platorius Nepos	long axis	narrow wall (2½ feet) east door
VI (?)		long axis (?)	broad wall (3½ feet) west door
II (?)		short axis	

that they were occupied by their garrisons as they were built. On the stone wall both milecastles and turrets were built with short wing walls ready to receive the curtain. Where the stone curtain was completed to the 10-foot gauge these wing walls are not noticeable as they are skilfully bonded to the curtain. The reduction in the thickness of the curtain, however, produced an ugly effect at the edge of the wing wall where the wall abruptly narrowed by two feet or more at a corner or 'point of reduction'. This point of reduction can be seen at both milecastles and turrets. Usually it takes the form of a vertical re-entrant extending through all the four or five feet of wall still standing but at some turrets the wing wall is so low that the narrow curtain wall rides up over it to meet the side walls of the structure. At these turrets no attempt was made to carry the wing walls up to the full height of the wall top but they were stepped down gradually to make bonding with the curtain wall easier (Plates 3 and 6).

The digging of the ditch apparently commenced while the structures were being erected; at Chesters, for example, the ditch was dug before work on the curtain was completed, but it is difficult to follow its progress in detail. One legion, VI Victrix, made a start on the curtain before it had built all its structures. XX Valeria Victrix, on the other hand, appears to have completed all its milecastles and turrets and the wall foundation before it started on the curtain. II Augusta as far as can be judged followed the same practice. Each legion divided the stretch of curtain allotted to it among its constituent cohorts and within each cohort among individual centuries. Each century, cohort and indeed legion marked both ends of its block of work by the erection of inscriptions. Sometimes all three appear on the same stone, sometimes separate stones are used. These stones are called 'centurial stones'. Since the War many of them have been found *in situ*. Unfortunately few have been found at the eastern end of the Wall, that completed before the fort decision, where there was no disruption in the work. Although more have been found in the central sector they are too few to determine just how much wall each century constructed, while there is the unknown factor of disruption introduced by the decision to build the forts. It is not even certain that the three legions were present in full strength. There is some evidence that not all cohorts were complete. Few stones recording the second, fourth, seventh and ninth cohorts of legion XX – adequate evidence for the other two legions is lacking – have been found. These are precisely the cohorts which, according to Vegetius' description of the legion's line of battle, contained the highest number of recruits. The major part of these four cohorts may have remained at the legionary fortress to train. These difficulties make it impossible to commence the study of the building of the Wall by examining the centurial stones; it is better to start with the allocation of the milecastles, turrets and curtain to the three legions.

The Building of the Wall

This evidence makes it now possible to follow in detail the building of the Wall. Assuming Hadrian, Nepos and VI Victrix arrived in Britain in 122, the decision to construct the Wall was probably taken in that year. Elaborate preparations in the way of surveying, summoning of the three legions from their respective bases and organization of the working parties and transport would have been necessary. All this may have taken weeks if not months and the building operations may therefore not have commenced until the following year. The first year's work seems to have been the construction of a short stretch of wall from milecastle 4 to about milecastle 7 with the bridge at Newcastle. The bridge would have considerably facilitated work at the east end, for the lowest bridge on the river previously was fifteen miles upstream at Corbridge. Two altars of legion VI have been found on the site of the bridge. This has been taken to imply that the legion constructed the bridge, but it is more likely that the bridge was built just before the legion arrived in Britain and they dedicated the altars to celebrate their safe arrival. There may have been time in 122 to construct this 3-mile stretch of wall and the bridge. It seems better to assign it to this year rather than assume that the surveying and other preparations took a whole year.

Another reason for postulating a short stretch of actual building in 122 is that the next stretch, from about milecastle 7 to milecastle 22, divides up fairly neatly into three legionary blocks, that is, three stretches of similar length containing the same ratio of turrets, milecastles and curtain wall. Although proof is impossible it seems reasonable that these represent a season's work for each of the legionary 'gangs', however constituted. This also accords with the completion of these sections and more under Platorius Nepos and before the change in plan.

The second season was the first full season, and included work on the stone wall, the turf wall and on the Cumberland coast. Firstly the stone wall. As already mentioned the stretch of Wall from about milecastle 7 to milecastle 22 falls neatly into three legionary blocks, each legion constructing about 5 miles of wall, with the attendant milecastles and turrets. All this stretch of Wall was completed to the broad gauge. On the turf wall there is only one recognizable legionary block, the most easterly 5 miles. Here there are long-axis milecastles and turrets with narrow walls and east doors, the hall-mark of legion XX Valeria Victrix. The next turret to the west, 54a, has broad walls and a west door, suggesting work by VI Victrix. Presumably the third block of work was done by II Augusta, and although there are no excavated structures in this length, a short-axis milecastle, 79, does fall in a comparable position on the western half of the turf wall. If each legion therefore built 5 miles of wall, as is most probable, the 31 miles of the turf wall would presumably have been divided into two three-legion blocks of 15 miles each, one three-legion block being constructed at the same time as the stretch from milecastle 7 to milecastle 22. The stone wall was built from east to west, but the turf wall may have been built from east to west, or from west to east. Progress on the Cumberland coast is much harder to determine. With no wall to construct work should have proceeded much more quickly and it is possible that half was completed in this season.

The next year will probably have seen the completion of most, if not all, of the turf wall and the Cumberland coast. On the stone wall the situation was very different. In this season there was a redistribution of the three working parties. XX Valeria Victrix continued building westwards from milecastle 22 at least as far as turret 27a, for that turret was started before Chesters fort, and had to be demolished to make way for it. They also presumably had to construct the bridge over the North Tyne at Chesters. The VI Victrix party was sent off to another major river crossing, that of the Irthing, and built eastwards from that point. Next

Table 5   The building of the stone and turf walls

Stone wall

Legion	VI	II	XX		VI	II	XX		(??)
Wall mile	49 Irthing	43	36b	27a N Tyne	22	17	12	7	4 Tyne

←——— completed by Legion XX ———→

Turf wall

Legion	II	VI(?)	XX(?)	II(?)	VI	XX	
Wall mile	80b Solway	75a	70	64b	59a	54	49 Irthing

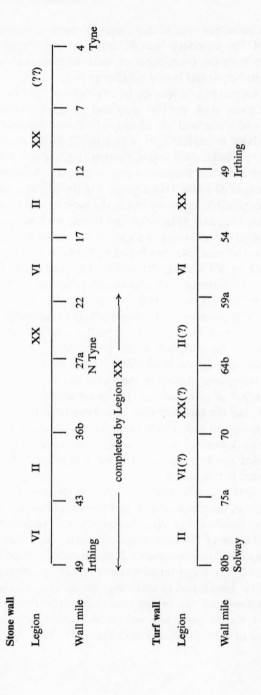

to them was II Augusta, the last structure of their allocation being turret 36b, later to be demolished to make way for Housesteads fort (the structures east of this turret are of legion XX type). It is from this phase of building that the inscriptions of Nepos at three of the milecastles come. Interestingly each legion seems to have been given a little more work to do than in the previous season, 6 miles of Wall or 5 miles and a bridge. This strengthens the supposition that 5 miles had been the allocation for the previous season. For reasons which are far from clear VI Victrix constructed two milecastles, 47 and 48, and possibly others which have not been investigated, to a larger size than those built in the previous seasons. This provided more accommodation in the fortlet, perhaps because these two particular milecastles are in the Irthing gap. However, many of the later stone milecastles built on the turf wall were larger than earlier stone milecastles and the increased size of milecastles 47 and 48 may be part of a general trend.

During the second full season, 124 on our reckoning, there was dislocation of the work. Between milecastle 22 and turret 27a, in the XX Valeria Victrix area, there are stretches of half-built or just-started broad wall, broad foundation with a narrower wall on top, a turret built to receive broad wall with broad curtain on the west side and narrow on the east, and so on. In the twelve miles eastwards from the Irthing the same phenomena recur: broad wall built, a few courses of broad wall laid, milecastles and turrets built to receive broad wall with narrow wall brought up to them. Legion XX seems to have constructed all its milecastles and turrets and the bridge over the North Tyne, probably completed laying the foundation of the curtain and built substantial sections of the curtain itself. The other two legions were well behind schedule. Legion VI had presumably erected the Irthing bridge and a very short stretch of adjacent curtain. It had begun but not finished its structures and made a start on the rest of the curtain. Legion II was even further behind. At least four of its milecastles and turrets were unbuilt while at the Housesteads milecastle, 37, only the gateway was erected; the milecastle was completed after the decision to narrow the Wall so that it was necessary to taper the north wall of the milecastle from the broad gateway to blend with the narrow curtain. Legion II seems to have done little more than lay the foundation of the curtain in places. This may have been due to the difficulties of working on the crags. The impression is that all three working parties were called away by some dramatic change of plan.

That change can hardly have been other than the decision to build the twelve new forts on the Wall. VI Victrix is attested building at Halton Chesters under Nepos while the similarity between the masonry of the II Augusta milecastle gates and the Housesteads fort gates suggests the same builder. The forts on the Wall appear to fall into two groups based on dimensions and shape; the forts of one group are longer and thinner than those of the other. Presumably VI Victrix was responsible for one group, and II Augusta for the other. XX Valeria Victrix is attested later building on the Cumberland coast. How long it took the two legions to build the twelve forts is uncertain. The task could be completed more quickly if the legions received some aid. A detachment of the British fleet was therefore drafted in to help construct certain of the fort granaries. The strength of the granary foundations in the forts of Benwell, Rudchester and Halton Chesters bears witness to the efficiency of the fleet engineers and builders, whose activities are recorded on an inscription discovered at Benwell.

Benwell and Halton Chesters were completed, or nearly so, before the departure of Nepos, that is by about 126. Great Chesters was completed in 128 or later. Wallsend ought to be earlier than Great Chesters as it projects, though like Great Chesters it is bonded in with the narrow wall. Housesteads, which is bonded in with the narrow wall on the north-west, may not be much earlier than Great Chesters, and Chesters appears to be bonded in with the narrow wall on both sides. Carrawburgh may also be bonded in with the narrow wall; it does not project and was built after the construction of the Vallum. The only fort with a more precise date is Carvoran, which was rebuilt in stone 136–8. It may have been a Stanegate fort up to the construction of Great Chesters but virtually nothing is known about its history. It may be assumed that Rudchester came early, along with Halton Chesters and Benwell. Newcastle is a problem. Little is known of the fort, and it does not fall into the spacing pattern. It could precede or follow this series; perhaps as a bridgehead fort it belonged to the first plan before the general transfer of forts to the Wall line. Even less is known about the forts in the west.

These forts, as has been stressed, were at first designed to lie astride the Wall where the land allowed. This placed them in a unique position: easy movement in and out of the fort to the north was provided by three double gates while ready contact was maintained with the province to the south by a double gate at the rear and two extra side gates. It was, however, soon realized that if a fort was actually on the Wall line fewer gates to the north were necessary. The main west gate of Halton Chesters fort, one of the first to be built on the Wall, was therefore blocked before it was completed as was, it seems, the east portal of the north gate at Housesteads, though the situation is not so clear here. Great Chesters, a primary fort but one of the last to be constructed, is completely south of, albeit still attached to, the Wall, though it could have projected. At Carrawburgh, too, the fort, a later addition to the primary series, was attached to the rear face of the curtain. A few years later when the turf wall flanking Birdoswald was rebuilt, the wall was realigned to come up to the north corners of the fort, not the south guard chambers of the side gates, demonstrating again that forts on the Wall line did not need three double gates to the north. This apparently led to the disuse and later blocking up of some gates. On the Antonine Wall all the forts were built behind the Wall, none projected.

The known structures in this uncompleted central sector of the Wall from turret 27a to the river Irthing, with one exception, conform to the milecastle and turret designs of legion XX, while inscriptions from the curtain wall in this area bear witness to the work of this legion. XX Valeria Victrix doubtless completed the construction of the Wall itself, though in the later stages it may have received some help from the other legions.

XX Valeria Victrix had between thirty-three and forty-eight structures to build – the exact number is not known – and about 20 miles of curtain. From the speed of its previous work this may have taken about four years. Certainly they were still at work in or after 128, for the curtain and the fort at Great Chesters bond together and an inscription ascribes the building of the fort to the years 128 to 138. Legion XX seems to have completed the chain of milecastles and turrets first. When most of these were built, and work was perhaps ready to start on the curtain, it was decided to reduce the thickness of the curtain from 10 Roman feet to 8 feet or less. The remaining structures and the rest of the curtain were completed at this reduced gauge, accounting for the unusual, and rather ugly, spectacle of conjoining stretches of broad and narrow wall. These points of junction are especially strange in the stretch of Wall eastwards from the river Irthing being built by VI Victrix before the fort decision. Here up to five courses of broad wall, including in places the offset course, had been laid. Instead of these dressed stones being reused in the narrow curtain they were left in position, the low broad wall forming a sort of step on the south side of the curtain. The new builders even sank new foundations for the narrow wall into the core of the existing broad wall, so deeply in places as to create a shallow gulley between the south face of the narrow wall and the top courses of the old broad wall. The narrowing of the Wall was undoubtedly to speed up work. But for the fort decision this stretch of wall from turret 27a to the Irthing could have been completed in 125; the building of the forts had added at least three seasons to the working period.

The burden of the Wall builders was further increased by the extension of the Wall 4 miles down the Tyne from Newcastle to Wallsend. On spacing considerations the new fort at Wallsend was one of the primary forts but the 4-mile length of Wall, with which the fort was bonded in, was built to the narrow gauge, probably late in the works programme. This stretch of Wall would have been nearly one year's work for one legion.

Completion of the Wall

While the forts were built and the curtain finished off the Vallum was constructed. The decision to add the Vallum was probably taken at the same time as the decision to move the forts up on to the Wall, or possibly a little later, but its construction may have proceeded at a faster rate than the building of either the forts or the curtain. In the Limestone Corner area the Wall and the Vallum are so close as to suggest that the latter was constructed first. This possibility receives some support from the fact that the fort of Carrawburgh, just a mile west of Limestone Corner, was constructed over the filled-in Vallum ditch while the fort is probably contemporary with the curtain. Also from Limestone Corner comes striking proof of the desire of the military command to complete the Vallum, for the Vallum ditch was dug for over a mile through solid rock while the Wall ditch was left unfinished. Help for the legionaries in this operation was forthcoming in this case from the *auxilia*, for an inscription from the south mound of the Vallum between turret 7b and milecastle 8 attests work by the *cohors I Dacorum*.

It is difficult to say when Hadrian's Wall was completed. Great Chesters and the adjoining stretch of curtain were not built until 128–38. The fort of Moresby on the Cumberland coast, built by XX Valeria Victrix, falls into the same period. The building of all the forts on the Cumberland coast may have been left until the completion of all, or most, of the Wall itself. Since a road was apparently provided in the first scheme from milecastle 50 TW north to Bewcastle it would appear that the outpost forts were planned from the first, though only built later. Perhaps they were to be built on the completion of the curtain but were held up by the fort decision. The last dated work on the Wall comes from the very end of Hadrian's reign. In 136/7 the fort of Carvoran, just south of the Wall three miles west of Great Chesters, was being rebuilt in stone. Either it had continued in use as a survivor from the Stanegate system or it had been abandoned only to be reoccupied towards the end of the reign. Also near the end of Hadrian's reign the rebuilding of the turf wall in stone commenced and the legions played a part in this work. The milecastles were built by VI Victrix and XX Valeria Victrix and they are all larger than the earlier stone wall milecastles, a modification probably resulting from earlier experience. Another change was the introduction of regular drains through the Wall. Hitherto these had only been placed at some points; now they were provided at regular intervals of 20 feet or so. One minor modification, started some years before when the stone curtain about milecastle 45 was being completed, was the eradication of the off-set. From now on all the curtain was built without an off-set; this particular stretch to the narrow gauge, 8 Roman feet thick.

Hadrian's Wall was being continually modified and improved throughout the life of its designer. Much of the Wall bears the imprint of that designer: the rigidity in the spacing of milecastles and turrets, the regular spacing of forts, the provision of three twin-portal gates north of the Wall for the forts, and the Vallum, another experiment not tried elsewhere. All these clearly show that the Wall was conceived by someone with little time to study the problem of the northern frontier in detail. Nevertheless Hadrian did create an enduring monument to his name and foresight.

The Wall as an Engineering Achievement

How great an achievement was Hadrian's Wall? Over a hundred years ago Collingwood Bruce supplied figures, not entirely correct ones, to an engineer of his day, Robert Rawlinson, who was used to working with navvies without the benefit of bulldozers on large engineering projects. Rawlinson produced estimates of 1,702,115 cubic yards of masonry, in his day costing £1,021,269. Each cubic yard entailed the movement of a ton of material – stone, lime and water – and this would have to be done by ox-drawn wagons.

Rawlinson reckoned each cubic yard required from quarrying to setting at the least the energy of one man per day – probably a very conservative estimate – so a force of 10,000 men would have taken 170 days to build the curtain alone, reckoned as 68 miles long, 16 feet high and 8 feet wide. The forts, milecastles and turrets were not taken into account by Rawlinson, nor were the forts on the Cumberland Coast, and the three outpost forts, whose existence was not then known. The nineteenth-century excavator could move twenty cubic yards of earth a day; Rawlinson only allowed his second-century counterpart eight cubic yards, and made no estimate of the increased labour occasioned by cutting through rocks, though compensating for this by taking no account of the lack of ditch on the crags. Seventy days was allowed for the digging of the ditch, and for the Vallum 46 days. His force of 10,000 would therefore have constructed the curtain, dug the ditch and thrown up the Vallum in 286 days. Rawlinson considered that work would be possible

15 The development of the Hadrianic frontier. a. 'Stanegate frontier';
b. Hadrian's Wall as planned; c. Progress achieved when the fort decision
was taken; d. Hadrian's Wall as completed

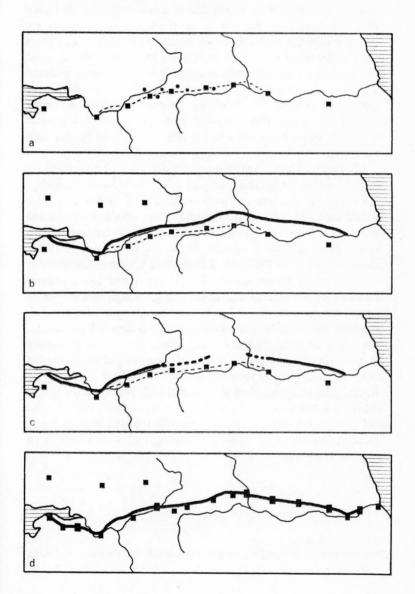

only 200 days of the year, so the operation would have been completed in a year and a half, two years allowing some leeway.

Although the stone wall was 45 miles long, not 68, and 10 feet wide, not 8, Rawlinson's estimate of a working force of 10,000 may not have been far wrong, so if the minor structures are brought into the calculations an estimate of almost three years for the first scheme may not be far out. This is remarkably close to the time which the archaeological and epigraphical material suggests. The construction of fourteen or fifteen forts must have greatly lengthened the building programme, and obtaining materials – more dressed stone and turf together with vast quantities of timber, nails and the like – must have further held up work.

Mr Hunter Davies has recently obtained from Laings a figure of £55 million for building the wall in reinforced concrete today. This was for a much narrower wall; a wall to Roman width would cost £80 million. No quotation was obtained for dressed stone, as a stone-faced wall's cost would be too astronomical to contemplate at today's prices – in 1850 a cubic yard of facing stone cost 12/-, in 1974 £10. Rawlinson's figures give some idea of the human labour involved, and the possibilities, Hunter Davies's of the size of the undertaking, though neither set of figures can be pressed too far. Bruce's specifications for Rawlinson were incorrect; Hunter Davies gives no details of his specifications. The undertaking was certainly vast, with special difficulties in providing the required quantity of water on the crags. On the other hand it must be remembered that it was not expensive for Rome. The army supplied the labour, with perhaps carting and other unskilled services imposed on the provincials. The quarries belonged to the state, or to any one with the skill to work them. Nevertheless the Wall as an engineering feat would have been notable in any age.

Table 6   The building of Hadrian's Wall

ORIGINAL SCHEME
Milecastles (and milefortlets), turrets (and towers), curtain (stone and turf), ditch

Stone Wall c. milecastle 4 – River Irthing (Willowford Bridge)

(i) c. milecastle 4–c. milecastle 7 (with bridge at Newcastle)

(iia) c. milecastle 7–milecastle 12	legion XX	3 legionary blocks
(iib) turret 12a–milecastle 17	legion II	built together
(iic) turret 17a–milecastle 22	legion VI	

(iiia) milecastle 22–turret 27a+	legion XX	3 legionary blocks built
(iiib) turret 36b–milecastle 43(?)	legion II	together under Platorius
(iiic) milecastle 43(?)–Irthing	legion VI	Nepos (122–c. 126)

This last 3-legion block had not been completed before the second scheme was started.

Turf wall River Irthing (Willowford Bridge)–turret 80b (?)

Milecastle 49–turret 53b or milecastle 54 constitute one legionary block of 15 or 16 structures, 5 miles, and it is possible that all the 96 or 97 structures on the turf wall were divided into 6 blocks of 16 structures, that is two 3-legion blocks. It is not possible to say whether the turf wall was built east to west or west to east, but the eastern end was completed under Platorius Nepos.

Provisional Scheme

(ia) River Irthing–milecastle 54	legion XX	3 legionary blocks built
(ib) turret 54a–turret 59a	legion VI	together under Platorius
(ic) turret 59b–turret 64b	legion II	Nepos (122–c. 126)

(iia) milecastle 65–milecastle 70	legion XX(?)	3 legionary blocks
(iib) turret 70a–turret 75a	legion VI(?)	built together
(iic) turret 75b–turret 80b	legion II	

Cumberland Coast turret 80b(?)–milefortlet 40(?)

This system of milefortlets and towers is probably part of the original scheme. Differences have been noted in the structures but it is not possible to make out any pattern yet.

Forts

(i) The auxiliary units were to be left in the forts behind the Wall on the Stanegate.

(ii) On the Cumberland Coast Maryport was probably occupied and continued to be held.

(iii) The outpost forts probably fall into the original scheme, for a road was provided now from milecastle 50 TW north to Bewcastle. However, they may not have been built till later: Bewcastle was possibly built between 124 and 130, Netherby and probably Birrens before 128.

(iv) A fort may have been planned (and built) at Newcastle to protect the new bridge.

(v) The fort at South Shields may have been planned (and built) now though it probably forms part of the second scheme.

Hadrian's Wall

SECOND SCHEME

Forts were moved up from the Stanegate onto the line of the Wall and the Vallum added to the south of the Wall.

Forts

(i) Primary forts: Wallsend, Benwell, Rudchester, Halton Chesters, Chesters, Housesteads, Great Chesters, Birdoswald, Castlesteads, Stanwix, Burgh-by-Sands, Bowness-on-Solway. Started under Platorius Nepos (122–*c.* 126).

II Augusta was probably responsible for: South Shields, Rudchester, Housesteads, Great Chesters.

VI Victrix was probably responsible for: Benwell, Halton Chesters, Chesters, Birdoswald and probably also Stanwix and Bowness.

These forts were probably all intended to project north of the Wall wherever possible. Not completed until 128–38.

(ii) The forts on the Cumberland Coast may also be primary forts: Beckfoot, Maryport (already occupied), Moresby (built by XX 128–38).

Vallum

The decision to construct the Vallum was contemporary with or postdated the decision to build the forts, though the actual construction of the Vallum may have preceded some or all of the forts. It diverges round Benwell, Halton Chesters, Birdoswald and Castlesteads, crosses the site of Carrawburgh, excludes Carvoran and ends at Newcastle not Wallsend.

Stone wall

Completion of milecastle 22 to Willowford Bridge over the Irthing by XX, with some help, not finished before 128–38. After most of the milecastle gates and the turrets had been built in this sector the gauge of the Stone Wall was reduced from 10 Roman feet (broad) to 8 Roman feet or less (narrow), and the remaining structures and curtain completed. (Turret 44b is the only narrow wall structure known.)

FURTHER MODIFICATIONS

The Wall was extended eastwards for 4 miles to Wallsend in narrow gauge.

Before all the primary forts were completed it was decided that it was not necessary for the forts to project north of the Wall. Great Chesters was therefore built behind the Wall (128–38).

Carrawburgh added behind the Wall.

Carvoran rebuilt in stone 136–7.

The turf wall from the Irthing to just west of milecastle 54 rebuilt in stone under Hadrian. The Wall around Birdoswald was realigned so that the fort no longer projected. The rest of the turf wall was probably completed in stone about 160.

Table 7 A draft chronology for the building of Hadrian's Wall

Date	Stone wall	Turf wall	Cumberland Coast	Forts	Vallum	Bridges
122	milecastle 4–milecastle 7			Newcastle (?)		Newcastle
123	milecastle 7–milecastle 22	milecastle 49–turret 64b (?)	turret 80b–milefortlet 20 (?)	outpost forts planned (and commenced ?)		
124	milecastle 22–turret 27a milecastle 43–Irthing	milecastle 65–turret 80b (?)	milefortlet 20–milefortlet 40 (?)			Willowford Chesters
Dislocation by fort decision						
	structures turret 27a–milecastle 43	continuing (?)	continuing (?)	primary forts commenced	commenced	
125	continuing	continuing		continuing	continuing	
126	reduction in gauge of curtain (?) continuing work on Wall milecastle 22–Irthing			continuing	continuing (?)	

77

Table 7 – cont.

Date	Stone wall	Turf wall	Cumberland Coast	Forts	Vallum	Bridges
Governorship of Platorius Nepos ended (?)						
127	continuing			continuing	continuing	continuing (?)
128–38	completion of curtain { extension to Wallsend			completion of primary forts (Great Chesters behind Wall)		
				Carrawburgh added behind wall		
				Cumberland Coast forts completed		
		rebuilding in stone commenced		outpost forts completed (by *c.* 130 ?)		
136–7				Carvoran rebuilt in stone		

Three

The Antonine Wall

The Move North

Hadrian's Wall was scarcely completed – in fact it was probably undergoing extensive renovation in the turf wall sector – when it was abandoned shortly after the death of its designer in 138. The new emperor, Hadrian's adopted son Antoninus Pius, immediately decided on a new forward policy in Britain. He sent a new governor, Quintus Lollius Urbicus, with orders to reoccupy southern Scotland and construct a new Wall across the Forth–Clyde isthmus.

The occasion for this change of policy is not certain, but a Greek travel writer, Pausanias, writing about 176, mentions in his *Description of Greece* a disturbance in Britain which may be relevant. He comments that Antoninus never voluntarily involved the Romans in warfare but on two occasions he did make war. The first was against the Moors, the second was in Britain. He states that the emperor deprived the Brigantes of most of their territory because they had taken up arms and invaded the Genounian 'district', whose people were subject to the Romans. There are two problems here: the Brigantes lived within the province and so could hardly be deprived of territory, while the location of the Genounian 'district' is not known. However, the name of the Brigantes is sometimes used instead of Britons, in the same way as English is wrongly used for British today, and so might be taken to mean in a general way the tribes beyond the frontier. Whatever the explanation the event was probably connected with the reoccupation of southern Scotland since no other war in Britain is recorded under this pacific emperor, and this is

16 The Antonine Wall (land over 600 ft stippled)

the only war for which he took a salutation as victor (*imperator*). It seems incredible that Pausanias should have referred to some other troubles otherwise unknown and passed over this war in silence.

Moving the frontier of the province 100 miles further north implies that Hadrian's Wall was not a success. On the other hand its replacement by another Wall suggests that this failure was not absolute. Was it perhaps out of touch with the main centres of resistance to the Romans, hence the move forward? Hadrian's Wall would then be a tactical success but a strategic failure.

More than a logical reappraisal may have been made. It has been argued that military men chafing under the restrictions imposed by Hadrian won this advance as a concession from Pius. Equally however Hadrian may have ignored obvious weaknesses in his brain child. There is a further consideration. Pius' succession to Hadrian was not secure. He lacked military prestige, and he or his advisers may well have felt that a victory would strengthen his position, just as Claudius had in 43, and Britain may once more have seemed eminently suitable for a triumph. Certainly the abandonment and dismantling of the Wall, Hadrian's most impressive monument to his defensive policy, would have appealed to the generals who were frustrated opponents of Hadrian's ideas. However the advance in Britain is so out of character with the rest of Pius' reign that it should have some connection with Pius' own problems. A relatively short war and a spectacular advance, piloted by the emperor from his palace, as Fronto represented it, would have political advantages in Rome far outweighing any long-term disadvantages for frontier control in Britain.

In any event the move north was carried out with enormous speed, for the preparations for this move started in 139. In this and the following year inscriptions were erected at Corbridge, where Dere Street crosses the Tyne, recording the construction of buildings by legion II Augusta under the supervision of the governor Lollius Urbicus. Archaeological evidence suggests not just that these buildings were granaries but also that the whole fort was reoccupied after a period of abandonment. This abandonment had presumably been caused by the building of Hadrian's Wall; now that the Wall in turn was being evacuated

Corbridge on the road to the north was required as a supply base for the new campaign.

The duration of the campaign is not known but it clearly took place between the reoccupation of Corbridge in 139 and 140, and the acclamation of Antoninus Pius as *imperator* in 142 and the issue of commemorative coins then or in the following year. The campaigning must have ranged through lowland Scotland and into Strathmore, but no marching camps belonging to this period have been recognized, whereas other camps have been attributed to the campaigns of Agricola in the first century and Septimius Severus in the third. The construction of the new Wall commenced in the governorship of Lollius Urbicus, but may have been completed under his successor.

The Abandonment of Hadrian's Wall

Hadrian's Wall was presumably not abandoned until the Antonine Wall was completed. It does not seem to have been deliberately destroyed, but simply rendered open to traffic, both military and civilian. The milecastle gateways were opened, possibly the gates removed completely, for there is evidence at some sites of damage to the gate pivots, and the Vallum slighted. In certain areas the north and south mounds were backfilled into the ditch to form causeways at regular intervals of 45 yards. It seems best to assign the slighting to this period; analysis of vegetation remains below a crossing on Cockmount Hill suggests that the ditch was only open for a short time. But if the Wall itself was abandoned the Wall forts may not have been. Inscriptions at two forts, Chesters and Benwell, have been taken to indicate that the auxiliary garrisons were replaced at this time by legionaries. Their interpretation is however uncertain. A diploma of 146 from Chesters may imply a normal auxiliary garrison was there at that time. A difference in the treatment of the forts and the Wall is possible because their functions were completely different. The purpose of the Wall was to control the movement of people; the forts had a military function independent of the Wall. When the Wall was abandoned the forts retained their military functions, and were perhaps still garrisoned.

The Scottish Lowlands

The units to garrison the new forts constructed in the Scottish Lowlands and on the Antonine Wall were withdrawn from Hadrian's Wall and from forts in the Pennines, such as Slack, Brough-on-Noe, Binchester and Ebchester – the last two stations were replaced by a new establishment at Lanchester about half-way between them. More units may also have been withdrawn from Wales at this time. These new forts, often placed on or near the sites of earlier Agricolan foundations, lay mainly along the two trunk roads leading north to the Antonine Wall, Dere Street taking the eastern route while to the west the road passed up

17 North Britain in the first Antonine period (about 150). The open square indicates that occupation at this time is not certain

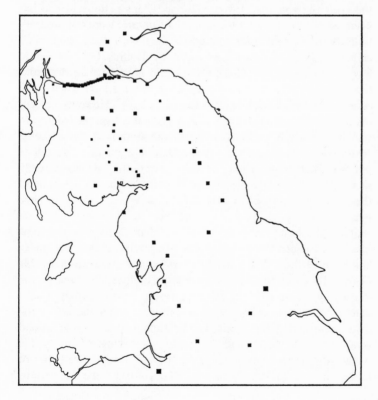

Annandale, with a loop up Nithsdale, and down Clydesdale. One of these new forts was at High Rochester, the Roman Bremenium. The first-century fort there was replaced by a new establishment under Lollius Urbicus and many, or all, of these forts may have been built, or at least started, in the same governorship. The purpose of these forts and fortlets was to police and control the inhabitants of Lowland Scotland and the Borders, the most troublesome of whom apparently were the tribes of the Selgovae and the Damnonii.

Forty years ago it was suggested that a method employed to bring peace to the northern frontier at this time was to draft the newly conquered barbarians into the army and transport them and their families to the Upper German frontier. This suggestion is based on the first appearance there in 145–6 of at least ten *numeri* of *Brittones*, many bearing subsidiary titles taken from the river by which they were stationed. This is unusual and has been taken to imply that the *numeri Brittonum* were not ordinary military units but communities of men with their wives and children. The tribesmen conquered by Lollius Urbicus would have no legal rights and therefore could have been so drafted – the same happened in reverse some thirty years later when 5,500 conquered Sarmatians were sent to Britain. However, recent excavations by Dr Dietwulf Baatz at Hesselbach on the Odenwald sector of the Upper German *limes*, the station of the *numerus Brittonum Tripputiensium*, have cast doubt on this. He points out that the type of garrison of the fortlet in the 140s was already in residence by 130 and probably earlier. Indeed on the basis of the building history of the site alone this type of unit could have been at the fortlet from its foundation at the end of the first century. It seems unlikely therefore that there was any new influx of Britons in the 140s. This theory has also come under attack in Britain. Extensive field work and excavation by Mr George Jobey in Northumberland and Dumfriesshire and by the Royal Commission on the Ancient Monuments of Scotland have demonstrated the existence of a substantial population in the area between the two Walls at this time. Indeed in the second century the population may have been increasing. Certainly it is improbable that it was reduced by transplanting entire tribes of barbarians to the continent. On the contrary the barbarians stayed at home and throve under the *Pax Romana*, extending their existing farms and constructing new homesteads to cope with the increase in population.

The Antonine Wall

The Antonine Wall had one great advantage over its predecessor: it was 37 miles long, only half the length of Hadrian's Wall. In many ways it was similar to Hadrian's Wall. An examination of the Antonine Wall and a comparison with its predecessor will illustrate the function and purpose of Hadrian's Wall both in the reign of Hadrian and when it was reoccupied on the abandonment of the Antonine Wall.

The most obvious difference between the two Walls is that the Antonine Wall was of turf. The turf rampart, certainly 10 feet high, possibly as much as 12 feet, was built on a heavy stone base usually 14 feet wide. This turf rampart was only two-thirds the width of its predecessor on Hadrian's turf wall, thus saving materials and time, while the greater stability of a stone base would have allowed the Antonine Wall to be the same, or almost the same, height. The stone base may also have resulted from other experience. Hadrian's Wall, as has already been noted, suffered from a drainage problem; when the turf wall was rebuilt in stone the number of drains through the curtain was increased to allow water ponding up beside the Wall to drain through it. It is not known if, or how regularly, drains were provided on the turf wall; certainly drainage through it would have been difficult. A stone base made the turf superstructure more stable and at the same time made the provision of culverts easier.

One important question which remains is why turf should have been used for the Antonine Wall at a time when the turf wall of the abandoned Hadrian's Wall was being rebuilt in stone, unless the long drawn-out building of Hadrian's Wall created a desire for a quicker result. In fact on an empire-wide basis the use of stone was unusual, the other frontier barriers of this period being turf, earth or timber. However, the original intention may have been to build the Antonine Wall in stone. The fort of Balmuildy, one of the first on the new Wall to be constructed, was provided with stone walls and stone wing walls just like the milecastles on

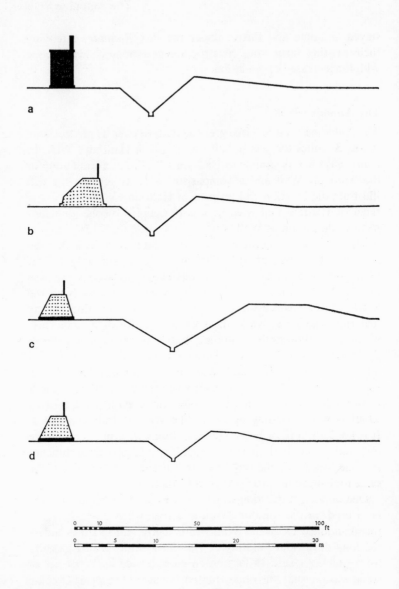

18 Sections across the two Walls. a. Hadrian's Stone Wall; b. Hadrian's Turf Wall; c. The Antonine Wall, eastern sector; d. The Antonine Wall, western sector. Scale 1 in. = 36 ft (1:432)

Hadrian's Wall. Stone wing walls would not bond with a turf rampart – which incidentally had not yet been built – and interpreted strictly should mean that the Wall would be of stone. In that case only while work was actually proceeding were plans changed and the Wall built in turf.

If the wall itself was slighter than its predecessor the ditch to the north was not, though again there are hints of modifications during building. In the eastern half of its length, that part usually considered to have been dug first, the ditch was normally 40 feet wide and about 13 feet deep, except in front of the forts, and was separated from the rampart by a berm 20 feet wide. In places, due to the local topography, the distance between the rampart and the ditch was much wider; on Croy Hill it reached 100 feet, while at Kinneil, for no apparent reason, the width of the ditch was only 18 feet and the berm 24. In its western half the ditch nowhere exhibits the uniformity of the eastern half. Its width varies from 19 to 36 feet while its depth can be as little as 6 or 8 feet. The berm is more usually nearer 30 feet than 20. The reason for these variations is not understood, though the immediate impression is of reduced efficiency; the legionaries may have been getting tired of their task.

It has been suggested that the greater width of the berm on the Antonine Wall was to allow the army more room to corral the enemy between the rampart and the ditch. However we have already seen how unlikely it was that either Wall was used in that way. More probably the wider space was for structural reasons. The north wall of a turf-wall turret had collapsed into the ditch on Hadrian's Wall and probably made the army more cautious, though that collapse seems to have been caused by a local geological phenomenon. The material from the ditch was thrown out on to the north side to form a mound, usually termed the upcast mound or the outer mound. This earth would, of course, be of no use in the construction of the rampart.

Another feature ran along the whole length of the Wall, a road, known today as the Military Way. This road, about 18 feet wide, was placed a little to the rear of the rampart. It was an innovation. Hadrian's Wall was built when the Stanegate was already in existence and there may have seemed no need for a new road. On the Antonine Wall no such road existed. Again, however, the opportunity may have been taken to remedy a deficiency realized, but not remedied, on Hadrian's Wall.

The Builders

The rampart was constructed, and presumably the ditch dug, by soldiers of the three legions which had built Hadrian's Wall less than twenty years before; some soldiers may have taken part in both operations. The legions marked the completion of each length of the Wall by the erection of commemorative plaques or distance slabs. These were highly decorated, a far cry from the centurial stones of Hadrian's Wall, almost as if the soldiers were making up for the less spectacular nature of the new Wall by these vivid records. On several of the stones appear captive or slain barbarians, on others Victories, while the *suovetaurilia* – the sacrifice celebrating the end of the victorious campaign – appears on the finest, that from Bridgeness; all are evocative reminders of the success of Roman arms.

Eighteen distance slabs have been found, the last as recently as 1969, and part of a nineteenth. They demonstrate the presence on the Wall of the whole of II Augusta, but only detachments of the other two legions, VI Victrix and XX Valeria Victrix. The legions divided the Wall between them, building mostly in lengths of 3, $3\frac{2}{3}$ or $4\frac{2}{3}$ miles, always measured in paces.

Mr G. S. Maxwell has recently suggested, on the basis of a study of the temporary camps used by the Wall builders, that these lengths were in turn subdivided. In the eastern $4\frac{2}{3}$-mile stretch constructed by legion II Augusta there are four temporary camps, two towards either end of the length. He argues that these are bases from which the legionaries issued to construct this stretch by working from both ends to the middle. Possibly two gangs worked on the rampart and the other two on the ditch. Elsewhere the evidence is less clear but the arrangements seem similar. The four camps assigned to the second legion vary in size from 4 to 8 acres and between them may have held as many as four, possibly even six cohorts. Further west a camp of either VI Victrix or XX Valeria Victrix was as large as 11 acres, though most were in the 5- to 6-acre range. Since all three legions appear to have constructed a similar length of Wall it is probable that some four to six cohorts, or 2000 to 3000 men, of both legions VI and XX were present on the Wall. The remaining cohorts of II Augusta were presumably allotted other tasks, and indeed the legion is attested constructing the fort at Balmuildy under Lollius Urbicus.

Although no temporary camps are known at the west end more than half the distance slabs come from the last four miles. These demonstrate that the Wall here was divided into six short lengths, each less than a mile long, and each measured in feet not paces. Sir George Macdonald argued in his study of the distance slabs that this stretch was constructed last, building having started at the Forth. Nothing has been found to disprove this theory, though it does not completely explain the anomalies on the Wall.

The Forts on the Wall

Forts were regularly placed along the Wall. Sixteen are at present known and another three presumed on spacing grounds. The distances between the forts vary considerably. Bearsden was, for example, $2\frac{3}{4}$ miles from Balmuildy to the east, but only $1\frac{1}{2}$ from Castlehill to the west. The forts were more closely related to the local topography than those on Hadrian's Wall and the intervals between them varied accordingly. On average, however, the forts were just over 2 miles apart.

In size they range from tiny Duntocher with an internal area of half an acre to Mumrills, $6\frac{1}{2}$ acres internally and larger than most forts on Hadrian's Wall. The forts had from two to four ditches and although most had turf ramparts, between 12 to 20 feet wide, two – Balmuildy and Castlecary – had stone walls. In general this is in keeping with Hadrian's Wall where the forts on the stone wall, and Birdoswald east of the Red Rock Fault, had stone walls while those on the turf wall appear to have had turf ramparts.

The internal buildings also varied little in their materials and construction from their counterparts on Hadrian's Wall. The principal buildings were of stone, the barracks, stables and store-houses of timber. Although most barrack-blocks on Hadrian's Wall appear to have been built of stone, the surviving walls were

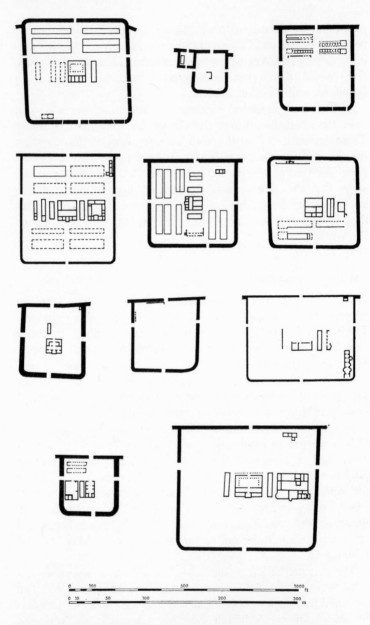

19 The Antonine Wall forts, early Antonine plans. From top left to
bottom right: Old Kilpatrick, Duntocher, Bearsden; Balmuildy, Cadder,
Bar Hill; Croy Hill, Westerwood, Castlecary; Rough Castle, Mumrills.
Scale 1 in. = 400 ft (1:4800)

probably only sill walls as a base for a timber superstructure, while recent excavations at South Shields have furnished evidence of wholly timber barrack-blocks in the Hadrianic period.

In their internal arrangements, however, the Antonine Wall forts display none of the uniformity of the Hadrian's Wall forts. At Croy Hill, for example, a granary was placed in the *praetentura*, while a large part of the *praetentura* at Cadder apparently was left empty. At several sites the bath-house was placed within the fort; elsewhere it lay outside the fort but within the annexe. In keeping with the later practice on Hadrian's Wall none of the forts lay astride the rampart but all lay to the south, though in all but two cases (Carriden and Bar Hill) still attached to the Wall.

The one way in which the lay-out of the forts was more rigid than on Hadrian's Wall was the direction in which the forts faced. On the earlier Wall the forts were designed for whole units and were only part of the Wall for convenience. Most lay astride the Wall and therefore faced north. The other forts – Housesteads, Great Chesters, Bowness and probably Stanwix – all appear to have faced east. The Antonine Wall forts faced north with the single exception of Cadder which faced east. Often the principal buildings, which determined the position of the main gate, lay across the long axis, unlike those on Hadrian's Wall where the central range lay across the short axis. The overall impression is of much more flexibility in siting, planning, and designing the forts on the Antonine Wall than was evident on Hadrian's Wall twenty years before.

The legionaries played a part in constructing the forts as well as the wall. Part or all of Croy Hill, Bar Hill, Auchendavy, Cadder, Balmuildy, and possibly also Carriden and Castlecary were probably constructed by legionaries, for legionary building stones have been found at them. Although these stones are undated it is usually presumed that they belong to the first period of building. They attest the activities of all three legions. However, unlike on Hadrian's Wall, the auxiliaries seem to have helped. The headquarters building and possibly more of Rough Castle was built by *cohors VI Nerviorum* while at Castlecary *cohors I Tungrorum* was at work and at Bar Hill *cohors I Baetasiorum*. These three units were building under Antoninus

Pius; the inscriptions may date to the original building of the Wall early in his reign or to a later rebuilding towards the end of the reign. Since none of the inscriptions specifically refer to restoration of the building it seems best to assign them to the earlier period. The weight of the evidence suggests that most of the work fell on the shoulders of the legionaries with the auxiliaries acting in a secondary capacity, possibly concentrating on the buildings inside the forts.

One experiment on Hadrian's Wall, the Vallum, was not repeated. Instead, the forts were provided with a new feature, annexes. These lay to one side of their fort, usually the east, and were often almost as large as or even larger than the forts themselves. Annexes are found outside many forts from the first century onwards. They are absent on Hadrian's Wall presumably because they were rendered unnecessary by the Vallum, which served as an elongated annexe running the entire length of the Wall. The bath-house when outside the fort was usually within the annexe. Timber buildings have been found in some annexes, Mumrills, Cadder and Bearsden for example, but neither the purpose nor date of these buildings is known. It is highly unlikely that civilians were allowed to build houses and shops in the annexes. These enclosures had a military function, as had the Vallum, and would accommodate equipment and stores which could not be housed in the forts. Civilians were not allowed in the area between the Wall and the Vallum, the 'Hadrianic annexe', and there is no reason to suppose that the Antonine annexes were treated differently. Excavation, admittedly not very extensive, at Mumrills, Rough Castle, Castlecary, Bar Hill, Bearsden, Duntocher and Old Kilpatrick has produced no evidence of civilian buildings in the annexes though the excavators of the annexe at Camelon, just north of Watling Lodge fortlet, did suggest that buildings there were used by civilians.

Minor Structures

Fortlets have been discovered between certain of the forts. Three are at present known, a fourth preceded the fort at Duntocher, and more may yet be found. These fortlets are a little

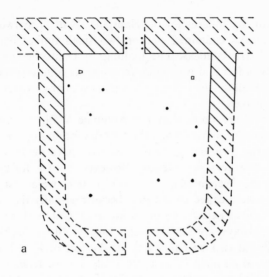

a

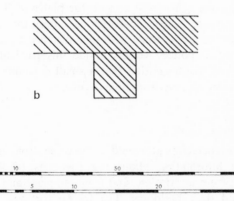

b

20 Minor structures on the Antonine Wall. a. Wilderness Plantation
fortlet; b. Bonnyside East beacon-platform. Scale 1 in. = 36 ft (1:432)

larger than the milecastles on Hadrian's Wall. The two excavated examples contained one or two small timber buildings,
probably barrack-blocks. The building at Duntocher measured
36 feet by 18 feet and is so close in size to its counterparts in the
Hadrian's Wall milecastles as to suggest a similar garrison, that is
about eight men.

No turrets are known on the Antonine Wall. Turrets were
built on Hadrian's Wall when the forts lay behind on the Stanegate, and the forts on the Wall itself may have made many of
these watch-towers superfluous. However, a new feature was
provided, the beacon platforms. When these were first recognized they were called expansions because visually they appear
to be southward expansions of the rampart. Only six are known
and they always appear in pairs, two on the west brow of
Croy Hill and two on either side of the fort of Rough Castle.
The one at Bonnyside East, a few yards west of Rough Castle,
was excavated some years ago by Dr K. A. Steer and found to
consist of a turf platform on a stone base 18 feet square. The
base was attached to the rear of the wall and the platform was
presumably the same height as the wall top. Around the base
was found a considerable amount of burnt wood and burnt turf
presumed to have come from fires on the platform. The spacing
and position of the beacon platforms have been thought to suggest that they were concerned with long-distance signalling. The
discovery of two pottery vessels beside this particular beacon
platform led to the suggestion that a small detachment of men
might have camped there from time to time.

The Garrison of the Wall

Such a small detachment would have come from one of the
Wall forts. Information about the garrisons of these forts
derives both from inscriptions and from the plans and layouts of
the forts and their buildings. The largest fort was Mumrills,
which was garrisoned by the *ala I Tungrorum*, the only cavalry
unit attested on the Antonine Wall. Inscriptions at Castlecary,
eight miles to the west, record the *cohors I Tungrorum milliaria
peditata*, which as we have seen helped to construct the fort, and
the *cohors I Vardullorum milliaria equitata*. Both are large

infantry units, the latter also containing cavalry, and the only units of this size to be attested by name on the Wall. The only sizeable areas of Iron Age settlements known for twenty miles north of the Wall lie at the east end of the Campsie Fells just north of Castlecary, and this may account for the presence of the milliary units there. The position of Mumrills close to the road which led north through the Wall at Watling Lodge may have governed the nature of its garrison. Inscriptions record the presence of several quingenary (500-strong) cohorts on the Antonine Wall, at Rough Castle, Bar Hill and at Castlehill. The size and number of barrack-blocks at Old Kilpatrick at the west end of the Wall suggest a *cohors milliaria peditata*, while Cadder and Balmuildy may have been garrisoned by quingenary cohorts. At another fort, New Kilpatrick at Bearsden, possible cavalry barracks have recently been recognized. Many sites along the Wall have produced inscriptions recording legionary detachments – for example, Westerwood, Croy Hill and Auchendavy. Although the inscriptions are not dated they may belong to the first period of the occupation of the Wall. Some forts, such as Westerwood and Croy Hill, are in any case too small for a complete auxiliary unit, as are others, Rough Castle and Castlecary, where such units are specifically attested. Clearly part of these units must have been permanently outstationed, possibly at the smaller forts along the Wall; the only one of these forts extensively explored, Duntocher, does not appear to have a headquarters building, suggesting that it was the home not of a unit but only a detachment.

It is difficult to distinguish any general policy governing the garrisons of these forts. Different types and sizes of auxiliary units are mixed together with legionary detachments apparently at random. Two points do stand out, however. Firstly, very little cavalry is attested on the Wall. Only one *ala* is known to have served on the Wall, one *cohors milliaria equitata*, and two *cohortes quingenariae equitatae*, one probably succeeding the *ala* at Mumrills later in the second century, though there may be cavalry barracks at Bearsden. In comparison one *cohors milliaria peditata* is attested and three smaller peditate cohorts, while legionary detachments, presumably composed completely of infantrymen, served at a further three forts. Finally the lay-out and barracks of a further three forts suggest that they too were occupied by infantry cohorts, one of milliary size. Only one-seventh of the troops on the Antonine Wall may therefore have been cavalry compared to a quarter on Hadrian's Wall. This emphasis on infantry may suggest a different strategy of frontier control, though alternatively it may have been in response to local terrain and conditions. The valleys of the Kelvin and the Carron in the Roman period would have been very boggy and unsuited to cavalry, while the countryside was probably densely wooded, again not ideal for cavalry.

The total infantry and cavalry garrison of the Antonine Wall was only slightly less than that of Hadrian's Wall, which was twice as long. Put another way, the garrison of the new Wall was proportionally nearly twice as large as its predecessor. The strengthening of the frontier line under Antoninus Pius reflects not just the local situation but also the general nature of the Antonine reoccupation of Scotland. The Scottish Lowlands were now controlled by more forts and fortlets than either before or later and more than was usual in other similar areas, for example north England or Wales. The impression is that the Roman army moved north in great strength. The fact that some of these sites, both forts and fortlets, were abandoned within a few years suggests that the army may have overestimated the problem in the 140s and placed a greater occupation force in the Scottish Lowlands than was really necessary.

The second point is that the weight of the Wall garrison lay towards the west. Six of the eight western forts of known size were large enough to hold complete auxiliary units compared to only three out of the seven in the east. This was probably due to the closeness of the Campsie Fells and the Kilpatrick Hills north of the Wall to the line of the barrier, while to the east the Wall was protected by outpost forts as far north as Bertha on the Tay. These forts presumably did not act as advanced warning stations but protected and controlled friendly tribespeople in Fife and around the head of the Forth, the area which later became part of the kingdom of the Manau Goddodin. The style of their houses suggests strong connections between the tribes in Fife and those south of the Forth at this time. The south shore of the Forth was also protected by forts during the Antonine period, though no

Table 8 The suggested original garrisons of the Antonine Wall forts

	Acreage	Garrison
Carriden	*c.* 4·2 (?)	
Kinneil	small (?)	
Inveravon	small	
Mumrills	7·2	*ala I Tungrorum*
Falkirk	small (?)	
Rough Castle	1·5	part of *cohors VI Nerviorum quingeneria peditata*
Seabegs	small	
Castlecary	3·9	part of *cohors I Tungrorum milliaria peditata* (or of *cohors I Vardullorum milliaria equitata* or vexillation of legions II and VI)
Westerwood	2·3	vexillation of legion VI (?)
Croy Hill	2	vexillation of legion VI (??)
Bar Hill	3·6	*cohors I Baetasiorum quingenaria peditata*
Auchendavy	*c.* 3·3	vexillation of legion II (?)
Kirkintilloch	(?)	
Cadder	3·3	*cohors quingenaria peditata*
Balmuildy	4·3	*cohors quingenaria peditata* or part of a unit
Bearsden	2·7	the garrison probably includes cavalry
Castlehill	*c.* 3.4	*cohors IV Gallorum quingenaria equitata* (or later)
Duntocher	0·66	part of a unit
Old Kilpatrick	4·7	*cohors milliaria peditata*

complex system such as the Cumberland Coast scheme is known. Eleven miles beyond the eastern end of the Wall lay the fort of Cramond at the mouth of the little river Almond, where no doubt a thriving port grew up. Nine miles further east was Inveresk, the base, apparently, of a complete *ala quingenaria*. The west flank of the Wall was protected by a fort at Whitemoss, Bishopton and two fortlets at Lurg Moor and Outerwards.

The picture of the Antonine Wall which has now emerged is very different from that of the Wall which it replaced. Although the turf barrier itself was much slighter than the stone wall of Hadrian, it was much more heavily garrisoned. Although only half as long, it had seven more forts than Hadrian's Wall, and a garrison almost its equal in size. Surprisingly, however, neither east nor west flank of the Wall was as strongly protected as the flanks of Hadrian's Wall. No regular system of milecastles is known, and no turrets at all, though the beacon platforms are a new feature. The Vallum is not replaced but a new linear feature appears, the Military Way. The Wall, it has been thought, also contains no evidence for the major changes in plan which characterize the building of Hadrian's Wall. A recent re-interpretation of the evidence suggests that this is far from the case.

Changes in Plan

Two series of forts on the Antonine Wall have long been recognized. One series precedes the construction of the rampart. Balmuildy, the only fort to have produced inscriptions of Lollius Urbicus, Mumrills, Old Kilpatrick and probably Castlecary fall into this group; so does the fort of Duntocher, but the complex building history of the site places it in a class of its own. Other forts are later than the rampart: Rough Castle, Westerwood, Croy Hill, Cadder and probably Bearsden. Two forts, Carriden and Bar Hill, lie detached from the rampart, so their position in the building programme is unknown, while the relationship of the other forts to the rampart has not been determined. Of the fortlets, Duntocher precedes the rampart, while Wilderness Plantation is contemporary with the rampart. These differences have long been considered to reflect the time-lag between the construction of the rampart and the forts – the rampart was built from east to west and the eastern forts are either contemporary with or later than the rampart while the western forts usually precede it. There may be a more fundamental reason for these differences.

The forts which precede the rampart, Mumrills, Castlecary, Balmuildy and Old Kilpatrick, are large and widely separated from each other. Mumrills and Castlecary are 9 miles apart, Castlecary and Balmuildy 15 miles, Balmuildy and Old Kilpatrick 9 miles. The central 15-mile stretch may have been broken by a fort: although Auchendavy, 8 miles from Castlecary and 7 from Balmuildy, may be a candidate, Bar Hill, more asymmetrically placed but on a high eminence with a fine view to the west and north, and detached from the Wall, is a stronger possibility. Its position behind the rampart may suggest its construction before the rampart; the fort would surely have been simply attached to the rear of the wall, if the wall was already there. At the east end of the Wall the large fort of Carriden nearly 8 miles from Mumrills probably belongs to the same series.

Both the excavated fortlets also seem to belong to the same scheme. At Wilderness Plantation the Wall and the fortlet are of one build, clearly demonstrating their contemporaneity. The other fortlet at Duntocher actually preceded the rampart, and was in turn succeeded by a fort before the rampart reached that point. The fortlet may therefore be taken to belong to the first series of structures. Although no other fortlets have been examined, the presence of a primary fortlet, Wilderness Plantation, between two forts, one a primary fort and the other a secondary, and the replacement of another, Duntocher, by a fort strongly suggest that the original intention was to place these structures at mile intervals along the whole length of the Wall. It could therefore be argued that the blue-print for the Antonine Wall was based on Hadrian's Wall as it was abandoned, that is, on the second scheme for Hadrian's Wall. The running barrier was modified, being in turf not stone, a Vallum was not provided, though a road was, but the main features were similar. Forts were established at regular 8- to 9-mile intervals with fortlets every mile in-between; turrets may have been planned, but none have been found. These primary forts were designed for whole units, or at least were of a size to hold whole units; only Castlecary is too small to have held the milliary cohort which is attested building there.

The other forts on the Wall represent a modification of this plan. At Rough Castle, Westerwood, Croy Hill and Cadder, where the rampart had already been constructed, the fort was simply added to the rear of the Wall, the fort ramparts usually resting against the Wall rampart. Where the rampart had not yet been constructed, as at Duntocher, the fort (incidentally here replacing an existing fortlet) might still be built in anticipation of the rampart. It has been suggested that the so-called wagon

Table 9   The spacing of the 'primary' forts on the Antonine Wall

	Acreage	Distance between forts in miles
Carriden	c. 4·2	
		7¾
Mumrills	7·2	
		9
Castlecary	3·9	
		6
Bar Hill (?)	3·6	
		9
Balmuildy	4·3	
		9
Old Kilpatrick	4·7	

park at Rough Castle was a 'primary' fortlet in a relationship to the fort similar to that at Duntocher. The ditch had already been dug across the front of the sites of the secondary forts and so most of these forts had no causeways outside their north gates. Only at Rough Castle was a causeway, placed asymmetrically to the gate, provided. At Croy Hill, however, the undug section of ditch just to the east of the fort was presumably used as a causeway.

The number of forts along the Wall line was in this way increased from six to nineteen and the distance between them reduced from 8 miles to just over 2 miles. But although the number of forts was trebled the garrison of the Wall was not raised accordingly. Most of the new forts were smaller than the forts already built and incapable of holding complete units. Only three of the thirteen new forts, all towards the west, are known to be large enough to contain whole units. It is at these new,

21 The development of the Antonine Wall. a. Antonine Wall as planned;
b. Progress achieved when the fort decision was taken; c. Antonine Wall
as completed

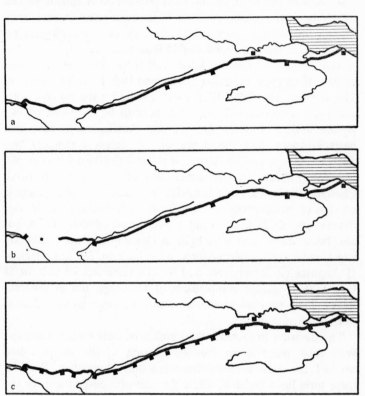

small forts that the legionary detachments are attested, apart
from Castlecary. Thus the increase in the number of forts probably only doubled the Wall garrison. It was, moreover, a startling
break with tradition. Not only on Hadrian's Wall, but also on the
Stanegate frontier, built forty years before the Antonine Wall,
the forts were about 7 miles apart. This is a simple development
from the earlier spacing of 14 miles, a day's marching distance,
and is found also on the Taunus frontier in Germany. The
Roman high command must have had a good reason for this
innovation, an innovation which entailed much extra work, but

it is now not clear. The spreading of troops thinly along the Wall line may suggest the presence of a hostile population in the area just north of the Wall, but no such population is known. In fact relatively few settlements have been discovered in this area, though this may in part reflect the lack of archaeological research rather than an actual void in Roman times.

The division of the Antonine Wall forts into two series may explain their great variation in size and lack of standardization. The forts of Hadrian's Wall itself, excluding the outpost forts and the Cumberland Coast, all appear to be the work of two legions and, at least in the size and dimensions of forts and barrack-blocks, and the depth of the defences (usually two ditches), have a certain degree of standardization: for example, 580 feet appears in the dimensions of four forts, Benwell, Chesters, Birdoswald and Stanwix. On the Scottish Wall there is no sign of standardization, mainly due, no doubt, to their construction by three legions and a number of auxiliary units, but also because the forts were built in two stages. Thus Balmuildy and Cadder, two adjacent forts, were built by the same legion, II Augusta (so it appears), and for the same size of unit, or at least with a similar complement of buildings, but at different stages. They bear no resemblance to each other in size, dimensions or barrack-blocks.

The decision to increase the number of forts on the Antonine Wall took place when the construction of the rampart had reached the area between Bearsden and Duntocher. Between these forts lies Castlehill, where the unit of measurement for the Wall changed from paces to feet. This may be the point reached when it was decided to add to the number of forts on the Wall, or if this was not the exact spot, that the change resulted from the fort decision. It is possible that most of the rampart-builders were redeployed to build the forts leaving only small detachments to complete the rampart. However, the new fort at Duntocher two miles to the west was apparently completed before the rampart-builders reached the site, which may imply that all the gangs were taken away to build the forts and some time elapsed before the rampart was completed; such a lapse of time would best explain the change in the unit of measurement from paces to feet.

The Building Programme

An attempt can now be made to reconstruct the building programme of the Antonine Wall. The easternmost length, built
by legion II, is 4⅔ miles long. This is very close to the 5-mile
lengths which frequently recur on Hadrian's Wall, and taking
account of natural geographical divisions the nearest convenient
distance to 5 miles. Since further west each legion always seems
to have been allotted the same length to construct it may be
presumed that legions VI and XX also built about 4⅔ miles of
the Wall. A convenient boundary on the west may have been the
fort of Castlecary overlooking the Red Burn, while in the centre
Watling Lodge fortlet provided a useful landmark. Each legion
seems to have been divided into gangs with their own temporary
camps. Eight of these camps have been found between Bridgeness and Castlecary. While the three legions were at work in this
area other soldiers had started building the primary forts. Old
Kilpatrick, Balmuildy and probably Castlecary were all built
before the rampart, while the excavators of Mumrills suggested
that work was actually proceeding on the fort when the rampart
builders arrived. II Augusta certainly built Balmuildy, and
possibly the others as well.

It may have been intended to divide the whole Wall into three
lengths of about 13 miles each, each in turn subdivided between
the three legions. But if that was the intention it was not followed
in the next length to be constructed. This stretch, which probably
had Castlecary as its eastern boundary, is apparently only 9 miles
long. The reason for this is uncertain, though Sir George
Macdonald linked it with the difficulty of digging the ditch over
Croy Hill and, we may add, Bar Hill. The next stretch, 11 miles
long, brought the Wall builders to Castlehill, 4 miles from the
Clyde. Here there is the puzzling change from paces to feet as
the unit of measurement, probably connected with the addition
of some thirteen new forts. All the primary forts may have been
completed by now but the extra work apparently required all
three legions. Some soldiers may have been left to complete the
wall, but the change in the unit of measurement implies a break
in the building programme and this is reinforced by the sequence

at Duntocher, where the new fort was built before rampart builders arrived on the site.

The original intention may have been to build the Antonine Wall in three years, with each legion allotted a complete year's work at a time, $4\frac{2}{3}$ miles or thereabouts in the first season. The decision to add more forts may have lengthened the building programme by a year or two. The construction of some fort buildings by auxiliaries suggests the pressure now on the army. The acclamation of Antoninus Pius as *imperator* took place in 142, and it is usually considered that construction started then. In addition to the Wall the army had to build the outpost forts and the new forts in the Scottish Lowlands. Only one of these forts, High Rochester, has produced an inscription, which demonstrates that the *cohors I Lingonum equitata* was responsible for the erection of at least one building in the fort, though an inscription recording work by XX Valeria Victrix has also been assigned to this period. The auxiliary units may have built their own stations, leaving the construction of the Wall to the legionaries.

The Antonine Wall was designed, built and garrisoned in the light of experience gained on Hadrian's Wall, and then modified to suit the special problems of building – and occupying – a Wall on the Forth–Clyde isthmus. The tactical purpose of the two Walls was the same: to control the movement of people into and out of the province at a convenient point (not necessarily the political or administrative boundary of the province). In the event of an attack on the Antonine Wall the army would move out to deal with the enemy in the open, just as they would on Hadrian's Wall. The Antonine Wall was presumably modified to create a frontier complex able to deal effectively both with the day-to-day difficulties of frontier control and the more serious dangers of a major attack. If the emperor and his advisers considered that the movement north and the provision of a new Wall would settle the disturbed conditions on the northern frontier they were mistaken. Sixty years were to elapse before peace came to the north.

Four

The Two Walls

The history of the sixty years from the building of the Antonine Wall and its associated structures in the 140s to the reign of Caracalla in the early third century is most confused. Certain events are known from literary evidence, and there is a sprinkling of building records and other inscriptions, though their relevance is not always clear. Some time in the century a second occupation of the Antonine Wall and a second occupation of Hadrian's Wall have to be fitted in. There is no consensus among scholars as to how a meaningful history of the Roman north in this period can be constructed. All that can be done is first to detail the evidence relating to events, real or imaginary, secondly to describe the structural evidence and the varying conclusions of ceramic and numismatic experts, and finally to put forward the interpretation that seems best to reconcile all the evidence.

The 'Brigantian Revolt'

The first event or non-event after the building of the Antonine Wall is the so-called 'Brigantian revolt' of the mid 150s. Several different pieces of evidence for the years 155 to 158 together have been taken to indicate a revolt of the tribe at this time. The uprising (it is said) commenced with the attack on the Genounian 'district' described by Pausanias and set the north aflame from Birrens in Dumfriesshire on the north boundary of the tribal territory to Brough-on-Noe in Derbyshire on the south before it was suppressed by the governor Cnaeus Julius Verus with the help of reinforcements from the continent landed at Newcastle, the only way the beleaguered garrison of the Wall could be reached. After the victory a special coin issue was struck, an altar dedicated to Mars the Avenger at Corbridge and the destroyed forts of Birrens and Brough-on-Noe rebuilt. All the evidence on which this story is based is, however, capable of more than one interpretation.

A coin issue of 155 portrayed Britannia, the personification of the province, seated disconsolately with her head bowed. This has been taken to imply a disturbance, possibly an invasion or revolt, put down shortly before. Her attitude may simply be ringing the changes from earlier coin issues of Hadrian and Antoninus Pius depicting the personification of the province, though her demeanour does suggest an unhappy event in Britain. This coin issue appears, from its distribution and workmanship, to have been minted in Britain. (The second reference to a victory is the dedication to *Mars Ultor*, Mars the Avenger, at Corbridge by an officer of VI Victrix during the governorship of Julius Verus (155–8). Re-examination of the inscription has eliminated the word *Ultor*, and this piece of evidence must therefore be discounted.) The reinforcements sent to the three legions of Britain from the two provinces of Germany may well have been to strengthen an army depleted by fighting; on the other hand Britain might have been experiencing difficulty in providing all the citizen recruits required by the legions and might have needed outside help. In this case, however, the Tyne would not be a very convenient disembarkation point for soldiers travelling to the three legionary fortresses.

The rebuilding of the two forts seems stronger evidence for a revolt at this time. Birrens was certainly rebuilt in 158 after destruction. The cause and nature of the destruction, though, are not known. The fort may have been sacked by an enemy, but the damage might have been done accidentally or even by the Romans themselves prior to a change in garrison; it is known that the garrison was changed at this time, while not infrequently forts were demolished by the retiring garrison and rebuilt by the new unit. Recent re-excavation, not yet published, may clarify events there. Brough-on-Noe was also certainly rebuilt at this time but unlike Birrens it had been abandoned for thirty or more years. The rebuilding of the fort may therefore have been occasioned not by unsettled conditions in the area but as part of a redeployment of units in north Britain.

Two other 'events' have been connected with this alleged revolt: the siege of the hill-fort at Burnswark near Birrens, and the destruction of the Roman fort at Newstead. On either side of the Iron Age hill-fort at Burnswark is a Roman siege camp and it has been considered that these were built and used in war-time. Recent excavations, however, suggest that this was not the case. The hill-fort had long been abandoned when the siege camps were constructed, while over the site of one entrance a gateway was laid out in plan using paving stones. Around this area were found many clay sling bullets. The camps themselves were proved to be semi-permanent, thrown up not in haste but apparently at leisure, with some of the facilities of a permanent fort such as paved streets, ovens and possibly even buildings. All this suggests that the site was the scene of practice siege warfare, the soldiers firing sling bullets from the massive ballista plat-forms in front of the gates of the south siege camp at the mock entrances laid out on the hillside, and no doubt storming the 'defences' as well. Moreover although the siege works have often been assigned to the 150s, it now seems probable that they are later, for the ditch of the Antonine fortlet which underlies the south camp had silted up and become overgrown before its rampart was thrown into the ditch by the builders of the camp. This suggests that the practice camps were not constructed until later in the second century, or even in the third century.

At Newstead the evidence is rather grimmer. During the course of the excavations carried out at the site before the First World War many pits were emptied. The Antonine pits were found to contain debris cleaned out of the fort, including damaged armour, tools, personal ornaments, and even human skulls; this has been interpreted as evidence for the sacking of the fort. But by an alternative interpretation it is rubbish, un-wanted odds and ends, and armour awaiting repair, all abandoned when the fort was evacuated and demolished by its garrison, which may not have been able to carry away all its equipment and accumulated possessions. The metalwork will have been buried not just to leave the site tidy but also to hide it from hostile tribesmen. For the same reason no doubt all the nails left when the fortress of Inchtuthil was evacuated seventy years before were buried deeply. The human skulls may also have had a less spectacular if no less gruesome explanation. On Trajan's Column can be seen Roman auxiliaries in action brandishing the heads of slaughtered Dacians, and even gripping these heads in their teeth as they fought. In another scene two such heads are fixed on stakes outside a Roman camp. The heads found in the pits at Newstead may therefore have been of British or Caledonian tribesmen killed in earlier wars and displayed as trophies in the fort. Clearly the material from Newstead cannot be taken as unequivocal support for the sacking of the fort at this time.

One final piece of evidence used for the Brigantian revolt is the passage in Pausanias' *Description of Greece* which relates how the Brigantes attacked the Genounian district and as a result were deprived of part of their territory. This is more likely to refer to events leading up to the reconquest of the Scottish Lowlands and the building of the Antonine Wall than to anything later in the reign of Antoninus Pius.

Nevertheless there may have been trouble, not perhaps connected with the Brigantes, in the 150s but in the past it may have been dated too late. If the coin issue of 155 is relevant it should celebrate a victory even earlier, before the governorship of Julius Verus. His activities, the drafting-in of experienced replacements from Germany direct to all three legions serving in the north (recruits would have gone to the depots), the rebuilding of Birrens and the reoccupation of Brough-on-Noe may have followed a hard-won victory north of Hadrian's Wall. In conjunction with an inscription from Hadrian's Wall showing rebuilding of the curtain in 158, the coin issue may suggest that Verus was withdrawing strategically to Hadrian's Wall. Repair work to the curtain of the Wall ought to imply reoccupation of the whole Wall. If so it is not impossible that the rebuilding at Birrens was connected with a change in function from a hinterland fort of the Antonine Wall to an outpost fort of Hadrian's Wall, while Brough-on-Noe may have been reoccupied by a unit returning from Scotland.

Literary and Epigraphic Evidence for the Later Second Century

Whatever the reorganization of the frontier forces at this time it was not successful in restoring, or maintaining, peace, for there was a difficult situation in Britain in the early 160s at the beginning of the reign of the next emperor, Marcus Aurelius, who succeeded his adoptive father in 161. At this time, his biographer states, war was threatening in Britain and Marcus sent against the Britons Calpurnius Agricola. The description is reminiscent of the scene facing Hadrian in Britain at his accession forty years before: Britain could not be kept under Roman control. This raises an interesting question of biographical criticism. At the opening of the reigns of four successive emperors, Hadrian, Antoninus Pius, Marcus Aurelius and Commodus, there is reference in their biographies or in the contemporary histories to a difficult situation in Britain. Although these may have been accurate – indeed in some instances there is corroborative evidence – it is also possible, if not probable, that this emphasis on the disturbed conditions which his hero inherited and forcefully dealt with is part of the stock-in-trade of the imperial biographer. Hadrian responded by visiting Britain and building a Wall, Pius by sending Lollius Urbicus to reconquer the Scottish Lowlands and build a new Wall, and now Marcus by sending to Britain Calpurnius Agricola. Nevertheless the writer cannot have created an event which did not happen; there must have been a germ of truth in his account. Certainly Britain was a difficult province to govern, for the best generals of the day were sent here in the second century. Sex. Julius Severus was governor of the province when called upon to deal with the Jewish revolt in 133, Q. Lollius Urbicus had a distinguished military record, as did Cn. Julius Verus himself. M. Statius Priscus, governor in 161 or 162, was recalled in less than a year to cross the Empire to take command in Cappadocia against the Parthians, while in the reign of Commodus P. Helvius Pertinax, governor in succession of four major provinces and a future emperor, was to be sent to Britain. For these men the governorship of Britain was the climax of their careers; they had previously served a long apprenticeship in both civil and military posts usually including a junior governorship of one or two of the Danubian provinces and also the senior governorship of Lower Germany. Little is known of the earlier career of Calpurnius Agricola, though he went on to govern the three united Dacian provinces, but it was doubtless similar.

Calpurnius Agricola was evidently concerned with Hadrian's Wall, for building inscriptions of his governorship have been recovered from the forts at Carvoran and Chesterholm, and also from Corbridge; he was also active in the Pennines, for building at this time is recorded at Ribchester and possibly also Ilkley. He can perhaps be seen as continuing the programme started by Julius Verus. His successor is also attested building on Hadrian's Wall, this time at Stanwix and Great Chesters.

Unsettled conditions apparently continued in Britain for the rest of the reign of Marcus Aurelius. The emperor's biographer records, apparently in the early 170s, that war was again about to break out in Britain. When in 175 peace was concluded on the Danube and the Sarmatians provided 8000 cavalry for the Roman army, 5500 were sent to Britain. They may have been required to support a hard-pressed provincial army, or Britain may simply have been an isolated place to which to send troops of uncertain loyalty.

If the nature of these disturbances is uncertain, those which afflicted the province in the early 180s are somewhat less obscure. Cassius Dio in his *History of Rome* records that

the greatest of the wars of Commodus' reign was fought in Britain. The tribes in the island crossed the wall that separated them from the Roman forts, doing much damage and killing a general and the troops he had with him; Commodus in alarm sent against them Ulpius Marcellus, who ruthlessly put down the barbarians.

This passage clearly indicates the nature of the troubles in Britain at this time, an invasion of the province, involving the death possibly of the governor himself, or one of the legionary commanders, and the destruction of his army. However, unfortunately the location of 'the wall' is not given, and we must turn to archaeological evidence to try to determine this.

Cassius Dio, or rather his epitomist, instead of narrating useful information tells us about Ulpius Marcellus' reputation as a martinet, with supporting anecdotes. It is perhaps no coincidence that the army of Britain was in a mutinous state in 185. Their resentment of an attempt by Commodus' favourite and praetorian prefect Perennis to replace their senatorial commanders by equestrians helped to lead to the downfall of Perennis, and they were still mutinous when Pertinax arrived to take charge of them in 185. Although he had some success after almost losing his life, he finally asked to be relieved of his command because of the resentment towards him nourished by the troops.

The next tribulation which befell Britain was a result of the murder of Commodus on 31 December 192. In the ensuing power struggle the governor of Britain, D. Clodius Albinus, was bound to become involved, as governor of one of the three major military provinces. In the final act of that struggle Albinus led his troops across the Channel to face Septimius Severus, governor of Upper Pannonia, who had made good use of his central position and the proximity of his province to Rome. In February 197 Albinus was defeated at a hard-fought battle at Lugudunum (Lyons) in southern France.

The following years cannot have been happy for Britain. Families in the military areas lost husbands, sons and fathers in the fighting while many of the province's leading families must have suffered as a result of their support for Albinus. Meanwhile the tribes north of the frontier were restless. Cassius Dio refers to the conditions which faced Virius Lupus, Severus' first governor:

since the Caledonians did not keep their promises and made ready to assist the Maeatae, and since at that time Severus was devoting himself to the Parthian war, Lupus was forced to purchase peace from the Maeatae for a great sum, receiving back a few prisoners.

It has been considered that in 196 Albinus withdrew the units garrisoning the Wall for his fight with Severus, allowing the northern tribes to attack and destroy the Wall. There is, however, no mention of this in the contemporary literature. Ten years later Herodian does record that 'the barbarians had risen and were overrunning the country, carrying off booty and causing great destruction...'. But neither Herodian nor Cassius Dio mention a single geographical place-name in their discussion, though the latter does state that 'the Maeatae live close to the wall which divides the island into two, and the Caledonians beyond them'. Unfortunately again which Wall is not made clear, for this would have been known by the people living at the time and reading the account. Because these references in the sixty or seventy years following the construction of the Antonine Wall are so brief the events of these years are obscure and likely to remain so. While new inscriptions may from time to time be discovered, new literary evidence is unlikely to be found. Meanwhile archaeologists and historians will have to rely on more imperfect tools for tracing the history of the second half of the second century, namely coins and pottery.

Archaeological Evidence for the Later Second Century

Excavation at many sites in the north of Britain has provided a considerable body of material relating to the history of individual stations and the frontier generally. This evidence consists of the structural sequence of buildings within the forts, and the objects found at the sites. The coins at least provide a clear *terminus post quem*, though few stratified coins have been found in north Britain. The pottery, which is more abundant, is not self-dating and has to depend on its relationship to contexts dated by inscriptions and literary sources. Where these are lacking in the second half of the second century the pottery is difficult to date. However, typology of the vessels and comparison of pottery from different sites, some securely dated, together with the detailed examination of the potters' stamps on Samian ware and *mortaria* (mixing-bowls), do allow some conclusions concerning the occupation of individual sites in relationship to each other. Nevertheless nearly all this evidence is open to more than one interpretation and in reconstructing the history of the northern frontier at this time this awkward fact must be borne in mind.

Any discussion of the northern frontier in the late second century must take into account two facts which archaeological investigation has now established almost beyond any doubt. The first is that both Hadrian's Wall and the Antonine Wall saw two separate periods of occupation in the second century, as demonstrated by the structural history of the forts and smaller sites on the two Walls. A third period has, it is true, been recognized at certain sites on the Antonine Wall; this occupation, if indeed it ever took place – preparations may have been made for a re-occupation which never happened – was ephemeral and may be discounted. The beginning of the first periods on both Hadrian's Wall and the Antonine Wall can be dated by literary and epigraphic evidence, but no such source is available for the commencement of either of the second periods, and we must rely on the more doubtful testimony of archaeology.

Archaeology does attest that both periods on the Antonine Wall ended in the destruction of the forts, and some of those on Hadrian's Wall suffered the same fate at the end of the second period in the second century. Excavation rarely allows the cause of the destruction to be determined. It could have been the result of the demolition of the fort by the Romans before abandonment of the site, or due to a successful attack by the enemy; it could also have been accidental. There are hints that the first destruction of the Antonine Wall was the work of the garrison before evacuation. Sir George Macdonald long ago suggested that the distance slabs had been removed from the Wall and carefully buried to prevent their desecration by the natives. More recently Dr K. A. Steer has pointed out that the east rampart of the fort at Mumrills had been demolished and thrown into the inner ditch at the end of the first period, while at Balmuildy the excavator concluded that the bath-house had been carefully dis-mantled and covered with a layer of clay. Recent excavations at Bearsden have demonstrated that the army demolished and burnt the timber buildings before evacuating the site. At other sites the situation is not so clear. Doubtless the action of the withdrawing units varied from site to site.

It also seems that the forts were not left abandoned for long. Evidence has been adduced at two sites, unfortunately not on the Antonine Wall but in the Scottish Lowlands, Newstead on Dere Street, and Crawford in Clydesdale, to demonstrate that the second occupation followed shortly after the first. At Newstead no silt or growth had been allowed to accumulate in the ditches of the first period before they were filled by the upcast from the three new ditches of the second period. At Crawford the fort was enlarged in the later period and this involved filling the earlier ditches, a task carried out most carefully. One ditch was packed with boulders at the bottom and then filled with cut turves and clay. There was virtually no silt in the bottom of the ditches before this process began. The subsoil on this site is gravel and the excavator was led to conclude that only a very brief interval separated the two periods. The Samian ware found at Newstead suggests that the fort was occupied continuously from about 140 until at least 180. A change of garrison may have occasioned the rebuilding of the fort within that period, which would explain the lack of silt in the ditches. There is, however, no such simple explanation for the situation discovered at Crawford. Only if it is assumed that the two occupations of the site are really phases both falling within the first Antonine period, or that the fort continued in use as an outpost fort of the reoccupied Hadrian's Wall, or that the silt was carefully cleaned out of the ditch before it was backfilled with more solid material, can the conclusion that the second Antonine period followed closely upon the first be refuted. None of these suggestions carries conviction. If Crawford was reoccupied after a short break then it is probable that so were the Antonine Wall forts, though no evidence has yet been found from the Wall to support this supposition.

The second 'incontrovertible' fact is established from detailed examination of the stamps of the Samian potters supplying the garrisons of the northern frontier. Mr B. R. Hartley has recently demonstrated that 95 per cent of individual die stamps appear on sites on one Wall only. This is a clear indication that the two Walls were never held at the same time, except for the minimum period necessary for the repair of the new Wall before the evacuation of the old. This must have been short for there to be only a 5 per cent overlap in the distribution of the stamps, bearing in mind that the same potters would have supplied both Walls.

This result should come as no surprise. It would make no sense to hold both Walls at the same time. Each Wall was constructed to control movement in and out of the province; manning a barrier within the province would be expensive in man-power and to no purpose. It would not divide and separate possibly troublesome tribes such as the Brigantes and the Selgovae; that would be done by the normal Roman forts garrisoning north Britain. Nor would a lightly held Antonine Wall as an advance defence for a strongly held Hadrian's Wall be in keeping with normal Roman frontier policy. It would moreover be extremely dangerous, for in the event of an attack on the northern Wall the nearest reinforcements would be one hundred miles to the south on Hadrian's Wall, with only small and isolated forts in between. No advantage could be gained by holding both Walls at once; when the one was occupied the other was abandoned. It is equally possible that at certain times neither Wall operated as a frontier barrier.

Mr Hartley also suggested that the Antonine Wall and the other Scottish forts, except Newstead and probably Cappuck, were abandoned by the middle years of the decade beginning in 160. His conclusion rests on the lack of stamps and decorated ware of potters believed to have worked in the period 160–200 and represented in two large groups of samian ware, the Wroxeter Gutter and the Pudding Pan Rock deposits. The former was from a pottery retailer's shop destroyed in a fire and was subsequently buried in the gutter of the street in front of the shop, and the latter from a ship wrecked on the Pudding Pan Rock off the coast of Kent on its way to London and gathered off the beach or dredged up in modern times. Neither collection can be very closely dated but they both fall into the last forty years of the second century. The absence of any similar material on the Antonine Wall does suggest that the Wall was abandoned not long after 160. The lack of stamped *mortaria* of the period 160–200 on the Antonine Wall supports this conclusion while Mr J. P. Gillam now considers that the coarse pottery confirms a date in the mid-160s for the abandonment of the Antonine Wall. The evidence from samian, *mortaria* and coarseware, the three different types of pottery in use on the northern frontier, is in agreement, but none of this evidence is self-dating and depends on a relatively small number of dated deposits interpreted by even fewer highly specialized scholars.

Numismatic Evidence for the Later Second Century

Numismatic evidence is not open to this qualification. The coins found on northern sites give clear and unquestioned dates, but dates of minting, not of loss. The latest stratified coin from the

Antonine Wall is of Antoninus Pius, was minted 154–5 and comes from a destruction deposit at Mumrills. Unstratified coins of a rather later date are known. A bronze *as* of Marcus Aurelius dated to 173–4 has been found near Mumrills, while from Kirkintilloch comes a coin of Commodus recorded by a nine-teenth-century antiquarian and from Bar Hill a coin tentatively assigned to the same emperor. Since these coins are unstratified they may not be relevant to the date of the abandonment of the Antonine Wall. They may have been dropped by a passing Roman patrol or by local natives at a much later date. Coins of Marcus and his son Commodus are absent from other Roman forts in Scotland, apart from Cramond on the Forth, which was reoccupied under Severus, and Newstead, always a special case, as it was occupied for some years after the abandonment of the Antonine Wall. However, an important coin-hoard has been found at Rumbling Bridge in Kinross-shire. Although a few miles north of the Antonine Wall Rumbling Bridge lies within the area protected by the outpost forts. The hoard of 179 coins contains eight of Commodus, the latest a fairly fresh specimen minted in 186–7, but the reasons for its deposition and whether a Roman or a native buried it are unknown. The owner of the hoard could have obtained his coins from the Antonine Wall forts or from the outpost forts, though Newstead, held almost certainly until 180 and possibly beyond, sixty miles to the south, may have been the source. The hoard was within that part of Britain shielded by the outpost forts in the Antonine period and over which the army may have maintained surveillance and some sort of physical presence from the abandonment of these permanent bases to the fourth century. Quite possibly the coins have no historical importance at all and formed a hoard built up by a native farmer, merchant or even bandit and buried fortuitously at this time. Certainly the hoard does not prove that the Antonine system continued down to 186–7 nor do the unstratified coins from the Wall itself. The numismatic evidence does attest the occupation of the Antonine Wall down to 154–5, and the unstratified coins of later date hint at some continuing Roman presence in the Antonine Wall area.

Table 10 Events of the second century

Date	Emperor	Literary	Epigraphic	Numismatic	Archaeological
				Evidence	
119	Hadrian			Britannia issue	
122		Hadrian visits Britain and builds a Wall	Diploma: Nepos becomes governor July 122; building inscriptions		Wall built
139–42	Antoninus Pius	Pius conquers barbarians and builds Wall	Building inscriptions	Coin issue 142–4	Wall built
155				Britannia issue	
158			Hadrian's Wall and Birrens building inscriptions		
161	Marcus	British war threatens	Building inscriptions on Hadrian's Wall and in hinterland		

Table 10 – cont.

Date	Emperor	Evidence			
		Literary	Epigraphic	Numismatic	Archaeological
162		Calpurnius Agricola sent			Scotland (apart from Newstead) abandoned; Hadrian's Wall and hinterland forts reoccupied
170–72		British war threatens			
175		5,500 Sarmatian cavalry sent to Britain			
180	Commodus	The barbarians cross a Wall			Destruction at Corbridge, Halton, Rudchester
184				Coin issue for British victory	

Date				
197	Severus	Defeat of Albinus at Lugudunum; Maeatae and Caledones restless	Building inscriptions in hinterland	
205–7			Building inscriptions on Hadrian's Wall and outposts	
208		Barbarians overrun province, emperor and sons arrive		
210		British victory		Coin issue for British victory
211		Caledones and Maeatae revolt; death of Severus		
213			'Loyalty' inscriptions; building inscriptions on Hadrian's Wall and hinterland continue into 260s	

The Second Occupation of the Antonine Wall

For the date of the abandonment of the Antonine Wall we must fall back on the ceramic evidence, which, with all its uncertainties, appears to demonstrate a date in the 160s. If this is accepted, how should the available literary and epigraphic evidence be interpreted?

22 North Britain in the second Antonine period (about 160)

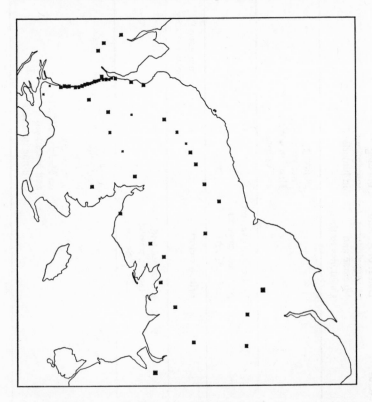

The inscription recording rebuilding of the curtain of Hadrian's Wall in 158 ought to imply reoccupation then. This reoccupation may have been a reaction to events in the early 150s, possibly ending in a victory for Rome commemorated by the coin of 155. In that case the activity of Julius Verus prepared for reoccupation. The rebuilding of Birrens and Brough-on-Noe would then be part of this plan and foreshadow the later activity of Calpurnius Agricola after the final return to Hadrian's Wall in the mid 160s. The building activity at Chesters under Pius may also date to this time. However, this involves the abandonment of the Antonine Wall, and yet the evidence from Crawford forces us to postulate a quick return to Scotland. The policy of Verus must then have been reversed, perhaps soon after 158. The army did not return to Scotland in the same strength. Many of the sites in the Lowlands were abandoned, including most of the fortlets in the south-west of Scotland and all the stations in the Nith valley. The garrisons of South Scotland were now all

23 The Antonine Wall in the second Antonine period. Open squares indicate forts abandoned or reduced in garrison

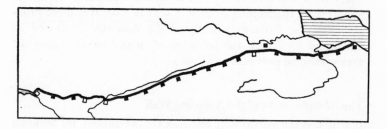

based on the two main roads leading north, Dere Street and the Annandale–Clydesdale route. The primary purpose of the units in these forts now appears to be in support of the Antonine Wall rather than as 'police' controlling the local population, though doubtless this and the protection of communications continued as part of their duties. The Antonine Wall itself also saw a reduction in the size of its garrison. The fort at New Kilpatrick, Bearsden appears to have been abandoned, while the *cohors milliaria peditata* based at Old Kilpatrick was probably replaced by a *cohors quingenaria peditata*. The excavator of a third fort, Balmuildy, also suggested that its garrison in the second Antonine period may have been smaller than in the first.

Although other forts were reoccupied at only two sites can the new garrison be shown to have been the same size as its predecessor; at one of these, Mumrills, the only *ala* stationed on the Wall was replaced by a *cohors quingenaria equitata*. North of the Wall the garrison of Ardoch was seemingly reduced.

This reduction in Scottish garrisons may have had several causes, working separately or more likely together. Troops may have been needed elsewhere, in the Pennines and Wales. Controlling the tribes of the Scottish Lowlands may have required fewer units than in the first Antonine period, maybe because the earlier occupation had been in massive strength to ensure Pius his easy victory. In that case the second Antonine occupation may have been a more sober, and sensible, reaction to the problems the army had to face. Perhaps fewer units were employed in the Scottish Lowlands because the army only intended to return for a short period in preparation for a final return to Hadrian's Wall; however, this is unlikely. The army would hardly rebuild so many forts and fortlets – possibly as many as thirty – with the intention of abandoning them in a year or two. It is more probable that the Romans reoccupied the Antonine Wall and its hinterland forts with the intention of finally incorporating the area within the province.

The Abandonment of the Antonine Wall

If that was the intention it was quickly overturned, for within a few years all the forts north of Hadrian's Wall were abandoned with the exception of Newstead and the chain of stations linking it with the province, and the western outpost forts. Whatever the enigmatic third period on the Antonine Wall means it did not involve the reoccupation of the Wall and its accompanying forts. Although permanent garrisons were withdrawn from central and south-western Scotland the army did not lose all interest in this area. The continuing occupation – in strength – of Newstead on the north side of the Cheviots points to a considerable interest in the tribes of this frontier region, and there is a hint that Newstead was not the most northerly base. Late Antonine Samian ware has been found at Castlecary on the Antonine Wall as well as at Newstead and Birrens. Although

Castlecary can produce only one stamp paralleled in the late-Antonine Wroxeter Gutter deposit, this isolated find does receive support from an altar discovered at the site. The dedication to Mercury, found just outside the fort, records the erection of a shrine and statue by soldiers of VI Victrix who were citizens of Italy and Noricum (Austria). The most straightforward way that soldiers from that part of the Empire could have entered VI Victrix is by transfer from II Italica, the one legion of Noricum, raised in Italy in 165. (Only new legions recruited Italians – most Italian recruits entered the Rome units such as the praetorian guard or the urban cohorts.) That would date the inscription within the period 165 to 190, probably later rather than earlier as the number of Noricans is large enough to warrant special mention. Moreover it is unlikely that soldiers could have been spared from the Danube until after 180; indeed it is possible that the soldiers were sent to make up losses suffered in the invasion of the early 180s when not only was a Roman general killed but also his army. However, this is speculation; the troops may have arrived some years earlier. Nevertheless the altar does attest a continuing Roman interest as far north as the Forth–Clyde line after the mid 160s. This altar, if correctly dated, is the only inscription from the Antonine Wall certainly later than the reign of Pius.

The continuing Roman preoccupation with the land – and the tribes, the Caledonians and the Maeatae – north of the Forth in the late second and early third centuries certainly may imply that the Antonine Wall was held until the end of the century. Speaking of the Severan campaigns of 209–11 Cassius Dio says that 'the Maeatae live close to the wall which divides the island in two, and the Caledonians beyond them'. The Maeatae lived just north of the Forth – their name is commemorated in the place-names of Dumyat and Myot Hill in Clackmannanshire – and so the Wall which they lived beside was the Antonine. This, together with the inscription from Castlecary, is the best evidence for the continuing occupation of the Antonine Wall in the later second century. But it is not unequivocal proof of a late date for the abandonment of the Wall. It directly contradicts pottery evidence, which is unanimous in suggesting a date in the mid 160s, and the lack of epigraphic and numismatic evidence later than the 180s. Castlecary may have been held for some time as an advance base. It was an important fort in the first and second centuries, lying on the watershed of the Carron and Kelvin valleys, possibly beside a natural route north.

Why was the Antonine Wall abandoned about 163, only twenty-five years after it was built, and only six or seven years after its reoccupation following a brief break? The reason does not seem connected with the local situation. The army experienced no difficulty in controlling northern England and southern Scotland and the withdrawal cannot be connected with a need to strengthen control over the Pennines. Nor did the hostile attitude of the Caledonians force the Romans to withdraw – it is inconceivable that Rome at the height of her power would be forced into a 'strategic withdrawal'. The reason for the abandonment of the Scottish Lowlands must be closely connected with the reason for its occupation twenty-five years before. If the move into Scotland in 140 was a sop thrown to Trajan's marshals or a scheme to gain Antoninus Pius easy military prestige then the withdrawal after Pius' death could follow recognition by Rome that the need to hold Scotland had passed. Calpurnius Agricola was sent to Britain soon after the accession of Marcus and Verus. Before his departure from Rome he must have been briefed on the situation in Britain and what the emperors wished done there. During the course of his governorship it would appear that the army was withdrawn from Scotland and many of the Pennine forts rebuilt. It is difficult to escape the conclusion that this reversal of policy was decided not by Agricola on the spot but by the emperors and their advisors in Rome, who had recognized the Antonine occupation of Scotland for what it was. If so, the abandonment of Scotland in 158 may have been decided by Julius Verus on his own initiative, a decision reversed almost immediately on the direct orders of Pius, who had a vested interest in the sole conquest of his reign and the victory which set the seal on his peaceful succession.

The Reoccupation of Hadrian's Wall

The overall nature of the reoccupation of the frontier complex in the mid 160s is fairly clear. Hadrian's Wall itself was put back into working order much as before. The forts were repaired and reoccupied, usually by a unit of similar size and type to the one which had left it twenty years previously. The milecastle gates were replaced, the barracks repaired and the turrets rebuilt. The rebuilding was quite extensive, possibly because the Romans

24 Forts on Hadrian's Turf Wall rebuilt in stone. From top left to bottom right: Bowness, Burgh-by Sands; Stanwix, Castlesteads. Scale 1 in. = 400 ft (1:4800)

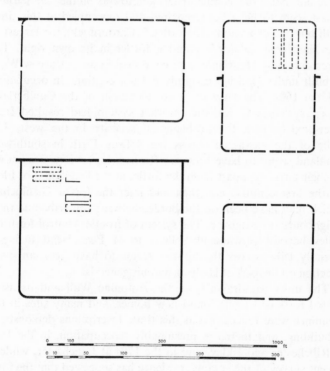

themselves had used the Wall as a convenient quarry for building stone. This is presumably why the curtain itself was rebuilt in places in 158. Work on the curtain in the west probably included the completion of the rebuilding of the turf wall in stone. The Vallum was cleaned out and the silt dumped on the south berm forming an extra mound (the 'marginal mound'). One addition to the frontier complex, a road, seems to have been made at this time, resulting from experience gained on the Antonine Wall. The discovery of side roads linking turrets abandoned some years later with this road, the Military Way, suggests that the road (clearly not part of the Hadrianic plan, for in places it overrides or runs along the top of the north mound of the Vallum) was built at this time. But if the Wall was reoccupied as before, and even improved, other parts of the frontier complex were not. None of the milefortlets and towers on the Cumberland Coast seem to have been repaired and reoccupied at this time, with but one exception, milefortlet 5 (Cardurnock), the largest of the Hadrianic milefortlets and a fortlet in its own right. The three definitely Hadrianic forts continued in use – Burrow Walls if built under Hadrian certainly did not continue in occupation till the 160s. The large-scale abandonment of the Cumberland Coast system was realistic for that system had resulted from over-anxiety with the problems of security in the west. The tribe of the Novantae across the Solway Firth in south-west Scotland seems to have been pro-Roman, for no forts are known in their territory, apart from the fortlet at the Gatehouse of Fleet in the first century, and then and later the fort a Glenlochar, which may have been on the border between this tribe and their neighbours the Selgovae. The system of frontier control for forty miles beyond Bowness-on-Solway to St Bees Head facing a friendly tribe across the Solway seems to have been an over-reaction on the part of Hadrian and his generals.

The units withdrawn from the Antonine Wall and its associated forts had to be found new homes, and many sites in the Pennines were reoccupied at this time. Inscriptions demonstrate rebuilding, and therefore presumably reoccupation, in the 160s a Ribchester and Ilkley, and in the 170s at Lanchester, while a recent survey of the ceramic evidence has suggested that the forts at Ambleside, Bainbridge, Binchester, Chester-le-Street, Ebchester, Lancaster, Manchester, Old Penrith and Templebrough were all reoccupied at this time. The renewed activity at these forts, spread over the whole of the north of England from Derbyshire to the Wall, does not imply any local disturbance but simply the need to find bases for the returning units.

25 North England about 170. The open squares indicate that occupation
at this time is not certain

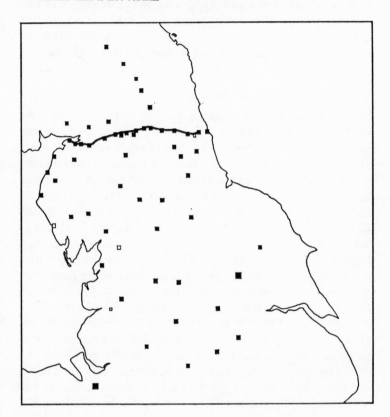

The return to Hadrian's Wall in the 160s did not break all
contact with the area to the north, as seems almost to have
happened under Hadrian. In the west Birrens and Netherby
certainly continued to be held, and therefore presumably Bewcastle also. In the east, as we have seen, the hand of the army
stretched even further north. Newstead was rebuilt about 160
and continued in occupation for another twenty years or so. The
forts on Dere Street linking it with the Wall presumably were
also held (Risingham alone has produced clear evidence for a
garrison in these years). Patrols may have maintained surveillance

127

over an area almost coterminous with the abandoned territories, if the evidence from Castlecary is accepted. This system of out-post forts, and the patrolling which must have accompanied it, heralds the later 'third-century' organization which lasted un-changed almost to the end of the Roman period in Britain.

The Invasion of the Early 180s

Britain was unsettled throughout the 170s but in the early 180s trouble erupted spectacularly. A Roman general was killed and his army massacred when the barbarians crossed the Wall. Which Wall was crossed is not recorded and some scholars have suggested that the peculiar wording of the passage – 'the wall that separated them from the Roman forts' – may imply that the unoccupied, but not forgotten, Antonine Wall was crossed. However, there does appear to have been damage to Hadrian's Wall at this time. The fort at Halton Chesters seems to have been destroyed, its neighbour Rudchester, and also the station of Corbridge two miles to the south. But none of the three other forts where excavation has taken place recently, South Shields, Carrawburgh and Housesteads, can be shown to have suffered damage at this time. Some milecastles and turrets exhibit signs of repair perhaps following destruction by enemy action, or as part of a general overhaul of the frontier complex, possibly over a period of years. There is an altar at Kirksteads between Stanwix and Burgh-by-Sands by a legate of VI Victrix recording success-ful operations beyond the Wall. It may have been dedicated at this time, but it could equally well have been set up at any time in the second half of the second century.

Ulpius Marcellus, sent by Commodus, retrieved the situation, and his victory was celebrated in 184. Marcellus also seems to have made changes in the military dispositions. Mr Hartley's study of the Samian ware has led him to conclude that it was now that the great base of Newstead was abandoned. Risingham on Dere Street may also have been given up at this time for an inscription erected over the south gate of this fort twenty-five years later records the rebuilding of this gate and the adjoining length of wall, which had fallen down through old age. It is diffi-cult to envisage an occupied fort with its gates and walls in ruins,

26 Hadrian's Wall and its outpost forts. a. about 170; b. about 190

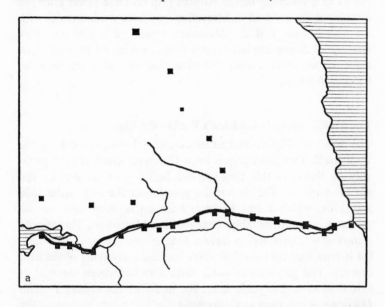

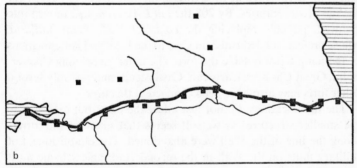

so the fort may have lain without a garrison for the last years of the second century. However, a similarly worded inscription dated to 221 comes from Chesters, where the unit had been in garrison at least fifteen years, so the continued occupation of Risingham cannot be ruled out. Unfortunately nothing is known of High Rochester, the next fort along Dere Street, at this time. The abandonment of Newstead, and possibly also of Risingham,

129

points to a lessening of the Roman grip on Dere Street after the disaster of the early 180s. Marcellus may have made treaties with the Caledonians and the Maeatae; a passage in Cassius Dio's *History of Rome* implies such a treaty, which might have been made either at that time by Marcellus or ten years later by Clodius Albinus.

The Modifications to Hadrian's Wall in the 180s

The hand of Ulpius Marcellus can also be recognized on the Wall itself. Two inscriptions from Chesters, which should probably be dated to this time, record building at the fort by the *ala II Asturum*. This is not the garrison of the fort in the 160s and 170s, which seems to have been an infantry unit, so the garrison was presumably changed by Marcellus. The *ala II Asturum* was destined to have a long connection with Chesters, for it remained for over 200 years into the early years of the fifth century. The garrisons of other forts may have been changed at this time or a few years later, for in 205–7 the *cohors I Aelia Dacorum* is recorded at Birdoswald, the fort it was to occupy for the next two centuries. By 208 the *ala I Asturum* had moved into Benwell, possibly replacing the *cohors I Vangionum milliaria,* whose prefect had dedicated an altar to the local god Antenociticus in the temple just outside the fort. The units garrisoning Chester-holm, Great Chesters, Carvoran, Castlesteads and possibly several other forts may also have been changed at this time.

The modifications did not just affect the forts, but extended to the smaller structures as well. It seems that many of the turrets along the line of the Wall were abandoned. The establishment of military units on the Wall in the second Hadrianic scheme must have made many of these observation posts redundant, although none seem to have been relinquished. All the ones investigated seem to have been put back into working order on the return to Hadrian's Wall in the 160s, unlike their counterparts on the Cumberland Coast, but reoccupation may only have been half-hearted. So little pottery of this period was found in turret 33b that the excavators felt the reoccupation was only very brief or spasmodic. The same can be said of the next turret to the west, 34a, while 35a, a mile further on, too may have gone out of use in the middle of the second century. This paucity of pottery at many turrets suggests that other sites may follow the same pattern. Some of these structures exhibit traces of blocking in their doorways. After an initial brief reoccupation in the 160s the turrets may have gone out of use and the doors been built up. Later in the century more drastic alterations were carried out at these turrets and at others. The structure was demolished, sometimes removing almost all trace of it, and the curtain wall built across the recess on the north side of the turret. Pottery dropped during this operation helps to date it to the later years of the second century or the early years of the third. The recess may have been built up because, after years of neglect, the first floor of the turret, essential to maintain communication along the Wall top, was becoming unsafe, if indeed the whole structure was not dangerous by this time. In some areas turrets were abandoned wholesale: in the central crags sector of the Wall no turret between 33b and 41b inclusive is known to have been retained though a few miles further west turret 44b in a splendid signalling and observing position did continue in use. Elsewhere the pattern is more irregular; in the Irthing–Birdoswald area, for example, some turrets were abandoned, others retained, with no discernible pattern. Some of the milecastles and turrets which did continue in use may have been abandoned during the third century; certainly few survived into the fourth.

The milecastles did not go untouched at this time. Every milecastle where investigation has revealed sufficient surviving evidence had one of its two gates narrowed so that it was only passable by pedestrian traffic. Usually the north gate was treated in this manner, but sometimes the south, while the north gate of milecastle 22 between Halton Chesters and the Portgate was blocked completely. However, only one milecastle, 27, seems to have been abandoned at this time, though the interiors of few milecastles have been examined and published. These alterations, like the changes to the turrets, follow realistic assessment of the situation on the Wall. There was an overprovision of milecastles – and gates – at the beginning so these changes were probably no more than an adaptation of the structures to meet the real situation.

The Mid 180s and After

Ulpius Marcellus, sent by Commodus to retrieve the situation in Britain, may have restored the frontier defences but he was not able to solve all the province's troubles. This disturbed state of affairs in Britain makes the history of the next twenty years correspondingly obscure. It is not until 213 or so that the mists shrouding the events of these years clear and the organization of the frontier defences can be better understood. Marcellus' victory over the barbarians was celebrated in 184 but in the following year the British army, now probably under a new governor, mutinied and their complaints led directly to the downfall of the senior army officer, the praetorian prefect, Perennis. P. Helvius Pertinax was appointed governor of Britain and tried to restore discipline, but without success. A legion mutinied again and in the disturbances Pertinax was almost killed. He retired prematurely from his command at his own request. The lack of building inscriptions dated to the reign of Commodus is not confined to Britain but is general to the empire. Perhaps the damnation of his memory after his murder resulted in the smashing of the inscriptions bearing his name. This makes unsafe any conclusions based on their absence in Britain. Be that as it may, the last years of his reign were not conducive to good and stable provincial government, while his assassination on the last day of 192 led to a civil war which lasted four years.

While the governor of Britain, D. Clodius Albinus, was preparing for his challenge to the new emperor, L. Septimius Severus, he cannot have been too concerned with the northern frontier. He was playing for higher stakes: if he won the empire he would have enough troops to settle any frontier trouble, and if he lost it would no longer be his concern. However, he may have made or renewed treaties made some years before by Ulpius Marcellus with the northern tribes, the Caledonians and Maeatae, to help safeguard the frontier. Immediately after Albinus' defeat in February 197, while the garrisons of some or all of the Wall forts may have been absent on the continent or reduced to a care-and-maintenance staff, these tribes may have invaded the province and caused extensive damage on Hadrian's Wall. While there is no definite evidence of this the Maeatae were clearly causing

1 Aerial view of the central sector of Hadrian's Wall looking east, with the Wall following the crags on the left and the Vallum running behind the Wall on the right

2 Milecastle 37 (Housesteads) from the air. Within the fortlet the small barrack-block is visible

3 Turret 48a (Willowford East). A point of reduction shows clearly on the extreme right

4 Model of a milecastle. The main features are: arched gateways with double
doors front and rear, tower over north gate, small barrack-block, steps and ovens

5 Model of a turret. The main features are: two storeys, flat crenellated top
and access to Wall top

6 The curtain at Planetrees. Here the Wall is reduced in thickness from 10 Roman feet to 6 Roman feet. The foundation, incorporating a drain, had already been laid

7 The Narrow Wall at Cuddy's Crag looking east

8 The diploma (grant of privileges) of 17 July 122 given to a man discharged by Pompeius Falco, the previous governor, the present governor being A. Platorius Nepos. The names of both governors and of the units discharging men can be picked out.
Each of the two leaves measures 6½ ins. by 5¾ ins.

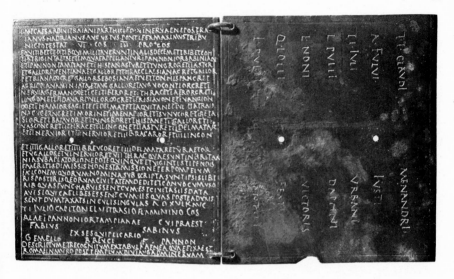

9 The Rudge Cup. Of mid-second-century date, this appears to portray the Wall as a running frieze, with the names of the forts above. Its diameter is 4 ins., and its height 3 ins.

10 *Above* Aerial view of the Antonine Wall at Rough Castle looking east. The fort lies to the right of the rampart and ditch, with the fortified annex immediately beyond

11 *Opposite above* Trajan's Column. The legions build: bridge-building, turf-cutting and carrying, ditch-digging. Ready-cut turves lie not far from stacked arms

12 Trajan's Column. The legions build: ditch-digging and turf-carrying. The ropes holding the turf on the soldier's back are clearly seen

13 Trajan's Column. The auxiliaries fight: mail-shirted auxiliary cavalry and infantry secure heads as trophies; one uses a bow. An irregular fights bare-chested with a club

14 Trajan's Column. The auxiliaries fight: auxiliary infantry, including one archer and a club-wielding irregular (some weapons supplied in metal have vanished). Jupiter hurls his thunderbolts (a rain-storm in the enemies' faces?)

15 One of the rear rooms in the headquarters building at Chesterholm. The screen to one side of the entrance would have been balanced by a second, the groove for which is visible

16 The tribunal in the *basilica* of the headquarters building at Chesterholm. The lower two of a flight of steps can be seen to the left of the dais

17 *Above left* The east granary at Corbridge. The floor of stone slabs is supported on dwarf walls to allow the free circulation of air below it

18 *Above right* The north granary at Housesteads. Here the floor was of timber supported on individual stone pillars

19 *Opposite above* Housesteads from the air looking north. Within the walls, complete with gates and towers, may be seen the central range of buildings, two granaries, headquarters building, and commanding officer's house

20 *Opposite below* Chesterholm from the air looking south. The fort platform, with the headquarters building in the centre, is visible on the left. The buildings of the *vicus* line the road leading out of the west gate. In the bottom centre lies the fort's bath-house

21 *Opposite above* Chesters from the air. Five of the six gates may be seen. In the centre of the fort lies the headquarters building, flanked by the commanding officer's house and bath suite, to the right of which parts of three barrack-blocks are visible

22 *Opposite below* Chesters bath-house seen from the north-east with the changing room in the foreground

23 Benwell fort lies astride Hadrian's Wall. In the centre is the headquarters building, to its right the courtyard house of the commanding officer and to its left a pair of granaries. To this side of the commanding officer's house is the hospital. The other buildings are barrack-blocks, storehouses, probably stables and a workshop

24 A pair of barrack-blocks at Chesters looking towards the officers' quarters

25 The east gate at Birdoswald

26 The simple apsidal temple of the god Antenociticus at Benwell

27 The head of Antenociticus

28 Turret 33b (Coesike). The blocking in the doorway dates to the second century. Later the turret was demolished down to the lowest four courses and the recess on the north side built up. Beyond this blocking can just be seen the original inner north wall of the turret

29 The Vallum crossing at Benwell looking north towards the fort. The ditch is shown dug to full depth, and to the north several periods of road are displayed as a series of steps

trouble, for Cassius Dio states that Severus' new governor Virius Lupus was forced to purchase peace from the Maeatae for a great sum, receiving back some prisoners, when the Caledonians did not keep their promises but made ready to assist the Maeatae. It is not recorded precisely what the Maeatae were doing but it clearly involved hostilities with the Romans. Possibly the Maeatae had attacked one of the pro-Roman tribes of the Scottish Lowlands, they may even have crossed the Wall, but it is perhaps unlikely that they destroyed the frontier complex and the forts of North Britain wholesale at this time; Severus, across the Channel in Gaul, made no move to come to Britain but instead turned east to fight the Parthians. This war was of his own choosing and it seems probable that he would have come to Britain if he was needed. Nevertheless the statement by Dio is unmistakable evidence for unsettled conditions on the northern frontier, which seem to have continued for some time. Nearly ten years later, again according to Dio, Severus was angry at the thought that, although he was winning wars in Britain through others, he had shown himself no match for a robber in Italy. The victories of these years may be commemorated in the dedications to Victory at Benwell on the Wall and at Greetland in Yorkshire, though the former may have been erected in 207 on the anniversary of the Parthian victory won in 198, and the latter, since it is dedicated to the goddess Victoria Brigantia, for the putting-down of a more local disturbance.

While fighting these wars Severus' governors still found time to rebuild at many forts. Ilkley, Bainbridge, Bowes, Brough under Stainmore and Greta Bridge in the Pennines all underwent repair; inscriptions on Hadrian's Wall at Chesters, Housesteads and Birdoswald are testimony to the work of army maintenance staff while Risingham and High Rochester north of the Wall have yielded building stones dated to these years. More building activity is recorded on these inscriptions than at any time since the construction of the two Walls, and it has long been taken as evidence that the forts of the north of England had recently suffered destruction. However, a long period of building continued until about 240 and over the forty years affected a score of sites from Yorkshire to High Rochester. Work over such a long period cannot have been occasioned by enemy action but rather by two other considerations: the need to undertake necessary repairs to forts occupied for some years, and a desire to improve facilities at these now-permanent stations. Hence the building inscriptions at two sites, South Shields and Chester-le-Street, record the bringing of water into the fort, while at Netherby a cavalry exercise hall was built. Chesters, Chester-holm, Great Chesters, Lanchester and some years later Lancaster all received major repairs after they had been occupied for some years.

Severus in Britain

Although the Romans were winning victories in the middle years of the first decade of the third century, in 208 the tide again turned against them. Herodian states that the governor wrote to Severus 'that the barbarians had risen and were overrunning the country, carrying off booty and causing great destruction, and that for effective defence either more troops or the presence of the emperor was necessary'. Severus responded by coming to Britain himself with more troops. The emperor brought his two sons, Caracalla and Geta, with him. Both Herodian and Cassius Dio are in agreement that Severus wished to get his sons away from the flesh-pots of Rome where they were being corrupted by the 'luxuries and pleasures of the capital'. Indeed Professor A. R. Birley has gone so far as to suggest that their father engineered the request from the governor of Britain as an excuse to give them a taste of military life and discipline. However, Cassius Dio states that Severus intended to conquer the rest of the island and emphasizes this by his remark that the emperor almost reached the end of the island. The costly and far-reaching preparations made by Severus for the campaigns suggest this was his intention even before he arrived in Britain, which would be consonant with his general policy of expansion to solve frontier difficulties.

Preparations were put in hand for the forthcoming campaigns. At Corbridge on the traditional invasion route into Scotland they included the rebuilding of a granary. South Shields at the mouth of the Tyne saw the construction of twenty new granaries in addition to the two already standing within the fort. This energetic work suggests preparations not just to serve for the duration of a single campaign but afterwards to supply a new garrisoning force in Scotland. A supply base at South Shields demonstrates that the campaigns were to be supplied by sea, and now or within a short time the fort at Cramond on the Forth was reconditioned, presumably as a link in the supply line. As far as land communications were concerned Risingham and High Rochester on Dere Street had already been occupied – if indeed they had ever been abandoned – and Mr Hartley has suggested that Newstead may also have been reoccupied for a time.

27   South Shields. a. about 130; b. about 210. Scale 1 in. = 400 ft (1:4800)

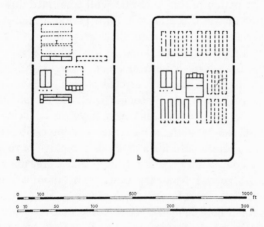

The imperial family with an army consisting of part, possibly most, of the praetorian guard and legionary vexillations arrived in Britain in 208. While Geta was left to gain experience in administration in south Britain Severus and Caracalla moved north. The Caledonians and Maeatae sued for peace, but Severus would have none of it and sending their envoys home prepared for war. The campaign was probably mounted in 208 and during its course the Roman army reached, according to Dio, almost the end of the island. The series of marching camps assigned by Professor St Joseph to this season, the 63-acre camps, only extends as far north as Montrose so it would appear that Severus' efforts

135

were concentrated on the Maeatae. The barbarians answered Rome's might with guerrilla tactics and Severus lost many men before they capitulated and, in the words of Dio, ceded 'not a small part of their territory'. Severus and his sons assumed the title Britannicus, while Geta was promoted to Augustus. The epithet Britannica was added to the titles of legion VI Victrix. Construction of the new legionary base at Carpow on the Tay may have started at this time. Less than 30 acres in size, it was too small to hold a complete legion, and may have been designed for legionary detachments, possibly from II Augusta and VI Victrix, the two units which built the fortress. The establishment of a base here emphasizes that Severus intended to reoccupy Lowland Scotland at the minimum.

If the occupation of the Antonine Wall continued down to the first years of the third century the third period on the Antonine Wall, apparently nothing more than preparations for a new occupation, may perhaps be dated to the end of Severus' reign. It may have been then that a detachment of legion XXII Primigenia from Upper Germany erected a commemorative slab, probably at Falkirk, on the Antonine Wall; but this site is on the invasion route and so the stone may have no connection with the repair of the Wall. It is moreover not impossible that the inscription was erected during a previous campaign or rebuilding.

After the conclusion of peace Severus and Caracalla returned to York, the nearest legionary base. Some months later they heard there that the Maeatae had revolted. While they were preparing for a new campaign news came that the Caledonians had joined the revolt. Severus was too ill to join his army – he had been carried on the previous campaign in a litter – so Caracalla was left in command. The series of marching camps, 130 acres in size, assigned to this season stretch as far north as Stonehaven, a few miles further north than was apparently reached in the previous campaign. But Caracalla was more concerned with securing army support than prosecuting the campaign, according to contemporary writers, and the death of his father at York on 4 February 211 brought a speedy end to the fighting. Caracalla signed a new treaty with the barbarians, withdrawing from their territory and abandoning some forts. He then joined his mother and brother and returned to Rome, the centre of power.

An inscription recording building activity at Carpow in 212 or perhaps a little later suggests that Caracalla's abandonment of his father's conquests may not have been as abrupt as his contemporaries imply. A series of inscriptions erected in the forts of north Britain in 213 emphasizing the army's loyalty to Caracalla may have been necessary after his murder of his younger brother Geta, whose interests, according to Herodian, had been protected by the British army; they also may point to the army's disquiet at the recent abandonment of Severus' costly-won conquests. The disgrace, and possible execution, of a governor of Britain in 213 emphasize the unsettled state of the army. It has also been suggested that the troops from the two Germanies attested at Piercebridge under Caracalla or his successor may have been brought over to stiffen the loyalty of the British units, but this is unlikely four years after 213.

The Scottish Lowlands in the Third Century

The frontier defences after the final abandonment of the Scottish forts were very different from those when the Wall was built nearly 100 years before. Although the Wall itself no doubt retained its bureaucratic function of frontier control the weight of the military units defending the province was moved north to the outpost forts. Four such forts appear to have been occupied now – High Rochester and Risingham in the east, Bewcastle and Netherby in the west. Thus the farthest-flung outposts in the east, Cappuck and Newstead, were abandoned, though third-century inscriptions found at Jedburgh near Cappuck demonstrate a military presence there at this time, while in the west Birrens, one of the original Hadrianic outpost forts, had been given up. These forts were the bases of perhaps the most versatile auxiliary units in the Roman army, the thousand strong mixed infantry and cavalry units, the *cohortes milliariae equitatae*. Only five such units are attested in Britain and in the third century four were north of the Wall in these forts. In the east Risingham and High Rochester had additional support in the form of *exploratores*, scouts, while Netherby was actually called Castra Exploratorum. These troops must have patrolled the Cheviots and southern Scotland; in fact the parent forts were so

137

small that they could not have held the whole garrison if present at the same time.

The Ravenna Cosmography, a list of places in the Roman world compiled at Ravenna in the seventh century, records various meeting places, *loca*, in North Britain. These include the *locus Maponi*, *locus Manavi*, *locus Dannoni*, the *Segloes* and the *Tava*. The first was clearly connected with the god Maponus, whose shrine may have been at or near the stone known as the Clochmabenstane on the northern shore of the Solway; the near-by town Lochmaben also preserves the name. The meeting place of the Manau may also have been connected with a stone, in this case the Clackmannanstane, which now lies in the market place of Clackmannan on the north side of the Forth, while Slamannan to the south of the river also commemorates the name. The full name of the Manau was the Manau Goddodin, Goddodin deriving from the Votadini of Ptolemy, who apparently had their capital at Traprain Law in East Lothian. In the seventh century A.D. the seat of the tribe, or kingdom as it then was, had moved to Edinburgh. Possibly in the third century the Manau were a sept or division of the tribe living at the head of the Firth of Forth. The Dannoni are clearly the same as the Damnonii, who seem to have been centred on the lower Clyde valley, and the Segloes the tribe named as the Selgovae by Ptolemy. These are all tribes or place names within the territory recently relinquished and the inclusion in the list of the Tay, the northern limit of the province in Antonine times, suggests that although withdrawing permanent garrisons the army intended to maintain surveillance over this area. Similar arrangements to those in North Britain are known on the Danube, where meeting places were agreed with various tribes in areas evacuated by the Romans but still subject to their control. These included the fixing of where these tribes should assemble and when, and that such assembly should only be in the presence of a Roman centurion.

Hadrian's Wall in the Third Century

The establishment of a broad zone of defence in advance of the Wall was accompanied by changes on the Wall itself. The building-up of the recesses in many turrets rendered obsolete as observation posts by the presence of military units on the Wall can probably be dated to these years. The Vallum also appears to have gone out of use at this time. In the peaceful conditions of the third century it seems to have been simply forgotten about: civilians were allowed to build houses and shops between the Vallum and the forts, even filling in the ditch and levelling the mounds where it suited their purpose. This process may even have started before the end of the second century, at least at Benwell, where the pottery recovered from the filling of the Vallum ditch would support such a date.

The Fort Garrisons in the Third Century

Although many turrets were abandoned, milecastles had their gates narrowed and the Vallum was built over, the forts continued in use and their garrisons were strengthened. Four cavalry regiments are now attested on the Wall as opposed to only one or two in the Hadrianic period. Most fort garrisons contained an element of cavalry, indeed only three or four forts are known not to have contained at least some cavalry. At many sites the normal auxiliary garrison was strengthened by the addition of irregular units or *numeri*. The *cohors I Tungrorum milliaria* stationed at Housesteads, for example, was supplemented by the *cuneus Frisiorum*, a cavalry unit, and the *numerus Hnaudifridi*, Notfried's regiment. Often the fort could not hold the troops technically stationed there and many soldiers must have served away from base, unless there was accommodation in the *vicus* outside the fort; barrack-like buildings have been recently excavated immediately outside the west rampart of the fort at Chesterholm. Although it has been suggested that these were married quarters, provided possibly by the army, it is equally possible that they were barrack-blocks. With these extra troops and units the garrison of the Wall was 10,000 men, some 2000 more than in the Hadrianic period. Approximately a third of these were cavalry, compared to about a quarter of the Hadrianic garrison, while the garrison of the outpost forts was doubled to 4000. The increased strength of the Wall garrison gave not only greater protection to the province, but also strong additional support to the outpost

Table 11 The garrison of Hadrian's Wall in the third century

Fort	Garrison
South Shields	*cohors V Gallorum quingenaria equitata*
Wallsend	*cohors IV Lingonum quingenaria equitata*
Newcastle	*cohors I Cornoviorum quingenaria peditata*
Benwell	*ala I Asturum*
Rudchester	*cohors (Frisiavonum?) quingenaria peditata*
Halton Chesters	*ala I Pannoniorum Sabiniana*
Chesters	*ala II Asturum*
Carrawburgh	*cohors I Batavorum quingenaria equitata*
Housesteads	*cohors I Tungrorum milliaria peditata, cuneus Frisiorum, numerus Hnaudifridi*
Chesterholm	*cohors IV Gallorum quingenaria equitata*
Great Chesters	*cohors II Asturum quingenaria equitata, vexillatio Raetorum gaesatorum*
Carvoran	*cohors II Delmatarum quingenaria equitata*
Birdoswald	*cohors I Aelia Dacorum milliaria peditata, venatores Bannienses*
Castlesteads	*cohors II Tungrorum milliaria equitata*
Stanwix	*ala Petriana milliaria*
Burgh-by-Sands	*cohors I Germanorum milliaria equitata, cuneus Frisionum* (later *numerus Maurorum Aurelianorum*)
Drumburgh	(?)
Bowness-on-Solway	*cohors milliaria*
Beckfoot	*cohors quingenaria* (?)
Maryport	*cohors milliaria* (?)
Moresby	*cohors II Thracum quingenaria equitata*
Netherby	*cohors I Aelia Hispanorum milliaria equitata, exploratores*
Bewcastle	*cohors milliaria*
Risingham	*cohors I Vangionum milliaria equitata, numerus exploratorum, vexillatio Raetorum gaesatorum*
High Rochester	*cohors I Vardullorum milliaria equitata, numerus exploratorum*

forts. In effect the establishment of the forward patrolling system moved forward the military zone and the Wall forts took over the support duties of the earlier hinterland forts. Indeed this, and the peaceful conditions prevailing, allowed the garrisons of many hinterland forts, in Durham, Yorkshire and Westmorland especially, to be withdrawn towards the end of the third century. The strengthening of the cavalry element on the Wall gave not only more mobility in the case of an impending invasion, but also allowed these troops to participate to greater effect in the patrolling of the area to the north of the Wall.

This system of frontier control, which was to last well into the fourth century, is often attributed to the emperor Caracalla but there is strong evidence that it was established before the death of his father Severus in 211. The auxiliary units garrisoning one of the outpost forts, Risingham, and two of the Wall forts, Chesters and Birdoswald, in the third century were in residence in 205–7 when they were rebuilding or repairing the forts, while by 213 the auxiliary garrison of Risingham had been joined by the irregular troops, the *Raeti gaesati* and the *exploratores*. There are building inscriptions of this date at High Rochester and Housesteads but unfortunately both are fragmentary and the name of the units missing. The altar to Victory erected at Benwell in the governorship of Alfenus Senecio, 205 to 208, mentions the *ala I Asturum*, the third- and fourth-century garrison of the fort. Thus at several sites, and possibly all – for no fort can be shown to have changed its garrison in the years following 207 – the unit which was to be stationed there for the next 200 years was in residence by the middle of Severus' reign, before his campaigns against the Maeatae and Caledonians. There is the possibility, already mentioned, that the garrison of Chesters, the *ala II Asturum*, was there in the early 180s. If that was the case other forts might have received their third-century garrisons at this time. Probably the other major modifications to the Wall, which were to last through the rest of its history – the abandonment of the turret system and the narrowing of the milecastle gateways – were made at this time. Perhaps these years saw a thorough rethinking of the purpose and function of the Wall, though not perhaps a complete overhaul of its installations, which came some years later under Virius Lupus, Valerius Pudens and Alfenus Senecio, Severus' governors.

The units on the Wall then were in position before Severus' campaign and possibly since the 180s. There was a milliary cohort at Risingham before Severus came to Britain and the other milliary cohorts may have taken up their positions. Is there any evidence to suggest that the system of basing scouts on the outpost forts commenced before the campaigns? If so all the elements in the 'Caracallan' organization were in place before 208. There had always been individual *exploratores*, which simply means scouts, in the Roman army, for patrolling was always important. Units of *exploratores* develop first in the second century, as the frontiers settle down. What is special about the 'Caracallan' system is that *exploratores* known by the fort name, for example the *exploratores Habitancenses*, are attached to the outpost forts. At Netherby the evidence is its name, Castra Exploratorum. But the name itself comes from the Antonine Itinerary, a collection of routes prepared for special journeys by Caracalla and others, and the route in which Castra Exploratorum appears begins at Blatobulgium (Birrens), which was abandoned by at the latest 211–12. If it took some time for this name to become established the *exploratores* must have been stationed at Netherby for some time before the death of Severus. The Ravenna Cosmography, which names the *loca* which the *exploratores* are generally taken to have supervised, names ten forts on the Antonine Wall, possibly those occupied in the second period. Although it cannot be shown that the material in the Cosmography was collected at one time this does suggest that the *loca* were already established at a time when the Antonine Wall forts and a number of other places in Scotland appeared on Roman road maps. It is perfectly possible therefore that the *exploratores* had taken up position and were exercising their supervisory duties from an earlier period than Caracalla, perhaps from the 160s.

Seen in this context the campaigns of Severus mark a complete break with his governors' policy of overhauling the system based on Hadrian's Wall; this had been pursued since perhaps the 180s when the last changes in the garrisoning of the Wall took place, on lines that had been laid down in all probability in the 160s when the outpost forts on the east were held for the first time. After the campaigns of Severus Caracalla simply reverted to this system.

The Development of the Frontier from Hadrian to Caracalla

The system of frontier control and defence which had been established by the early third century did not materialize out of thin air; it was the result of many years, rather decades, of experiment on the northern frontier. Hadrian's Wall in the 120s had been added to an existing network of forts and roads which covered the north of England. These forts controlled the local population and also supported the units in the front line in the event of an enemy invasion. The movement of people into and out of the province was supervised by a chain of forts, small forts and watch-towers stretching across the Tyne–Solway gap, at that time the most northerly dispositions of the army. It was presumably the failure of this system of frontier control which led to the construction of the only effective substitute in the absence of a natural barrier, a Wall: a barrier indeed, but a non-defensive barrier, for Hadrian's Wall was not a medieval town or castle wall. Its position was a matter of historical and geographical accident. It was not in the best situation geographically, which was later occupied by the Antonine Wall, nor politically, for the northern limit of the British tribes (who on the whole may have been friendly and not too troublesome) – as opposed to the fiercely anti-Roman 'Caledonian' or Pictish tribes – also followed the Forth–Clyde line.

Hadrian's Wall was a non-defensive barrier and no military units were placed on it at first. This was quickly remedied and thereafter army units were always stationed on the Wall, be it Hadrian's or the Antonine. The Wall was to control movement into and out of the province, and allow the peaceful economic exploitation of the northern part of the province, but it was not the provincial boundary. Three outpost forts north of the Wall protected that part of the province isolated by the Wall. These forts were not advance warning posts or forward patrolling bases, for there was no reason to provide these on the west and not on the east.

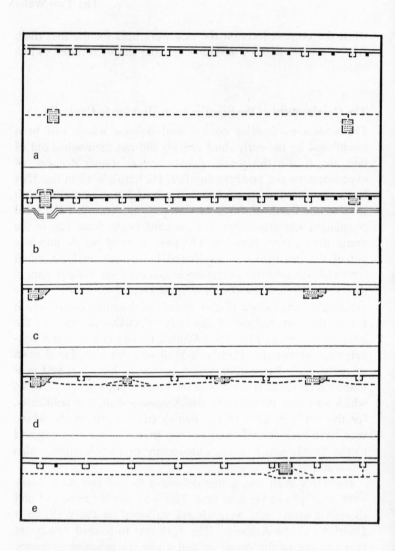

28 Diagram to illustrate the development of the mural frontier:
a. Hadrian's Wall as planned; b. Hadrian's Wall as built; c. Antonine Wall
as planned; d. Antonine Wall as built; e. Hadrian's Wall in the third
century

The Antonine Wall broadly follows this pattern. The forts were more closely integrated with the Wall, but neither now nor at any time until possibly the later fourth century was the Wall used to protect the army from an invasion. If attacked the army would move into the field to deal with the enemy in the classic Roman manner: the forts were only on the line of the Wall for convenience; the troops were not there to police the frontier, though once on the Wall this might have become part of their duties. The line of the Antonine Wall was much more strongly defended than Hadrian's Wall had been; indeed proportionally the garrison was almost double, though the cavalry content of the forces was reduced considerably. This is in keeping with the occupation force in the Scottish Lowlands, which was much stronger then than earlier or later. Outpost forts again protected Rome's interests beyond the Wall, though this time they lay to the east not the west; they extend so far north that the Wall clearly falls within the province.

In the second Antonine period the garrison of the Wall was reduced, a number of hinterland forts and fortlets abandoned, and the normal pattern for a frontier occupation reestablished after the abnormal conditions of the first Antonine period; the situation, whether real or imaginary, which had led to such strong reaction in the 140s had disappeared and with it the emphasis on local patrolling and control. The establishment of military units actually on the Wall line in Hadrian's reign must have reduced the importance of watchtowers and milecastles. While no turrets are known on the Antonine Wall, milecastles do appear, though only four are at present known. When Hadrian's Wall was reoccupied about 160 the milecastles and turrets seem initially to have been recommissioned though the Cumberland Coast system was to a large measure abandoned. During the following years some of the Wall turrets may have been abandoned, but in the main everything was as before. This was not true of the forts in advance of the Wall. There is no evidence that the western outpost forts were abandoned at this time but there were new stations on the east. When the rest of Scotland was given up the fort of Newstead and the stations along Dere Street linking it to Hadrian's Wall were retained. These allowed the army to exercise much closer control over events north of the Cheviots, a difficult task for troops based sixty miles to the south.

This system formed the basis of the third century organization. Risingham and High Rochester on Dere Street were now held and a base or station further north near Cappuck, while the most westerly fort, Birrens, was abandoned. Essentially, however, these sites did not protect local friendly tribesmen, but, as their garrisons clearly proclaim, provided the forward bases for large, mobile, wide-ranging auxiliary units and scouts who patrolled an area as far north as the Tay – if the witness of the Ravenna Cosmography is to be believed.

While the army was groping for a military solution to frontier defence, and arriving at one which effectively ignored both Walls, a similar process of reappraisal was continuing on Hadrian's Wall itself. This led to the large-scale abandonment of turrets and the narrowing of milecastle gateways. This reappraisal was long overdue, for the system of turrets and milecastles was rendered meaningless by the addition of forts to the Wall and had only survived through inertia. Attention was now focused on the units stationed in the Wall forts. Although these garrisons were increased they still did not equal, in relation to the length of the Wall, the garrisons of the Antonine Wall. (If the outpost forts are taken into account, however, the total garrison of Hadrian's Wall in the third century was not much less, relatively speaking, than the garrison of the Antonine Wall at its height.) This is in part because the advance patrolling system had moved the military zone forward and changed the units on the Wall from front-line to second-line troops, which they were to remain until the rise of the Picts in the second half of the fourth century led to the abandonment of the outpost forts.

The system of frontier control and defence which was to survive for close on 200 years was thus born out of many years of experiment and change under energetic governors of a province containing the largest army in the empire. It saw the invasions – and counter-invasions – of the reign of Severus and the reoccupation of Scotland considered and abandoned. Any modifications in these years seem to have been slight and have left little mark in comparison to the abrupt changes of policy every twenty years or less during the second century. The third century received a legacy which it saw no reason to reject. Indeed it was more difficult to alter than before. Under the Severi the single province of Britain was divided into two, perhaps in two stages. From this time on the governor of Lower Britain no longer had three legions at his disposal. The division left the senior governor, that of Upper Britain, with two legions, while his colleague commanded only one legion together with the auxiliary troops based in the forts of North England. The change was undoubtedly political, to rob the governor of Britain of the command of a three-legion province by dividing it. Its effect on the northern frontier was to remove much of the initiative for direct independent action from the governor immediately responsible for the defence of the province's most vulnerable frontier. However, throughout the third century the governors of Lower Britain, based at York, were not tested, for peace reigned on the northern frontier. In contrast with the great governors of an undivided Britain in the first two centuries the governors of Lower Britain seem of mediocre quality. There is no hint of any disturbance in this area until the 270s, when Aurelian took the title of Britannicus, suggestive of a British victory, or simply of the recovery of the provinces after the fall of the secessionist Gallic empire. The units garrisoning the Pennine forts were removed in the later years of the third century, and, as we shall see, some of the Wall forts themselves run down. The system of frontier defence and control does not by itself seem to have been responsible for this era of peace: in its embryonic state it had not prevented the invasion of the early 180s, nor when fully grown the disturbances of the early 200s. Perhaps the reason is more in the enemy it faced. Possibly the northern tribes tired of incessant war, possibly Severus and Caracalla had given them a thrashing which cowed them for several generations. It is more likely that they were kept happy, and therefore under control, by Roman diplomacy, including not just effective supervision of the meeting places, but also perhaps subsidies to the northern tribes.

Five

The Army of the Wall

The Legions

At the time of the building of Hadrian's Wall the Roman army was perhaps at the peak of its efficiency. The backbone of the army remained the legion, approximately 5000 heavy infantry-men trained and disciplined to break the enemy in hand-to-hand fighting in set-piece battles. From the citizen body of Rome in arms, with the weapons and armour that each could afford (the richest on horseback), fighting campaigns between seed-time and harvest, the legion had evolved into a body of infantry, with a very small cavalry contingent, armed and armoured in a standard fashion, trained to the highest standards of single combat and disciplined to react to orders and carry out manoeuvres even in the midst of battle. These men were for the most part volunteers even before the end of the Republic, following the reputation of individual generals. As a fighting force the legions had reached perfection under Caesar. The first emperor, Augustus, gave the legions permanent existence as units (previously they had been disbanded after campaigns) and recognized that soldiering had become a profession by providing a grant on retirement, in land or money, which under the Republic had been done only by individual generals. The length of service was laid down, and by the time of Hadrian it was twenty-five or twenty-six years (legionaries were only discharged in alternate years).

Recruiting was still limited in theory to Roman citizens. In the west apart from Italy many of the inhabitants of Gallia Narbonensis (Provence) and Baetica (southern Spain) were Roman citizens, and as the citizenship spread through various means

148

(the settlement of legionary veterans in the provinces, grants of citizenship to groups and to individuals, particularly auxiliaries on or before discharge) so did the sources of recruits multiply. In Britain there was only one early colony of veterans settled as a group, Colchester, and only two other such colonies, at Lincoln and Gloucester, in the late first century; also probably few early grants to towns (Verulamium may be an exception). British-born auxiliaries probably did not serve in their home province before the 80s. Thus only in the second century would there be many British-born Roman citizens eligible for the legions. In the second and third centuries all legions tended to recruit from their own provinces, especially the areas close to forts and fortresses; auxiliaries and legionaries alike usually settled close to the stations where they had served for twenty-five years, and their sons often joined the army. This almost certainly happened in Britain also, though the evidence is not so clear as elsewhere. Certainly the legions were not mainly composed of Italians, still less of 'Romans' in the sense of inhabitants of Rome (a sense in which Roman citizen had long ceased to be used) after A.D. 100 at the very latest.

The legion was organized into ten cohorts. Originally these were the same size, but at some time not later than the mid 80s, in all probability under the Flavian emperors, the first cohort had been doubled in size for reasons which are obscure. Cohorts II–X comprised six centuries each, cohort I five centuries each of double strength. The century, according to a Roman writer of the second half of the second century A.D., was eighty men strong, despite its name. On this basis cohorts II–X represent approximately 480 men each, cohort I 800, 5120 men in all, including 120 cavalrymen, who were carried on the books of the centuries. These figures are establishment strengths, and the true numbers must have fluctuated.

The officers of the legions need sufficient attention to explain their mention on Wall inscriptions. The supreme commander within the province was the governor, the *legatus Augusti pro praetore*, who commanded the army as well as being head of the civil administration (excluding finance, separately controlled by the procurator, who reported directly to the emperor) and supreme civil and criminal judge under the emperor. The governor of Britain, which had the largest provincial army, would normally be a man of proven military ability, though the system of selection and the career were geared to administrators rather than generals. Such a man would command a legion (*legatus Augusti legionis*) in his early thirties, with his only prior military experience being as senior tribune on a legionary commander's staff (*tribunus militum legionis laticlavius*) in his late teens or early twenties. The five junior tribunes were from a different social class and are discussed in connection with the auxiliary commands which were entrusted to them (see pp. 194–6). The legionary cohorts had no commanding officers. The grouping of centuries into cohorts had as its goal tactical purposes only. The only men exercising command under the legionary legate were the centurions. Probably it was the senior centurion in a cohort who took command in battle or on duty on detachment. There was no administration at cohort level, though the cohort was useful for the division of work, as when building the Wall. The cohorts bore their numbers, but the centuries were normally known by the names of their centurions.

The senior centurion of the legion was called the *primus pilus*, and his century *centuria p.p.* From the *primipili* were recruited the prefects of the camp. Each legion had a prefect (*praefectus castrorum legionis*), who ranked third in the legionary hierarchy, after the legate and the senior tribune, had heavy administrative responsibilities, and was the only officer above centurion level with a long career in the army behind him, normally more than thirty years. As an officer frequently in charge of construction gangs he is mentioned occasionally on inscriptions from the Wall area.

The legions did not garrison Hadrian's Wall. Nevertheless many inscriptions testify to their presence when they built it and played some part in the rebuilding in the 160s. During the troubled second century detachments of the legions, vexillations 500 or 1000 strong, and often the whole fighting force of the legions, that is all but the administration and training sections, were up in the north. Detachments of the sixth and twentieth seem to have moved to Corbridge in the 160s, though not to fight, but to carry on the industrial activities that were continued there in the third century by detachments of legions II and XX, transferred from the southern province of the now divided Britain. Legionary centurions appear on the Wall not infrequently, particularly as temporary commanders of auxiliary units, as do the *beneficiarii consularis*, men drawn from the legions but on the staff of the governor.

The Auxiliary Troops

It was the regiments of the *auxilia* that garrisoned the Wall. The legions had developed into almost exclusively infantry units, trained primarily for the set-piece battle. But this left a variety of essential tasks to other troops. The great lack was cavalry. Although the cavalry of Rome and her enemies, without the stirrup till the third century at least, was not able to break disciplined infantry, it was of inestimable value in the pursuit after victory, when the highest casualties were inflicted, or when the opportunity to outflank the enemy or to attack him from the rear occurred as they did at Mons Graupius. It was invaluable also for scouting. Cavalry was drawn from non-citizens inside and outside the empire, in the first century A.D. especially from the Gauls and Spaniards, later from the Danube lands. Other specialists were slingers and archers. The slingers from the Balearic islands were particularly noted, and the archers from Crete and the Middle East. Finally there was a need for infantry, to patrol, scout, take prisoners, plunder and burn (to name some of the activities shown on Trajan's column).

These 'aids' to the legions had originally been recruited and officered in a variety of ways, fighting in their national costume with their traditional weapons under their own leaders or Roman officers. As early as the late Republic there are signs however that the cavalry was being formed into stable units, and from the time of the emperor Tiberius (A.D. 14–37) the names of cavalry units appear as regularly on inscriptions as those of the legions. On Trajan's Column the cavalry appears in more or less standard uniform and equipment, in contrast to the Moorish light horse, who are distinctive in appearance and dress, representing the old-style type of *auxilia*, now distinguished as *numeri*, units which were neither regular *alae* (cavalry regiments) nor *cohortes* (infantry units). The infantry regiments were formed into regular

151

named units with standard equipment more slowly than the cavalry; again the process is complete by the time of the Column, which is our best guide to the appearance of the first army to garrison Hadrian's Wall. The slingers remain distinct on the Column, as do the archers, and also some club-men appear, who seem like the Moors to be specially recruited irregulars fighting in their own fashion (Plates 11–14).

Again the Column confirms what is implied by the battle of Mons Graupius in A.D. 84 and earlier battles, that the *auxilia* had reached the stage where they could very adequately fight battles with the legions held in reserve; in contrast they had been relegated to the wings in the battle against Boudicca in A.D. 60. On the Column it is the auxiliaries who scout, bring in prisoners, burn villages, and fight most battles. The legionaries build forts, construct bridges, make roads, and come into the fight only for big battles and specialized siege-warfare. The contrast holds good for the Wall; the legions build the Wall and its forts (with some assistance from the auxiliaries), but the garrisons are auxiliary. Particularly in Britain, where the legionary fortresses lay well back, frozen in the positions appropriate for the 70s, the auxiliaries would be the first troops in action, especially in defence.

Who were the auxiliaries, and how were they organized? Detailed discussion of recruiting may be reserved for later. Here the differences between auxiliaries and legionaries may be summarized. From Trajan's time the auxiliaries served for not more than twenty-five years; they were normally non-citizens, though the proportion of citizens tended to grow. Usually they were recruited locally, wherever they happened to be stationed, so any distinctive character derived from the original recruiting-ground rapidly disappeared, though the odd survival may be seen: the curved Dacian sword appears on stones set up by the *cohors I Dacorum* at Birdoswald long after Dacians will have disappeared from the unit. The great reward for the auxiliaries on discharge was the grant of Roman citizenship to themselves and their children. There is no evidence that they shared in the grants of land or money on discharge received by legionaries, and they received less pay than the legionaries. On the other hand there were better opportunities for promotion for the citizen who volunteered for an auxiliary unit; the life was less hard and the discipline and training less stringent than that of the legionary; there was more excitement possibly; and local recruiting made it easier for son to follow father into an auxiliary regiment, rather than go off to the legion for which his citizenship, gained through his father, now qualified him. In the course of the second century the distinction between legions and auxilia became less and less that between citizen and non-citizen units, and rather simply one of pay and training.

Roman Army Organization

The auxiliary units were organized into six basic types, which seem to owe much to precedents set by the legions. The basic infantry unit was the cohort, which like the legionary cohorts II–X was made up of six centuries. As there is no clear evidence for the strength of centuries, it seems best to assume a paper strength of 80, as in the legion, giving a total of 480, which fits nearly enough the description 'five hundred' (*quingenaria*) applied to these cohorts. Such was the *cohors quingenaria peditata*.

The cavalry regiment was made up on slightly different principles, as the basic sub-unit was not the century but the troop, the *turma*. There were sixteen *turmae* in the *ala*, the cavalry regiment, and its total strength is given by the Roman author and provincial governor Arrian as 512. This gives a strength of 32 men in a *turma*, including apparently the two senior officers under the troop commander, the *decurio*, but not the decurion himself, who like the centurion is on a different level entirely from the men. If the two senior officers in each *turma* are ignored the total strength is 480, the equivalent of the infantry cohort in legion and *auxilia* alike, and four times the number of cavalry attached to a legion.

There was a third type of unit, the *cohors equitata*, containing both infantry and cavalry. The term 'mounted infantry' must be avoided; mounted infantry dismount to fight, and it is clear that the horsemen in these units were trained to fight as cavalry, albeit second-class cavalry. These cohorts were made up of six centuries of infantry and four *turmae* of cavalry. If the same strengths applied as in the legion, *ala* and *cohors*, this would be 480 infantry plus 128 cavalry, 608 in all. Some have felt that as this mixed unit is called *quingenaria* also the numbers should be adjusted to produce this figure; perhaps centuries were 60 strong, producing 360 infantry plus 128 cavalry, 488 in all. Documents give a total of 546, 417 infantry and 119 cavalry, in the *cohors I Hispanorum veterana quingenaria* in the first decade of the second century, and 505, 363 infantry and 114 cavalry, in the *cohors I Augusta praetoria Lusitanorum equitata* in A.D. 156. In the former the cavalry total is correct but the infantry fall between 60 and 80 men per century; in the second unit the cavalry are almost full strength, and the infantry below strength for 80 but about right for 60. The figures clearly demonstrate that actual numbers could differ widely from theoretical strength.

Larger versions of all three types appeared under the Flavian emperors, between A.D. 69 and 96. It is tempting to suppose that they were modelled on the changed organization of the first cohort of the legion; for the first cohort of the legion had five double centuries by the mid 80s at latest, and the new infantry unit, the *cohors peditata milliaria*, ten centuries. Should we suppose that the centuries in the auxiliary unit were now 100 strong, so ten centuries would justify the title *milliaria*, one thousand strong? But the legionary first cohort is also called *milliaria*, although the legionary centuries in the first cohort were not altered to one hundred strong. A unit with ten centuries might be called milliary whatever its numbers; the auxiliary unit of six centuries was called *quingenaria*. The *cohors milliaria equitata* also had ten centuries of infantry, and in addition eight *turmae* of cavalry. With a century strength of 80 and a *turma* strength of 32 the total approximates well enough to one thousand, 1056.

The *ala milliaria* is an interesting problem. Possibly the last of the six to be established, it had 24 *turmae* instead of 16. This may have seemed the right combination, like 10 centuries for 6, but equally one-and-a-half is a recurring fraction in Roman affairs (among other things it is a recognized pay-grade) and five-thirds is sometimes used in its stead. Military units may have been intended not as double-size units but as one-and-a-halfers.

Table 12 Paper strength of Roman army units

Unit	Number of centuries	Men per century	Total infantry	Number of turmae	Men per turma	Total cavalry	Total
cohors legionis (II–X)	6	80	480				480
cohors peditata quingenaria	6	80 (100)	480 (600)				480 (600)
cohors equitata quingenaria	6	80 (60)	480 (360)	4	32	128	608 (488)
equites legionis				no turmae		120	120
ala quingenaria				16	32	512	512
cohors I legionis milliaria	5 double	80	800				800
cohors peditata milliaria	10	80 (100)	800 (1000)				800 (1000)
cohors equitata milliaria	10	80	800	8	32	256	1056
ala milliaria				24	32 (42)	768 (1008)	768 (1008)

This would explain why 10 not 12 centuries and 24 not 32 *turmae* were the bases of the new milliary units.

The milliary *ala* with its 24 *turmae* each of 32 men would then be 768 men. To make the title *milliaria* accurate a new *turma* paper strength of 42 must be supposed, giving a total of 1008.

In summary, it is the contention here that the six-century auxiliary *cohors* was formed on the analogy of the legionary cohort, and the *ala* was given sixteen *turmae* to produce a strength more or less the equivalent, and incidentally a multiple of the strength of the legionary cavalry. A mixed unit, a *cohors equitata*, was formed by adding a cavalry force one-quarter of an *ala*, and the equivalent of legionary cavalry strength. It was decided during the Flavian period to increase the centuries in the first cohort of a legion from six to ten, five double centuries under the five centurions of the first cohort (the sixth centurion post probably disappeared at this time). This increase of roughly 50 per cent was made also for the *cohors peditata* and the *cohors equitata*, and in the latter case the cavalry was doubled up to half-*ala* strength. The *ala* was increased by 50 per cent also, in numbers of *turmae*. It seems most likely that the paper strength of century and *turma* remained the same in all units, rather than that there were three different sizes of century (60, 80, and 100) and two of *turma* (32 and 42). The terms *quingenaria* and *milliaria* were used imprecisely, as the case of the *cohors milliaria legionis* shows. As the evidence available is indecisive both the view put forward here and the alternative, bracketed in the table on the previous page, are tenable.

The Army in Britain

Varying numbers of each of these six types of auxiliary unit were available to garrison Hadrian's Wall. There was only one *ala milliaria* in Britain, indeed no province had more than one. There are only two *cohortes milliariae peditatae* and five *cohortes milliariae equitatae* attested. There were at least fifteen quingenary *alae* in Britain at one time or another, and in A.D. 122 there were thirteen at least, which emphasizes how few of those available were stationed on the Wall itself. Quingenary cohorts as one might expect were more numerous, forty-nine, of which thirty-one, well over half, were *equitatae*, emphasizing how useful this composite unit proved to be.

In addition to the *alae* and *cohortes* there were the *numeri*. The term *numerus* originally meant a unit of any type. In the second century and later it was used in a specialized sense to mean a unit, not an *ala* or *cohors*, more akin to the old form of auxiliary troops. They appear to have been recruited from non-citizens, generally with little or no tincture of civilization. They did not receive Roman citizenship on discharge; they may not have served for a specified term. They fought in their own fashion, in their own style of dress. It is probably dangerous to ascribe to such units one form of organization, for they are essentially irregulars. The units on the German frontier, best known to us, appear to have consisted of four centuries. Their posts below the centurionate seem to correspond to the basic organization of the Roman army. *Numeri* appear on the frontiers of the empire, particularly those without clear river-boundaries, and these units may perhaps have been more frontier militia than fighting troops.

The Roman Fort

By the second century each of these units occupied a separate fort. The ancestor of the Roman fort was the Roman camp and its main features were common to both. The forts on the Wall retained their basic form throughout their history, even though changes in army organization in the fourth century affected the internal arrangement of certain buildings. The basic form was a defensive enclosure sufficient to protect troops resting or eating. In the marching camp for one night's rest a shallow ditch and bank with stakes planted in it sufficed. A large number of simple gaps in the enclosure served as entrances. Ditches could be widened, deepened, multiplied, banks raised and widened till they became true ramparts, surmounted by crenellated timber breastworks. The large numbers of gates remained as the essential characteristic of bases for troops accustomed to fight in the open. The siting of camps and forts is also characteristic. Impregnable and inaccessible positions are of no advantage to troops whose aim is to fight in the open, and flat or gently sloping sites with good access to water were preferred. It was no hardship to be overlooked from higher ground (as Risingham and Chesterholm were), as long as you were out of range of missiles. Forts tend to be about a day's journey apart, giving overnight protection to convoys and mutual support, and siting follows this almost mechanical spacing rather than local conditions; it is strategic rather than tactical.

The forts on the line of the Wall were quite normal forts with an extra pair of single-portal gates south of the Wall, if they lay astride it. Their walls were stone, backed by an earth rampart, implying perhaps a permanence that was to prove illusory. Apart from some rebuilding in stone under Trajan, mainly affecting the legionary fortresses, auxiliary forts in Britain had been built with earth and turf ramparts, reflecting perhaps the fluidity of the military situation. At the angles, and between the gates and the angles, rose towers. These were again translations into stone of the look-out towers on timber forts, which were simply platforms on stilts. Replacing timber posts by stone walls created ground floors, but there was no special use for them. The gates themselves were either flanked by towers or as at Housesteads were crowned by a massive gatehouse.

The fort gates on the Wall repay study. In their original form the four main gates were twin-portal, each with two doors opening inwards and closing against a raised threshold, with a central block. The doors were probably of oak, not hinged but pivoted, turning in iron collars let into holes top and bottom. Often there is a channel in the lower pivot stone, so that the upper door pivot can be thrust up into its hole, and the lower pivot can be guided in and dropped into position. Lead could then be run into the channel and around the collar, loose till this point, to make the door virtually irremovable. The doors occupied the front arches of the gateway, which was arched front and rear, with central piers between the two portals. The doors were secured by bars, their bottom edges screened by the raised threshold, and their sides concealed by projections of the side walls or central pier. They could only be broken down by an onslaught on the middle, the most difficult method. The doors lacked elaborate protection as they were not designed for passive defence, but were nevertheless no easy prey (Plate 25).

29 Fort gates. a. Birdoswald East; b. Housesteads West.
Scale 1 in. = 36 ft (1:432)

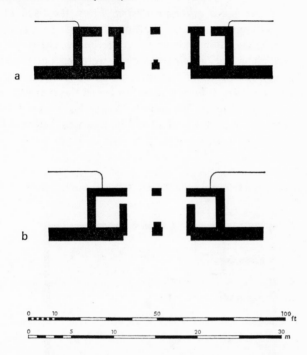

The gates and the internal roads of the fort were laid out according to a pattern that again derived from the old camp. The fort faced the enemy or the east. Its front gate was the *porta praetoria*, from which the *via praetoria* ran to the front of the headquarters building, the *principia*. In the camp the headquarters had been the commander's tent, the *praetorium*, but in the fort the commanding officer had separate quarters, in a spacious house, the *praetorium* still, with accommodation for himself, his family and slave household, flanking the headquarters building. On the other side of the headquarters building are generally found the granaries (*horrea*). Along the front of these principal buildings ran the *via principalis*, at right angles to the *via praetoria*, joining the main side gates, the *porta principalis sinistra* and the *porta principalis dextra*. Behind the principal

159

buildings and parallel to the *via principalis* ran the *via quintana*, which in six-gate forts served minor side gates, the *porta quintana sinistra* and the *porta quintana dextra*. From the back of the principal buildings, continuing the line of the *via praetoria*, ran the *via decumana*, ending at the *porta decumana*, the back gate, through which in ancient times soldiers were led out to execution. Between the buildings and rampart on all sides there was a wide space, the *intervallum*, which lengthened the range for anyone attempting to fire the buildings with missiles from outside. It also facilitated movement and assembly, and was occupied by a road, the *via sagularis*, running round the inside of the rampart.

30   Housesteads headquarters building probably as built.
     Scale 1 in. = 36 ft (1:432)

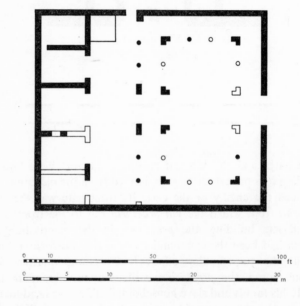

Fort Buildings

The buildings may now be described in more detail. The headquarters building combined a number of features from the camp, notably the tribunal on which the commanding officer took his

160

place, flanked by the standards, and the open space for assembly. It had developed into three main divisions, a courtyard, surrounded by verandahs, which were open under Hadrian, but later often divided into small rooms, a cross-hall (*basilica*), generally a nave with one aisle, lit by clerestory windows, and a rear range of rooms, the central one being the shrine of the standards. There was often a well in the courtyard. The cross-hall and court-yard combined could hold the whole unit. At one end of the nave stood a platform, on the left hand side facing the front of the building, in the correct position for the tribunal in the old camp. This would be used by the commanding officer. The aisle gave access to side-entrances to the building. At the back were generally five rooms, the central one being the shrine (*aedes*) where stood the emperor's statue, the standards, and other objects

31   Housesteads commanding officer's house. Scale 1 in. = 36 ft (1:432)

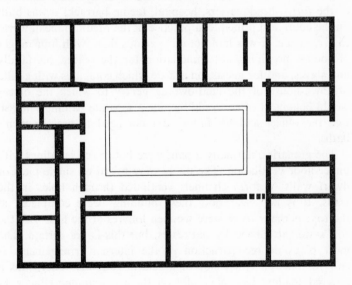

associated with the army's official religious activities. On either side were two rooms, normally interpreted as offices, on the tribunal side those of the *cornicularius*, the adjutant of the unit, and his clerks, on the other those used by the *signiferi*, the standard-bearers, who were also responsible for pay and savings. From the shrine there was often access to a strongroom where the money was kept, a feature which was sometimes original, sometimes a later insertion. The shrine and the two rooms flanking it were open-fronted, with central entrances flanked by low stone screens into which iron grilles were fixed. Through these grilles the standards and images could be seen and business with the soldiers could be carried out in the flanking offices across counters. The latter would have obvious advantages as their widespread use today shows. The offices at the extreme ends of the range, which could only be entered from the offices flanking the shrine, offered greater privacy (Plates 15 and 16).

The commanding officer's house, like so many of the buildings of the fort – headquarters, hospital, facing barracks – was built on the courtyard principle, a practice of the Mediterranean world to give shade. It was laid out on spacious lines, with four ranges of rooms, providing accommodation for the officer, his family and slaves, and for guests, on a scale which compares with a villa or town-house of the land-owning gentry to which the officer would belong. It often would include a separate bathing suite, so that the officer and his family did not need to use the men's baths.

The granaries, normally a pair, were buttressed buildings with under-floor ventilation. The floors were raised on single piers or dwarf walls to form channels ventilated through holes in the walls. It is not clear how these buildings were completed at the top; perhaps there were wooden louvres at the top, with the roof's weight carried by buttresses, but this is not certain. The most plausible reconstruction of the internal arrangements is rows of bins on either side of a central gangway. There was a covered loading bay, generally on the *via quintana* (Plates 17 and 18).

A hospital (*valetudinarium*) was a normal provision, certainly in *ala* forts and milliary cohort forts. It is in the row of buildings fronting onto the *via principalis*, or tucked in behind, communicating with the *via quintana*. Again the courtyard principle appears in ranges of wards with a central corridor or courtyard.

The rest of the fort, the *praetentura* in front of the principal buildings, the *retentura* behind, was given over to barracks and

32 Granaries. a. Halton Chesters; b. Housesteads.
Scale 1 in. = 36 ft (1:432)

a

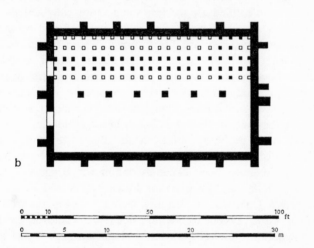

b

stables. The barrack takes us back vividly to the old tented camps. Instead of a row of bivouac tents, with a large box tent at the rampart end for the centurion, there is a long building, divided transversely into rooms corresponding to the old tents and holding a tent-group (*contubernium*). Each room available

163

was in fact subdivided into two, the front roughly corresponding to the old space for arms, the back to the tent, i.e. the sleeping-accommodation. At the rampart end a larger projecting block formed the centurion's accommodation, giving the building its characteristic L-shape. The normal practice was to house two *turmae* of cavalry in a similar block to that for an infantry century, with rather more elbow-room, eight rooms instead of ten, each holding 8 men (two *turmae* each of 32 men instead of a century of 80). There were two *turmae* officers to house; sometimes barracks were built with two projecting ends, one for each decurion – elsewhere the two decurions shared the end block. Barracks often faced each other, their verandahs divided by a central drain and path, again searching for shade. They backed usually on to other barracks or buildings, with so little space between that there must have been little light in the sleeping quarters, unless there was clerestory lighting (Plate 24).

Stables are something of a mystery. A number of buildings have been identified as stables, some more convincingly than others, but no one type of stable has emerged and no stable's internal arrangements are fully known. There would be extra horses for the officers in cavalry regiments, which would also need remounts, probably one to every two troopers. Were all these accommodated in the fort? A reasonable estimate is that the horses of two *turmae* would require as much space as the men, i.e. the equivalent of one century barrack-block.

There were probably stables in all forts, for even in infantry forts the commander and the centurions would have horses. There must have been accommodation for baggage animals, probably mules, and for oxen for drawing carts, and for the carts themselves. Chariots, incidentally, were not in general use in the Roman world, except for racing, but there would be plenty of other wheeled vehicles, from heavy wagons to gigs. Other buildings must have existed but are not yet easily identifiable. At some forts workshops and arms stores have been recognized. There was no central mess-hall; it is not clear where the men ate. Latrines were generally tucked into the back of the rampart. Also in the back of the rampart and in the guard-chambers of the gates and the lower storeys of towers (which had no essential function) were placed bread-ovens. In some forts though by no

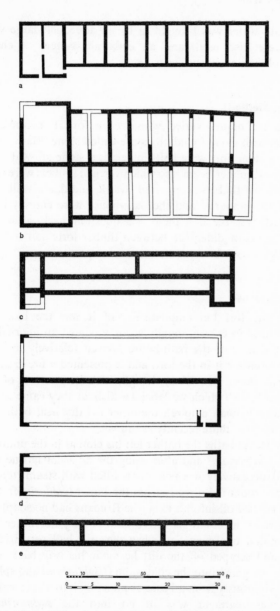

33 Barracks and 'store-houses'. a. Housesteads infantry barrack-block;
b. Benwell double cavalry barrack-block; c. South Shields cavalry
barrack-block; d. Halton Chesters 'store-houses' and barrack-blocks;
e. South Shields 'store-house'. Scale 1 in. = 60 ft (1:720)

means all, water was brought in by an aqueduct; large storage tanks were also used, and an elaborate system of channels carried off waste and surface water.

Building Methods

Building techniques varied within each fort. For convenience buildings with stone foundations are called stone. Many of these even in a stone fort were half-timbered; a stone sill-wall carried a horizontal timber beam into which vertical timbers were slotted. The vertical timbers supported wattle-and-daub walls. Only perhaps the granaries and the bath-house were entirely built of stone and over the first there is a question-mark, as has been seen. The major difference between timber forts and stone forts is the addition of the stone wall to the rampart.

The Bath House

Outside the fort but emphatically of it was the bath-house. Though later forts occasionally accommodated an internal bath-house, the idea of the bath-house arrived relatively late; there was no room for it in the fort, and it presented a fire-risk. It did become standard provision, though, with its two sets of baths, the steam baths (which we label Turkish, as they came to us via the eastern Roman empire), the other the dry heat baths which have come to us more recently as saunas.

In the steam baths the bather left his clothes in the undressing-room (*apodyterium*) and after using the adjacent latrine moved through successively warmer rooms filled with steam (*tepidaria*) to the hot room fed directly from the boiler (*caldarium*). On the way he rubbed oil into his skin (the Romans had no soap) and in the hot room he could get into a bath of very hot water. Steam was essential treatment and when the man had perspired sufficiently and scraped off the dirt he made his way back, closing his pores by going into the cold room (*frigidarium*) and splashing himself vigorously from a basin or plunging into a cold bath. The alternative treatment was to go into the *sudatorium* (or *laconicum*), the sweating-room, where the room was heated to a high temperature without any water or steam.

Bath-houses incorporated furnaces, with brushwood or char-coal fuel. They heated bronze boilers supplying steam and hot water, and circulated hot air underneath the floor (raised on pillars) and up through cavities in the walls. The hot air was

34 Chesters bath-house. Scale 1 in. = 36 ft (1:432)

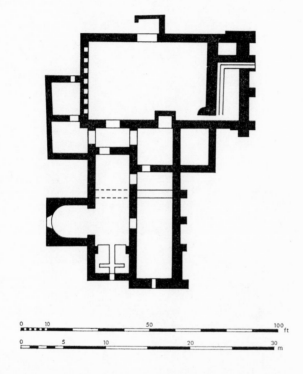

discharged into the open from just below the roof, in all prob-ability. These bath buildings must be distinguished from the hypocausts for underfloor heating, which appear for instance in the commander's house. Hypocausts required fewer box tiles as the temperature aimed at was lower; condensation was not a problem, so complete wall jacketing was unnecessary. The granaries also have underfloor passages, but for ventilation, not heating.

The other military feature outside the walls was the parade ground. Not many have been located, as they are conspicuous only where artificial levelling was necessary. All else – temples, inns, shops, brothels, private houses – though intended for and very largely financed by the fort's inmates, had no official status, although the commanding officer would exercise jurisdiction over them as they fell within the fort's territory.

Six

Life on the Wall

What has been described is the bare structure of the fort. What was life like within and without its walls? In discussing this there are two major difficulties. Firstly, although we are concerned here with auxiliary regiments, many of the literary and other documentary sources refer to legions. It is not always clear how far they apply to auxiliaries, who had lower standards of discipline and training and rather different functions. This point is re-emphasized in the chapter wherever it seems particularly relevant.

The second difficulty is that the *auxilia* were not as homogeneous as the legions. There were three distinct groups: the infantry, both of the purely infantry and the mixed cohorts; the cavalry of the mixed cohorts; and the troopers of the *alae*. The infantry, the lowest-paid, had the simplest training and lowest qualifications. The cohorts had a similar basic organization, but often used specialized arms and armour, the outstanding example being the units of Oriental archers. The cavalry of the mixed cohorts were paid more than the infantry, less than the men of the *alae*. They were not generally recruited directly from civilian life; infantrymen from the cohort were selected for training. On the march and in battle they were grouped with the *alae*; they did not fight with their cohort. The *alae* had a height qualification for entry, and were the best paid of all the *auxilia*. Their training was probably almost as exacting as that of the legionary. Their arms, equipment and clothing were elaborate, including the splendid sports helmets used by a number of senior troopers. Their status improved steadily till they replaced the legions as the striking force of the army in the third century.

Recruitment

The Roman army recruited auxiliaries locally from the very beginning except into the specialized units of Oriental archers. The legions did so more slowly in the west, where Italy, Provence and southern Spain provided a good reservoir of Roman citizens; in the east where there were fewer citizens men were recruited locally and given the citizenship on enrolment. As time went on local recruitment meant not simply recruitment from the province, but from the frontier region of the province. So a typical auxiliary on the Wall was born in the province, probably in the frontier region, possibly if not probably in the village outside the fort and fathered by a soldier of the regiment. Normally he would be a volunteer. The forced levy remained as a reserve power, but only in time of crisis or to remove the fighting force of a defeated tribe to a remote part of the Empire. The volunteer for auxiliary units would normally be a non-citizen, for a citizen could apply to the legions. By the middle of the second century more and more citizens, particularly the sons of auxiliaries, were entering the auxiliary regiments, which offered better opportunities for promotion, as long as citizens were in the minority in them, less exacting training and perhaps a more exciting life. The legionaries, kept out of the fighting line except in crises, experienced intensive training, heavier equipment, more numerous fatigues, stricter discipline and unexciting toil. It would be some time however before the number of citizens in the Wall area became considerable, the main source being the sons of veterans who by their service in the auxiliaries had gained the citizenship for themselves and their children.

Training

The volunteer signed on for twenty-five years. Like the legionary recruit he was between 18 and 23 in the majority of cases. He was given a medical examination and required to prove that he was free-born, neither a slave nor a freed slave, and of good character. He then took the military oath and was assigned to a unit where he underwent basic training for, according to the Roman writer Vegetius, a minimum of four months. Vegetius probably had legionaries in mind, but something similar though perhaps not quite so exacting would be required for auxiliaries. The men had to be physically fit, so they ran, jumped, learned to swim, felled trees and carried packs weighing up to sixty Roman pounds (about three stones). Cross-country marches were also on the training programme. The soldier learnt his foot drill, the military double pace of sixty inches not unknown to British infantrymen, and how to march in step six abreast maintaining correct dressing. Weapon drill and training involved practice with dummy weapons against wooden posts, working up to practising with covered points against human opponents. The recruits sweated away morning and afternoon, while the qualified soldiers only trained in the morning session. Double-weight wooden swords and shields helped to toughen the legionaries for the exhausting hand-to-hand fighting in which they specialized; auxiliaries did not escape similar training though perhaps less strenuous. Much of this training took place on the parade-ground, though there were covered exercise-halls for bad weather.

The recruits had to reach the required standards; failure might be punished by barley rations instead of wheat. Camp construction was probably included in their advanced training, though Trajan's Column shows legionaries doing all the camp construction and of course the building of roads and bridges. On campaign the auxiliaries were brigaded together with the legionaries, and camped with them. Training did not cease, at least in theory, on completion of basic training. Three times a month route marches of twenty Roman miles (just under 18½ English) had to be completed. The recruit had been trained to march this distance in five hours, which is about the British army pace of three miles to the hour, including a ten-minute rest. Apart from route marches all soldiers were expected to keep up their basic weapon skills by daily training.

Cavalry Recruitment and Training

The soldier in an *ala*, a cavalry regiment, had also to master the skills of horsemanship. The basic height qualification for entry to an *ala* was five feet ten inches (five feet eight inches English). On the whole men were not recruited directly into the cavalry contingents of the *cohortes equitatae*. They generally entered as infantry and were later selected for the better-paid cavalry section. The trooper was trained to mount, ride, jump ditches and walls, and to swim with his horse – all while wearing armour. He had to use his weapons, the spear (to throw or to thrust) and the sword, without the assistance of stirrups, it must be remembered. The *alae* practised close-order manoeuvres, and the sight of a regiment of 500 wheeling, with the elaborate trappings of men and horses, was a fine one. This was brought out by Hadrian in his speech to the *equites* of a mixed cohort when he reviewed the Roman army in Africa. It was difficult, he said, for the small body of *equites* of a cohort to impress when they appeared on display after an *ala*. Nevertheless it was an *eques* from a *cohors equitata* who swam the Danube in full battle kit in Hadrian's presence, and hit an arrow still in the air with a second one.

Pay

Basic training over, the soldier might reflect on his pay and prospects. As well as the basic requirements listed earlier, he needed letters of commendation to secure the unit he wanted and perhaps speedy promotion in it. The Roman world like most societies ran on a system of references, and commending men at every level for posts was not merely tolerated, it was part of the social fabric. All but the greatest and the humblest were both patrons and clients, looking after the interests of those who depended on them and expecting their support in return. To know some one who would speak or write for you, perhaps even just a soldier on an officer's staff, was worth much. Here again was a reason for soldiers' sons to do well in the army, especially in father's old unit. The hopes and fears of soldiers 'joining-up' are vividly portrayed in a number of letters that have survived.

The distinction between the men of the legions and the men of the *auxilia*, and among the *auxilia* between cavalrymen of the *alae*, cavalrymen of the mixed cohorts, and infantry of the cohorts, showed in pay scales. The legionary was at the top of the scale, the auxiliary infantryman at the bottom. The only precise figures are for the legionary; estimates of the auxiliary infantryman's pay vary between one-third of a legionary's and two-thirds or five-sixths. The former is preferred here, because it is easier to build a logical structure on it; we do not believe that a man in an *ala* was paid as much as or more than a legionary.

The pay structure for any unit of the Roman army was based on four divisions but only three pay rates: ordinary pay; ordinary pay with immunity from fatigues; one-and-a-half times ordinary pay; twice ordinary pay. The table gives the likely figures in *denarii* per year from Domitian to Severus, i.e. for the second century A.D.

Table 13   Soldiers' pay rates in the second century

	Basic pay	Pay-and-a-half	Double pay
Auxiliary			
Infantryman	100	150	200
Cavalryman in *cohors equitata*	150	225	300
Ala trooper	200	300	400
Legionary	300	450	600

The ambitious recruit would try to become an *ala* trooper or, failing that, an infantryman in a mixed cohort so that he could apply for selection as an *eques*. In any case he would next try for a job which gave him immunity from fatigues, by learning a trade or as a clerk on his commanding officer's staff.

Pay day was not a weekly event; in the Roman army pay was given out three or four times a year with accompanying splendour at special parades. Not all of it was passed across the table, or more probably the counter, to the soldier. From it was deducted a standard amount to cover bedding and food, for any items of clothing and odd items like camp dinner and burial club. There were charges also for weapons, a share of the cost of the tent each tent-group must have, and the cavalryman's horse, but these probably recurred but rarely after the first fitting-out. The horse made 'kitting-out' deductions particularly heavy for the cavalry-man, though the charge seems to have become standard, what-ever the horse's age or quality. Any credits or debits to the soldier after the deductions for the 'quarter' had been made were carried forward. The soldier could also save; the standard-bearers, who were in charge of pay, kept a record of his savings as well as his credits or debits. The *viaticum*, the three gold coins which were the equivalent of the 'Queen's shilling', was also retained, and not handed out to the soldier. The auxiliary could not hope for largesse from the emperor to add to his pay; this was apparently reserved for the citizen troops. The auxiliaryman's great reward was the citizenship, but that lay twenty-five years in the future for the recruit.

Promotion

The recruit then could set about improving his pay and prospects. The first move was to secure a post that carried *immunitas* (exemption from fatigues), such as a clerk (*librarius*) on the staff of the commanding officer (here a literate recruit had an advantage) or by doing general duties on his commander's staff (*beneficiarius*). The recruit could take up duties as a hospital orderly (*medicus* or *capsarius*) and learn simple first-aid and bandaging. The musicians, who signalled in battle or regulated the watches in camp and fort, also had immunity. The *tubicines* blew long straight trumpets and signalled the commander's orders. The *cornicines* with their curved horns picked up the messages and drew the men's attention to the standards, which signalled to centuries or *turmae*. The *bucinatores* were con-cerned with regulating the watches. The legion of course had many more trades and a number of officers had their own staffs.

For more pay and more responsibility the recruit would need promotion to junior officer in the century or *turma*. In the century his first post might be *tesserarius*, who appears to have had responsibility for passing on written orders to guard-posts and the like. Above him was the *optio*, the second-in-command of the century, and the centurion's deputy. Above him again ranked the standard-bearer, the *signifer*. He was responsible for trans-mitting orders and could therefore not take over if the centurion fell, but his responsibilities in battle and in administration – the century's finances were his special concern – were onerous. After holding one or more of these posts the soldier might receive a senior post on the commander's staff, that of *cornicularius* or adjutant, or of *actarius*, possibly the man in charge of records. From any of these posts he might reach the dizzy rank of centurion. From there he could advance to senior centurion of the cohort, *centurio princeps*. Only rarely did an auxiliary centurion get a transfer to the legionary centurionate. Nevertheless life as a centurion was a good life, in contrast with even the highest rank below him, as the scale of the centurion's quarters in an auxiliary fort shows. One other post below centurion ought to be mentioned, that of *custos armorum*, the man who kept the arms store, probably one in each century and in rank roughly equal to the *tesserarius*.

Table 14   Ranks, pay-grades and posts below the centurionate

Rank	Pay-grade	Post
Miles ⎫ *Immunis* ⎭	Basic	Clerks, musicians and other specialists, some junior staff posts
Principalis ⎧ ⎨ ⎩	Pay and a half (*sesquiplicarius*)	*Tesserarius*, *custos armorum*, *curator*, *actarius* and other staff posts
	Double pay (*duplicarius*)	*Optio*, standard bearers, *cornicularius* and other senior staff posts

Cavalry Promotion

Ranks in the *turma* were rather different. There, it would appear, the *optio* and *tesserarius* were usually termed *duplicarius* and *sesquiplicarius* respectively, literally 'twicer' and 'one-and-a-halfer'. This is a reference to their pay, and corresponds to the presumed pay of *optio* and *tesserarius* in all other units in relation to ordinary soldiers. There is an ancient tradition that the *turma* was originally commanded by three decurions, one being the senior, and this peculiar nomenclature may be an echo of that old situation. There is also a mysterious figure called the *curator*, probably connected with the horses, as well as a *custos armorum*. The prefect of an *ala* also had a *cornicularius* and an *actarius*, and the dream here was to become a *decurio*. The *decurio alae* outranked the *centurio cohortis*. Occasionally young men of rank sought direct commissions as *decuriones* in provinces without legions whose governors therefore had no legionary centurionates in their gift. Even if the *decurio* reached the senior post of *decurio princeps* – more difficult than *centurio princeps*, for there were more decurions in an *ala quingenaria* than centurions in a *cohors milliaria* – there was little chance of making the giant step to *centurio legionis*. So even senior officers generally stayed in the one unit; transfers from unit to unit at any level below the commanding officer seem to have been rare. Occasionally legionaries transferred to become junior officers in the *auxilia*, in the hope of later return to a legion as centurions, but it is difficult to estimate how common this practice was.

Duties

All this would lie some years in the future for the recruit. To reach a post in the century or *turma* might take seven years, a senior post on the commander's staff ten years, a centurionate or decurionate fifteen years. In the meantime life would be governed by training and duties. It would be comparatively simple to follow his progress if we could recover the individual file, carrying reports on his health and character, which every man had. In it would be filed letters regarding his entry into the unit. His duties would be recorded on a daily basis. In the daily report of the unit, giving the muster strength, he would be counted in. If he varied the tedium of life in the fort by getting on to a party going out for fuel, or on escort duty, his departure would be recorded, and his return if his absence was for more than a day. If he went on detachment duty for some time he appeared on a list of men who had left camp on more than one occasion.

Such detached duty might take a man far afield. Under Trajan, who inveighed against the practice, one unit had men outside its province collecting clothing and on guard-duty at mines, and inside its province men were detached for service in the governor's bodyguard, on the staff of the procurator (the emperor's man in charge of finance), on garrison duty, scouting and convoying animals. Such duties may have been a welcome break to the soldiers but must have played havoc with training. Still the records showed where the man was. Annually, and perhaps monthly, the total strength of the unit, with notes of permanent and temporary losses and gains, was sent to the provincial governor. The soldier's pay records were also diligently kept, and if he died in service account would be rendered to his heir.

Where did the recruit spend his time, and for how long was he on duty? How much free time and leave did he receive? These are questions that cannot be answered. There is evidence that things got slack in periods of prolonged peace. On the other hand diligent commanding officers could enforce a training programme. Apart from daily exercises on the parade ground the men might be taken out for a spell 'under leather' – tents were still standard issue in the third century – and they needed training for operations which would take the unit out into the field. Josephus, a Jewish writer who described the Jewish war of 66–70, lists a man's field-training equipment as saw, basket (for moving earth), axe, pick, strap, reaphook (for foraging), chain and rations: Trajan's Column shows *paterae* (mess-tins), cooking pots and string bags. Various sites have been identified as Roman training areas where practice camps were built, where cavalry could practise manoeuvring in broken country, with banks and ditches, and artillery practice be carried out against long-deserted hill-forts. As a variation 'attackers' could try to dislodge 'defenders' with clods of earth and similar non-lethal missiles.

When Hadrian was touring the armies of the Empire no commanding officer could let his unit neglect training, but few of his successors imitated his example. The Romans were well aware of the maxim that soldiers should be busy to keep them out of mischief, but not every commanding officer took notice. There were routine duties, attested for the legion and presumed for the *auxilia*, including mounting guard at the headquarters building and at the gates, cleaning centurions' kit, bath-house fatigues, including the laborious job of collecting brushwood or making charcoal, and cleaning out latrines. The soldiers also had to clean their own weapons and armour, gather fuel for their own cooking, and gather fodder for the animals. The cavalrymen had to attend to their horses; it is unlikely that (as has been suggested) slaves did this. Officers and some soldiers owned slaves, but there were no slaves attached to the unit. Despite this recitation of duties the auxiliaries escaped, for the most part at least, the back-breaking toil of road-building and quarrying that came the legionaries' way, and the laborious alternatives to fighting, such as the canal-digging and mining that some governors invented, again hit the legionaries hardest.

Recreation

Breaks for meals were taken at regular times as part of the Roman army day, but it is not clear where the soldiers cooked or ate. The ovens could only deal with certain types of food. Some have suggested that there were hearths for cooking on the barrack-block verandahs, but there seems to be no evidence for these; hearths, which may have been used for cooking, have been found inside barracks. Presumably hearths like ovens were usually placed against the rampart back. The barracks themselves were rather cramped but food would have to be eaten there or on the verandahs. In the British Army in the eighteenth and nineteenth centuries it was the normal practice for the men to eat in their barracks. When free at other times the soldiers no doubt lounged around outside and read the notices. These were probably posted in the verandahs around the headquarters courtyard, which may have been more like the market-place of the Italian town on which it was modelled than a sacred barrack square. The bath-house must have been a good place to skulk, perhaps one of the few warm places. Open fires have been found in the barracks at some forts, and braziers may have been used in others. Braziers may also have warmed offices (hypocausts were later provided there), but no doubt the soldiers were glad of their thick woollen cloaks over tunics and trousers.

The bath-house was outside the fort, and a short step away, once the civilians were no longer kept south of the Vallum, were the delights of the shanty town of the civil settlement, built in a better style in the third and fourth centuries. In the midst of a wilderness Rome set down 500 or 1000 men with money in their pockets. They wanted variety of food, wine or beer beyond the army ration, women and a change from army routine. That meant inns, shops, brothels, for immediate needs. Beyond that the soldiers wanted to set up homes. The Roman soldier could not marry legally, till the early third century at least, but could and did marry according to local custom, common-law marriages so to speak. On his discharge the children of this union would become Roman citizens by the same document that would grant citizenship to him. In the meantime the soldier, living in the fort, might have a wife and children living outside the fort. The state took no responsibility for them; they might be left abandoned by a movement of the unit (which in practice occurred less and less frequently). He could leave to them what possessions he had by will, orally if he wished, but they had no standing in Roman law till he received the citizenship upon discharge. Garrison changes in the second century must have made permanent unions difficult, and it is not till the third and particularly the fourth century that we find settlements of some size outside the Wall forts. Nevertheless at all times some unofficial wives and children lived, perhaps in squalor, outside the forts, and the soldier must have been able to spend some time with them.

Arms and Armour

Before passing on to other variations in the army routine, leave and the military religious calendar with its festivals and possible holidays, it is time to deal with the major variation in routine, fighting. There are few descriptions of fighting, particularly by auxiliaries; indeed fighting is an abnormal activity for a peace-time soldier. Even under war conditions it is rare for the majority of troops to be actively involved in fighting at any one time. Active campaigning in the second century need not occupy much of a man's service of twenty-five years, perhaps two or three summers in the field with hardly a sight of the enemy. Like the soldier in any other army the Roman soldier had little oppor-tunity to practise the killing for which he was trained. The auxiliary infantryman had as armour a helmet, iron or bronze, a mail or scale shirt, and an oval shield. This shield was flat, made of plywood covered with leather with a circular metal boss and applied metal rim. His offensive weapons were the spear, for throwing or thrusting, and the sword, a version of the *gladius* used by legionaries, two feet long and two inches wide, designed for thrusting with its long point, although it had cutting edges also. A dagger was also carried, no doubt useful as a scout-knife, and a last resort if the sword was lost. There are not enough accounts of auxiliaries in action to differentiate clearly their fighting methods from those of the legionaries. They could form a battle-line and did so increasingly though this was not their main function. They probably did not have such elaborate battle training as the legionaries, but had a greater variety of roles.

Variations in weapons and armour often relate to the fighting methods of the tribe from which the unit was originally raised. The most distinctive group was the Oriental archers, who used a composite bow, in the middle wood, on the outside sinew, on the inner side horn. When the bow is bent the sinew is stretched and tries to contract; the horn is compressed and seeks to expand. It was the normal bow of the Graeco-Roman world and the arrow shot was of no great weight and range; this helps to account for the relative ineffectiveness of archery against Roman heavy infantry. Archers sometimes carried axes and swords in case the enemy managed to close with them. Slingers were also used by the Romans, throwing both from hand and using slings, but they do not seem to have formed organized units. According to Vegetius some instruction was given to all soldiers in the technique of slinging.

Cavalry Arms and Armour

The *ala* trooper also wore a bronze or iron helmet and a mail or scale shirt and carried an oval shield like that of the auxiliary infantryman. His offensive weapons were the spear, used for throwing as a javelin or for thrusting as a lance, and the *spatha*, the long slashing sword, described by Tacitus as if it was the characteristic weapon of the *auxilia* but apparently confined to cavalry. His fighting potential was limited by the absence of stirrups, which allow the combined weight of man and horse to be used. Nevertheless there were heavy cavalry, notably the armoured cavalry (*cataphractarii*) where both horse and man wore armour. Some units were equipped with a heavy lance, the *contus*. On Trajan's Column the Moors appear as light horse, with apparently no armour, no saddle, simply a spear and shield.

Other units were partly or completely made up of mounted archers. One suspects that there may have been considerable variation in arms and armour from cavalry regiment to cavalry regiment.

One feature of cavalry armour calls for special attention. These are the sports helmets discovered from time to time. They are of iron or bronze, richly decorated, very light in construction, with face-masks. They were worn without body-armour and with light shields only. This equipment was reserved for special displays of skill, worn only by soldiers who held higher ranks or were accomplished horsemen. The elaborately moulded face masks, which are of male and female types, may have been used in a version of the Troy Games, pitting Greeks against Amazons in mock battle.

The horses seem to have been on the small side. The biggest horses from Newstead, the Roman fort on the Tweed, measure nearly fifteen hands, but the majority are below fourteen hands. The military saddle, made of leather, had no seat. It had horns stiffened with bronze for attaching the cloak and the shield. There was probably a cushion to protect the horse's back beneath the saddle. Saddle cloths, both over and under saddles, added colour and richness, and the harness was richly decorated with bronze medallions and pendants, as can be deduced from finds and sculptured representations. Here the cavalryman from the cohorts could not compete; he could not afford to. As Hadrian remarked, the quality of the horse and the arms, which may be taken to include trappings also, were in proportion to the pay.

Artillery

The use of catapults by the *auxilia* is not clearly attested; on Trajan's Column they are in the hands of the legions. They were used in defending camps, presumably by legionaries. E. W. Marsden holds that the *ballistaria* (platforms for catapults) erected at High Rochester about 220 were for *onagri*, the one-armed stone-throwers. There is little evidence for the use of this type of catapult before the fourth century. He further suggests that legionaries might have been specially detached to operate them, but this is uncertain. Until further evidence emerges it is best to regard the *auxilia* as operating normally without catapults; these when required in field or siege operations were provided by the legions in a combined force of legions and *auxilia*.

Rewards and Punishments

Military decorations were not available for the auxiliaryman or, to be more precise, for the non-citizen. They were reserved for citizens. Decorations could only be awarded to the auxiliary unit as a whole. Thus the *ala Petriana* was *bis torquata*, meaning that the *torques* that formed part of the standard decorations to the citizen soldier, legionary or praetorian, had been awarded twice to the unit as a whole, and may have been carried on its standards. Another award for bravery was to give citizenship to the soldiers of the unit; they continued to serve, and future recruits reaped no benefit from the award, but the decoration became part of the title of the unit, as, for example, the *ala Petriana civium Romanorum bis torquata*.

Roman military discipline was famous, draconian in its severity. But it is only fair to look at fact as well as theory. It was vital in the interests of all that the severest penalties be visited on men who endangered their fellows by running away, sleeping on sentry duty or other negligence in the presence of the enemy. Under peace-time conditions lesser penalties might be substituted for the full rigours of the law. When an army that had softened under such conditions had to be licked into shape one method was the old-time discipline, the famous instance being that of Domitius Corbulo, who had a man put to death for laying aside his sword while digging a ditch. More relevant to our soldier would be the beating, or flogging with a centurion's vine-stick, that awaited minor offences, or fines or extra duties. A centurion might find himself standing outside headquarters for hours unbelted or holding a measuring-rod. Reduction in rank or transfer to a position of inferior status, such as from *ala* to cohort,

cohort to fleet punished serious offences, and worst of all was *missio ignominiosa*, dishonourable discharge, with loss of the veteran's privileges (see below), and of the prize of Roman citizenship. The death penalty could be exacted for desertion, mutiny or insubordination, but extenuating circumstances even for desertion were normally allowed. Soldiers were valuable, and it was hard to see a comrade put to death. The most famous Roman punishment is decimation, the execution of every tenth man drawn by lot from a group guilty of cowardice in the face of the enemy; the 'by lot' emphasizes the man's responsibility for the conduct not only of himself but of his unit. Though the word has passed into our language with an exaggerated meaning, instances of decimation are rare. There were lesser punishments for such behaviour, such as compulsion to camp outside the ramparts, and barley rations.

Leave

Fighting and its rewards and punishments might have had little relevance for our recruit. He came in for the odd cudgelling by the centurion and extra duties, and survived. But if he rarely left the fort on campaign, and only occasionally on odd duties, did he get away on leave? Leave was a privilege and at one time centurions, in the legions at least, expected payment for granting it, till the emperors took over the responsibility of paying the centurions to waive this 'right'. Leave was granted, but how regularly and how it was arranged we do not know. One thing is clear; there was no help with fares home. At the end of his service a man, who had perhaps been recruited in another province (much might have happened in twenty-five years), had to find his own way home; most men preferred to stay near where they had served rather than travel home at their own expense after so long away. All the pressures were to stay, so that even those who had not been recruited locally might make a home for themselves and their citizen children close to the unit and their old comrades.

Roman Military Religion

The British soldier's life in peace time is closely related to the

183

week-end and the 48-hour pass. The Roman soldier had no week-ends, but he did follow a set religious calendar with festival days. It is likely but not certain that they brought him free time after the special parades. Otherwise one must conclude that there were no free days whatsoever. Rome was completely tolerant of all religions, provided that they were not inhumane in their practices (Druidism) nor suspect in their political loyalties (Christianity). It took no account of a man's private religious practice, but expected a soldier to join in imploring the blessing of the gods on the emperor and Empire. A unit of the Roman army collectively kept the festivals of the protecting gods of Rome, the ancient festivals of the city of Rome, remembered the birthdays, accession days and victories of the divine and living emperors and celebrated the festivals of the unit itself, those associated with the worship of the standards, which, even more than the standards of regiments today, had a mystical importance and sanctity. Rome had only the three centres of loyalty. The first was the city, nearly 900 years old in men's reckoning when the Wall was built. The second was the emperors, super-men whose achievements cast reflected light on their living successor, and some of whom had won a special place in the affections of the army. Germanicus, indeed, a member of the imperial family though never emperor (he died in A.D. 19) was still remembered on his birthday over two centuries later. Thirdly and finally, all the affection and loyalty that was associated with the unit itself was represented also. Great parades and festivities were associated with the calendar, which was observed by all units, with presumably little variation, and on some of these days the soldiers might hope for rest.

Many ceremonies took place on the parade-ground, where each year an altar was solemnly dedicated. Some were perhaps connected with the shrine, at the heart of the headquarters building and therefore of the fort, where the image of the emperor stood surrounded by the standards. Each century had a standard, similar to that of the legionary century, a tall staff decorated with flat discs, a cross-bar at the top and above it a hand or a spear-point in a wreath. The standard of a cohort is unknown. The animals on staves carried by soldiers, depicted on reliefs or found detached on military sites, may be emblems like those of the legions. The cavalry *turma* had a rather different and unusual standard, adapted for horseback, and the standard for the whole *ala* was a *vexillum*, a cloth flag. Also in the shrine perhaps stood statues of the guardian gods of Rome, and altars dedicated to them.

Personal Religion

Outside the official religion the soldier had a bewildering variety of deities to respect, for while it was impossible to worship all actively, none could be disdained. Native gods were not despised, far from it, for they were the local manifestations of divinities known elsewhere. Here only a brief catalogue can be given of the varities of religion available; there is more detail in Appendix 3 (pp. 259–70). There were first of all the gods of Greece and Rome, familiar to the soldier from the official calendar. There were the native gods, familiar to the soldier if he was a native or respected by him as powerful in their home territory. There were gods from overseas, similar in their basic characteristics to the native or Roman gods. Some came with units. Mars Thincsus was brought to Housesteads by German units; Dea Syria to Carvoran by a unit of Hamian archers, a specialist unit that did recruit from the original recruiting ground. Some order was brought into this galaxy by the process of syncretism, which saw in the native gods local manifestations of the gods known to Rome; thus Thincsus is known as Mars Thincsus, in his sculptured representation looks like Mars, and his fierce goddess companions become mild Victories. On the whole the native gods got the better of the bargain; their distinctive characteristics still remained, even though their features became classical, and they gained new worshippers without losing the old. Native gods like Coventina at Carrawburgh probably had a stronger grip than the gods of Greece and Rome, but men were asking for more, for a deeper knowledge of the gods, for a real hope of immortality and a strong ethical code, left mainly to the philosophers by the old gods. Religions moved in from the east, helped by the freedom of movement in the empire. Gods like Jupiter Dolichenus and Cybele found favour in this north-west corner of the empire, and after them came Mithraism and finally Christianity.

Health

What chance had the soldier in the auxiliary units of surviving for his twenty-five years and retiring? It has been estimated that of 100 recruits entering the legions at 18, half would perhaps be alive at 42 – a rather better expectation of life than for the comparable civilian. Insufficient evidence is available to make a detailed comparison for auxiliaries, but a number of points may be borne in mind.

The auxiliary fed reasonably well. Troops stationed in forts, not on active service, had a greater variety of food than is sometimes realized. The basic food carried on campaign was bacon fat, biscuit, sour wine (the 'vinegar' offered to Christ on the cross), corn (generally made into wholemeal bread or porridge) and also cheese. Meat was eaten when available. There was no prejudice against it but it was difficult to transport, alive or dead, along with the food for the march that could be carried, foraged, or supplied.

The diet in the fort could be varied, as animals could be kept on the land assigned to the fort, bought, or hunted. Ox, sheep, goat and pig all seem to have been popular. Milk and cheese could again be obtained from the unit's own herds, exacted or purchased. Oyster shells have been found on many sites, and there are remains of other shellfish, fish, chickens and other fowls and eggs. More expensive wines than standard-issue sour wine were brought in. A variety of local fruit was eaten. Soldiers' letters are often concerned with food, relations and friends being asked to provide further variety. It is a remarkable fact that there is no recorded complaint about the quality of the Roman military diet; the soldier fed better than or at least as well as many civilians of a similar social background. And the army is always the last to go hungry.

The auxiliary was reasonably clothed and housed. A leather tunic and leather trousers, with the heavy woollen military cloak, gave him adequate protection, and his footwear, the *caliga* or military boot, had points of superiority over the modern army boot. The barracks were at least comparable with the average civilian dwelling in town and superior to the stone huts of the native settlements around. They were unheated, unless braziers of charcoal were used, but the bath-house at least was warm. The water supply to the fort was well taken care of, surface water was carried away by an elaborate system of drains, and the bath-house and latrines helped to keep the army healthy.

Nevertheless men living in such large numbers were liable to epidemics, and disease always has been the great enemy of armies, far more than wounds. If the soldier did fall ill or was wounded there was a hospital at his own fort or perhaps at another not far away. Medical attention was available at three levels. There were medical officers, doctors who took the equivalent of a short-service commission. There were doctors of centurion rank, who made a career of the army; there is one recorded at Housesteads. Finally there were bandagers (*capsarii*) and orderlies (*medici*) who took care of the sick and did first-aid on the battlefield, ordinary soldiers who received some training and were immune from fatigue duty because of their trade. There were equivalents on the veterinary side, who were classed under hospital staff. A legionary hospital came under two *optiones valetudinarii*, and was a special responsibility of the prefect of the camp. Army doctors were particularly skilled in their treatment of wounds and surgery, as is shown by surviving descriptions, and the variety and quality of instruments that have been found. The richest evidence is for the legionary hospitals, but the occurrence of hospital buildings in auxiliary forts demonstrates that there was care for the *auxilia* also. The good general visited the sick and inspected the sick quarters, and there is evidence of a special diet for the sick and convalescents. There is also some evidence that medicinal herbs were grown in the hospital courtyards.

A soldier might need to be invalided out. If he was, with what was called a *missio causaria*, he did not automatically receive the privileges due to the man who served for twenty-five years; this was a matter for discretion.

Death

What if our soldier died? If he died on service his last resting-place was in a cemetery outside the fort, perhaps along one of the roads leading from it. Roman law strictly forbade the burial of the dead within an inhabited area. Though the location of some cemeteries on the Wall is approximately known, there has been little investigation. The soldier was cremated, or perhaps, from late in the second century, inhumed. Both rites continued side by side in the third century but after the late third century cremation tended to disappear. The ashes were placed in a container (urns, *amphorae*, glass jars, lead canisters, stone coffins and tiled tombs are all attested). The ashes of a legionary centurion might be carried home. The coffin for an interment was normally of wood, but stone, brick tile or lead were also used. The funeral arrangements were a private matter for the dead man's heir or heirs. Inscriptions in stone giving the name of the deceased and possibly some details of his career were expensive, so there are far more for legionaries than for auxiliaries, and among auxiliaries the higher paid are disproportionately represented. A man should not fear that his body be left unburied, a fate which practically every religion in the Roman world held in abhorrence. Special arrangements to ensure decent burial are known in the legions; they probably applied to the *auxilia*, although this is not attested. Christians too believed in proper disposal of the dead, by inhumation, not cremation, but they required nothing else in the grave, no goods for the next world, and on their inscriptions showed an indifference to their exact age, which on pagan inscriptions was sometimes calculated to the hour under the influence of horoscopes. The orientation of the body may also hint at a Christian burial.

Discharge and Retirement

In his twenty-five years the soldier whose fortunes we have been following rarely left the vicinity of his own fort, apart from a few skirmishes, practice marches and an escort or two; in the second century he might have seen a year or two's campaigning. Now an unusual honour awaited him. He was honourably discharged, but had to wait for the return from Rome of a small bronze tablet, listing the privileges now granted to him. That copy was taken from a great bronze tablet, set up in the heart of Rome, Rome that he had never seen but whose gods and god-emperors he worshipped and whose traditions and traditional festivals he inherited. On it his name duly appeared, along with all the others who were discharged that year in Britain or in his area of Britain, for it seems that Britain like other provinces was divided into legionary commands. The copy said that he was given Roman citizenship and *conubium*, the right to marry a woman and raise Roman citizens. If he already had an unofficial wife she became official. Any children born to him during service also received the citizenship. His wife did not receive the citizenship; if divorce or death ended the marriage she could not raise Roman citizens on her own account (a child derived its status from its mother). The privilege was limited to one union, that existing at the time of discharge or the first one thereafter. A further limitation was made in A.D. 140: children born during service were not made Roman citizens, only those born after discharge. The reason for this move can only be conjectured; possibly the aim was virtually to force such children to join the army. In this respect they were only being reduced to the same status as the children born to legionaries during service, for whom there was no retrospective provision. Legionaries once discharged had every right as citizens to contract formal unions, though they would have to marry citizens to beget citizen children, but nothing was done for their children born during service, who were also obliged to join the army to become citizens. There was no altruism for legionary or auxiliary, though it must be said that in granting citizenship to auxiliaries and their children Rome was more generous than any other ancient state – even if the privileges were anchored firmly to the advantage of army recruitment (Plate 8).

In any case the number of citizens joining the *auxilia* steadily increased. From this same period of the 140s the wording of grants of privileges to auxiliaries made clear that citizenship was being given to those who did not already have it. The auxiliaries rapidly became citizen soldiers, and a decree under Caracalla in the early third century making all but a few groups in the Empire citizens probably hardly affected the auxiliary recruiting grounds. Some time before (the last recorded example is A.D. 178) the issue of copies of a decree set up in Rome had ceased; probably non-citizens were now so rare in the *auxilia* that individual grants were made as and when necessary.

There was no grant of money or land to auxiliaries; that was reserved for the legions. Nevertheless the auxiliary had the prized gift of citizenship and the privileges given to army veterans, immunity from taxation and the expensive honour of municipal office. He had raised his family and descendants an important rung in the social ladder, and his sons would be well placed for a military career, which offered the best chances of advancement materially and socially. The veteran himself might not have much expectation of life, if the pattern for legionaries holds good for auxiliaries also. His savings might not amount to much, lacking the legionary's grant and extra donatives from the emperor; he would miss the regular food, standards of hygiene and medical care the army had given him. The figures for legionaries suggest that the veteran had a poorer expectation of life than the civilian, though while serving he had had a better one. The lack of inscriptions of veterans has led to the suggestion that veterans did not settle on the British frontier. As there is little positive

35 Chesterholm civil settlement in the third century.
    Scale 1 in. = 265 ft (1:3180)

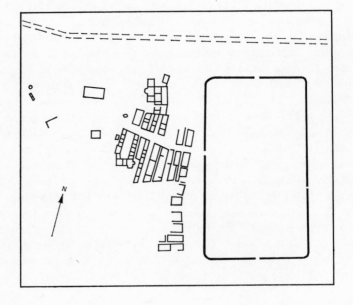

evidence that they settled elsewhere however it seems best to suppose the same pattern was followed here as on other frontiers, where veterans settled close to their forts.

The Civil Settlements

If the veteran did settle close to his fort he lived in the *vicus*, where his wife and family if he already possessed them had their home. It is still very difficult to say much about the civil settlements. They existed because of the forts. During the second century the Vallum kept civilians at a distance, but its abandonment in the third century allowed dependants of the unit and traders to build homes and shops right up to the walls. There seem to be signs in the third century of the regular laying-out of *vici*, with well-made structures, presumably half-timbered with stone sill walls. No *vicus* has reached the stage of excavation where anything like a complete plan is available, although aerial photographs of Housesteads reveal a large settlement and Chesterholm seems extensive.

Of the buildings in the *vici*, the bath-house was military and official. The temples, on the other hand, although created primarily for the officers and men of the forts, had no official position. They were privately financed. Attention has been drawn to the difficulty of identifying religious dedications by members of the *vicus* community, as opposed to soldiers or the families of fort commanders. The '*mansiones*' found at Corbridge, Benwell and Chesterholm raise problems. Are they overnight stopping-places for people travelling by the imperial post, a relay system of horses for official purposes, or are these merely inns, set up by private enterprise? Corbridge and Chesterholm, a day's journey apart on the Stanegate, both have such buildings, but either explanation would apply here. The other buildings, classed as shops and/or houses, give us fragmentary information, but as yet no chance of seeing the *vicus* as a whole. The publication of further reports from Chesterholm will help.

There is often evidence for industrial activity in the *vici*, but generally on a small scale, sufficient probably for the needs of the *vicus* and no more. Specialized manufactures such as bronze *paterae* (soldiers' mess-tins), fine footwear, glass and some mass-

36 Civilian houses. a. Housesteads; b. Chesterholm.
Scale 1 in. = 36 ft (1:432)

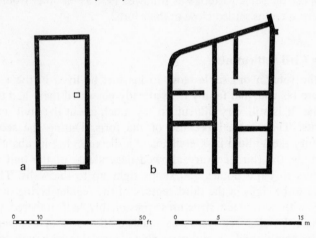

produced pottery were brought to the *vici*, but iron was smelted locally at Corbridge, Housesteads and Chesterholm. The wealth of iron objects shows the extent of the demand. Leather was another local material with plenty of uses. A cobbler's shop was identified in the *vicus* at Housesteads, and a rich variety of shoes and other leather goods has been found where conditions have preserved them, as at Chesterholm. Pottery could be produced locally, sometimes on a large scale as at Corbridge, and marketed widely. But in general it is difficult to demonstrate that industry supplying more than the local market existed. Even the military workshops at Corbridge, often described as supplying the Wall, cannot be demonstrated to have supplied more than the legionaries stationed there, though they may well have done so.

The legal status of these *vici* and the people living in them requires attention. Some generalities may help. Roman citizens were a privileged body of people, possessing rights and responsibilities. Citizenship was never a mere matter of where you lived, and Rome showed genius in making its citizenship a privilege accessible and even desirable to its former enemies. The people of Britain, like others who submitted to Rome, were regarded as persons who had surrendered unconditionally, with

192

no rights at all (*dediticii*) at first, but almost immediately they became *peregrini*, the normal word for non-citizens. They were not slaves or freed slaves. Though a freed slave could be a Roman citizen he was only eligible for certain sections of the army, and might be despised by the non-citizen freeman. Citizenship and social status passed through the mother, and must not be confused with legitimacy. The son of a Roman citizen mother was a citizen, if the father was free at least, whether or not they were married. This explains the cautious attitude of the Roman government to (non-citizen) wives of auxiliaries; it preferred to make her children citizens while denying the right to her. As the number of citizen men and even more of citizen women (daughters of auxiliaries) grew steadily situations must have become complicated, especially in the *vici*, the greatest concentration of Roman citizens in the province, apart from colonies and towns that had managed to obtain citizenship. It was probably a relief to all when the Constitutio Antoniniana under Caracalla made practically everybody citizens, though it is by no means clear that marriage during service for soldiers had become legal by this time.

The *vici* contained citizen veterans, their citizen children, and normally non-citizen wives (an increasing proportion of wives were citizens as the number of citizen women in the area rose). Their main industry would be the production of children for the army, with some return of money from serving members of the family. The veteran could hardly afford to buy land, unless he had done well with savings, but perhaps land titles did not matter too much in the Wall area; if you found unused land perhaps nobody bothered you. Some of the land belonged to the fort, and army herds grazed on it. Perhaps the veteran was allowed to feed his few animals on it. Alternatively he could turn his hand to supplying the needs of the community by working in metal, wood or leather.

The basic source of recruits was presumably the local population, though soldiering tended to become almost a hereditary occupation, so the army was to some extent self-reproducing. Traders and shop-keepers may have come from further afield, though this is clear only for the big towns at present, as the *vici* have still to yield much in the way of inscriptions.

These mixed communities of citizens and non-citizens came

directly under the jurisdiction of the fort commander, who acted as a sort of district officer. In the true Roman tradition these communities were encouraged to be self-governing. The community at Chesterholm was able to dedicate an altar as a body (to Vulcan the smith god), and the community at Housesteads made decrees. At Carriden, on the Antonine Wall, where the *vicus* had a life of no more than twenty years on present theories, the community also acted in a corporate way to set up a dedication. Thus some sort of organized communal life under magistrates flourished in these communities of in some cases thousands of inhabitants.

The towns of the Wall, Corbridge and Carlisle, and its port, South Shields, have yielded enough finds to hint at the variety and richness of life there, but we have hardly begun to see these settlements in plan. The buildings excavated at Corbridge before the First World War have not been touched since, apart from the area under guardianship, where in fact much of the later centuries has been removed, and our knowledge of the other two sites is fragmentary. They had presumably reached some level of self-government; Corbridge had walls, for which a special grant was needed, and from the third century Carlisle may have been a city-state in its own right, that of the Carvetii. The sculptures and inscriptions hint at a more cosmopolitan life than that of the *vici*. Gods are worshipped there which are not so far recorded in the settlements. Corbridge in particular had devotees of Eastern religions who set up altars in Greek, and shares with South Shields a record of a man from Palmyra, an oasis at the eastern end of the Roman world.

The Commanding Officers

Rather outside the busy life of fort and *vicus* stood the commanding officers, though their word was law in both worlds. In the second and third centuries these men were largely drawn from the equestrian order, made up of men just below senatorial rank with a property qualification and free birth. In the third century they were supplemented by men from the praetorian guard and legions who had held senior posts just below centurion level, men who might have gone on to the centurionate but who had entered the posts previously reserved for the equestrians. There should have been no shortage of equestrians, so it would seem that the army life was becoming unattractive for them, a phenomenon for which there is other evidence. The equestrian in the second or third century entered the army by assuming command of a quingenary cohort, *peditata* or *equitata*, his first military experience. His only preceding public service, if any, was as a town magistrate at 30, on the staff of a governor without troops under his command, or of a senior magistrate at Rome. In Roman eyes an officer was an administrator first and foremost, and a man who could run a city could run a unit too.

The officer, in his twenties or thirties, held his quingenary cohort for three or four years on average. He had obtained his post from the governor of Britain by a direct approach or more likely through an influential relation or friend. When relieved of his command by the arrival of his successor he would hope to be appointed by the same governor or a governor in another province to a tribunate in a legion, a pleasant change from the isolated cohort command, or if highly thought of he might be appointed to command a milliary cohort. There were fewer such commands than legionary tribunates. In any case a minor legionary tribune, one of five on the legionary commander's staff, could do less damage than a man in sole command of a milliary cohort; with the system of selection damage is what many officers may have done. There was also a substantial drop-out, for the approximate numbers of posts in the *militiae* (the different steps in the career) varied. There were about 270 as prefect of a quingenary cohort, but only about 30–40 as tribune of a milliary cohort and 141 as legionary tribune, so about one-third of the cohort prefects received no second appointment and gracefully returned to civilian life. The legionary tribune or tribune of a milliary cohort would hope to be appointed to a cavalry regiment as one of the 90 prefects of quingenary *alae*. At this stage if not before he certainly changed provinces.

Such appointments were made by the emperor, not the governor, and no equestrian officer held all three grades (*militiae*) in the same province, because of the political danger of a governor monopolizing the appointment of his officers, or the desirability of broadening the military experience of equestrian officers. Again there was a heavy drop-out, perhaps another 90 to whom no cavalry prefectures were offered. The pinnacle of the equestrian *militiae* was the prefecture of a milliary *ala*, only about ten such posts existing in the empire. Hadrian made this a fourth *militia*. In Britain there was only one such *ala*, the *ala Petriana* at Stanwix. The equestrian made his whole career in the army or went on to one of the posts in administration reserved for equestrians. Most of these posts were as financial heads in the provinces or departmental heads in Rome, or of branches of these departments responsible for a group of provinces; the only military posts were some governorships of provinces with auxiliary troops but no legionaries, and the command of the various fleets, including the British fleet. The Roman fleets were of minor importance, mainly concerned with convoying and supply of armies, and the suppression of piracy; only in the third century did attack by sea become a real possibility.

This means that any equestrian officer was unlikely to hold more than one command on the Wall itself, and unlikely to hold more than two posts in Britain. Equestrian officers were men on the move, only staying three or four years, separated socially by an immense gulf from their non-citizen men; even their officers, centurions and decurions, were overwhelmingly men promoted from the ranks. The commanding officers could have their wives and families and slaves with them, and though they might insist on thorough training for their unit they might have been little seen when off-duty. Hunting was probably their main recreation, unless they were fortunate enough to see some active service.

The Late Roman Army

Changes in the late Roman army affected the Wall garrisons. Information on the late army is far less than on the army of the Principate, a convenient term for the period from the first emperor Augustus, whose sole effective power dates from 31 B.C., to the late third century A.D. The changes in command (described in detail later) removed the garrisons of the forts on the Wall from the power of the governor, and placed them under a general, the Duke of the Britains. This probably happened at a date between 296 and 306, when the governor still appears on a military building inscription, and 337, when the emperor Constantine died. The only military duty then remaining to the civil governor was the supply of food to the troops.

The units in the Wall forts retained their names and identities throughout these changes, so that the Notitia Dignitatum, the last official document covering Roman Britain, lists them as they had been in the late second or early third century and apparently were still in or around 410, the date when Rome lost control of Britain. How far their internal organization was the same cannot be determined; there are no documents and insufficient archaeological knowledge of the fourth-century lay-out of the forts. All commanding officers of cohorts now bore the title tribune. The commanding officers of the *alae* and *cohortes* were directly commissioned from civilian life or had risen from the ranks, more probably from the new field armies than from the frontier troops. The division in the army was no longer between legions and *auxilia* but between frontier troops and field armies. Legions and *auxilia* alike had become tied to the frontiers and the differences between them had dwindled; now the Roman army recovered its lost mobility in field armies in which the dominant arm was cavalry. There was no field army proper in Britain, though the new units brought into the hinterland south of the Wall some time between the 260s and 410 (the most likely times being either the early fourth century or after 368), while still frontier troops (*limitanei*), may have had greater mobility than the Wall garrisons. A small field army was created in Britain under the count of the Britains, apparently in the very late fourth or early fifth century. Till then field troops were brought over from the Continent when they were needed, as they were in 360 and 368.

The later army was made up of conscripts, and sons of soldiers and veterans were legally obliged to serve. Attempts to evade military service were on the increase, but perhaps less in Britain than elsewhere. There may well have been more volunteers here, less resistance to conscription, and less danger. Pay was still received, and donatives from the emperor on accession and at five-yearly intervals thereafter. The old distinctions between citizen and non-citizen troops were dead; the rewards of legionaries and auxiliaries were alike. Allowances were good, for uniforms, boots and arms were supplied by the state; so were horses at first though this privilege was soon commuted for extra pay. Rations of bread, wine, meat and oil were provided by the praetorian prefect for the Gauls acting through the vicar of Britain and the governor of Britannia Secunda (later perhaps of Valentia). Promotion was by seniority. Decurions and centurions survived as posts in the old *alae* and *cohortes*; in the *vexillationes* and *auxilia* south of the Wall new names for posts emerged. Soldiers could marry during service; veterans had much the same privileges as under the Principate.

Life was probably little different on the Wall itself; perhaps only different in names of units in the hinterland. Citizenship and legal marriage were taken for granted; the former had cheapened in value as it had spread. Recruitment was compulsory and hereditary instead of being voluntary and virtually hereditary. The trend towards closer identification of garrison and fort continued, and the *vici* flourished. The soldiers were still better off than the peasantry, from which they came. Corrupt practices on the part of their officers might mean the sale of prolonged or indefinite leave to soldiers, and the collection of dead men's pay; discipline tended to become slack on the frontiers. Nevertheless the frontiers had to be defended, and the evidence is that the northern frontier was not broken, though it may have been by-passed. There is no general evidence for cultivation around the forts by serving soldiers till the fifth century, so descriptions of the Wall forts as manned by a farmer militia are unsubstantiated.

It must also be said that nothing suggests the presence of *foederati*, who bulk large in attempts to reconstruct the last days of Roman Britain. The first settlement of *foederati* was in 417, and it is an abuse of terminology to use the term earlier. These were whole tribes enrolled as allies of Rome, and living inside the frontiers. Small groups of barbarian prisoners of war, called *laeti*, were settled in the Empire as a source of recruits; none are known in Britain, but they may have been listed on a missing page of the *Notitia*. A number of men who call themselves Germans appear on the Wall, mostly on undated inscriptions, but these may have been volunteers enlisted in the regular units.

The units, then, had changed little in organization since the period when they came into being, but they had become even more permanently identified with their forts, recruiting on a hereditary basis, but still an efficient fighting force. The squalid living conditions in certain fort buildings may reflect partly change of use, partly in the days after the fort's regular garrison had ceased to function, and need not be interpreted as a sign of a catastrophic decline in the army's basic fighting efficiency.

The Local Population

Virtually nothing has been said or can be said about the people living in the immediate area of the Wall but outside the *vici*. It can be assumed but not proved that on the east the Wall ran through the territory of the Votadini, on the west that of the Brigantes. Their attitude to the Wall is not known, though the building of the Vallum implies that Rome had found belated reason to distrust the people to the south, the Brigantes. Most of our ideas about the attitudes of the tribes are founded on the pattern of forts occupied; this seems to imply south of the Wall little threat east of the Pennines, more in Cumbria. The Votadini north of the Wall seem to have been friendly on similar evidence, and because their major hill forts were apparently allowed to continue to be occupied. The Selgovae and the Damnonii are considered not to have been so well disposed to Rome.

Patterns in the life of the area were changing. Hill forts were abandoned, and in the east modern research has identified a characteristic settlement of stone-built huts defended by no more than a ditch and fence to keep out wild animals. This might reflect the imposition of the *pax Romana*. The size of settlements seems to have increased in the Roman period. The sub-rectangular form of these sites in south Northumberland might reflect planned and enforced settlement, but timber predecessors of the stone huts in these settlements have been found, suggesting that the form owes nothing to Roman example and precept. Normal Roman practice was to establish an empty zone in front of the frontier, five or even ten miles deep; the native settlements are no nearer than five miles to the Wall on the north, and in the area of the Wall itself there is only one, the second-century site at Milking Gap near Housesteads. However the army seems to have ended forcibly the occupation of this settlement. Rome built

199

37 The native settlement at Milking Gap. It probably started life as a single hut within a walled courtyard and later expanded into a settlement of five huts. Scale 1 in. = 36 ft (1:432)

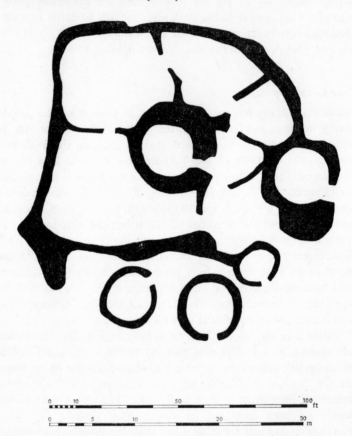

roads for military purposes which also opened up communications. The army was a voracious customer for meat, corn (there is evidence for ploughing in the Wall area) and leather, and some would be paid for above the quotas supplied as tribute. The army offered food, clothing, shelter and pay with security. It honoured local gods, providing for them shrines richer than had ever been seen. And the forts were a lure for men, and women, who had anything to sell.

These paragraphs are little enough to offer on life in the north. In the age-old toil of making a living four centuries of Rome were a very little thing. The fort garrisons and their dependants were an unnatural growth, only possible because of the external support of regular pay. When that ceased they withered and died. The peasants were the real people, the others only shadows. But the evidence works in reverse. It is possible to know much of the history of the Wall, something of the life that went on in and around its forts. The story of the native population is unwritten, only to be found on sites poor in material remains and especially artefacts, sites which it is impossible to date closely. At present they cannot be linked with the *vici*, except by analogies with other frontiers, or with the tribes known from geographical sources but not named in the surviving historical documents. Our attention is therefore concentrated on the Wall as it can be known through written and unwritten evidence, while acknowledging that its story will never be complete until it can be set in the context of the peoples it controlled and divided.

Seven

The Third and Fourth Centuries

The third century was a difficult time for the inhabitants of the Roman Empire. Inflation raged; civil war was endemic; the frontiers of the empire came under increasing pressure from the barbarian peoples beyond. Britain, however, only suffered the first of these ills. The civil wars passed her by and the frontier remained peaceful. One result of the civil wars, and the invasions from outside, was the remodelling of the army, though this may not have affected Britain in any way until the end of the century. In many ways in the third century her position as an island on the boundary of the empire served her well; she slumbered and her army relaxed while the rest of the empire suffered.

The chief reason for the army's relaxation was undoubtedly the stable condition of the northern frontier. From the beginning of the third century if not before, the four 1000-strong auxiliary units in the outpost forts together with scouts and irregular troops, supported by the 10,000 men stationed in the Wall forts, patrolled as far north as the Tay. They maintained a general surveillance over the tribes of this area – the Votadini, later to be known as the Goddodin, the Selgovae, the Novantae, the Damnonii and probably the Maeatae – and kept a watchful eye on their *loca* or meeting places. The reasons for peace in the third century are not easy to define, but peace there certainly was.

The Early Third Century

The first decades of the third century saw various improvements and repairs after years of neglect to the forts of the north of

202

England. At Chester-le-Street in 216 and at South Shields six years later new aqueducts were constructed to bring a fresh supply of water into the fort. Netherby saw the construction of a cavalry exercise hall in 222, and Great Chesters the rebuilding of a granary in 225. At Chesterholm a gate with its towers was restored from its foundations at about the same time, while at High Rochester the defences of this outpost fort were improved by the construction of ballista platforms. These repairs and renovations were carried out at many sites throughout the first half of the third century: Old Carlisle, Old Penrith and Whitley Castle in the hinterland; Birdoswald, Carrawburgh, Chesters, Chesterholm, Great Chesters on the Wall; and Netherby, Risingham and High Rochester to the north. Several sites have produced more than one inscription: at High Rochester building work was going on in 216, 220 and about 230 when two dedication slabs were erected; at Chesters in 205–7, in 221 and again a few years later; and at Carrawburgh in 211–17 and in 237. Some years later, probably in the early 240s, the headquarters building and the armoury, perhaps part of the same building, were restored at Lanchester after they had fallen down. At the same time another inscription from the same site records the rebuilding of the bath-house and *basilica* from the ground. The last inscription of this series is one at Lancaster of 262–6 attesting the restoration from the foundations of the bath-house and *basilica*, which had fallen down through old age. Most of these inscriptions date to the first thirty years of the third century and demonstrate clearly a time of great activity for the army – the soldiers were hardly being allowed to relax in their barracks.

In the early third century the conditions of the army were improved in a more tangible way, by increasing pay. Previously pay had been increased at widely spaced intervals of a hundred years and more – under Caesar, Domitian and Septimius Severus. Now pay was raised again by Caracalla after just a few years. Severus, according to Herodian, about 197 also allowed the soldiers to marry. The passage stating this is not unambiguous, since the Greek word for a wife also means a woman; if true the action was probably no more than another step in recognizing that soldiers had unofficial wives and children. It does not mean that wives and families were introduced into the forts, nor that soldiers moved out into married quarters. Centurions had always been allowed to marry but there is no archaeological evidence of their wives living with them within the forts. A recently discovered inscription at Westerwood on the Antonine Wall does show that a centurion of legion VI Victrix had brought his wife and family with him from York.

It has been considered that Severus Alexander went beyond Septimius Severus in his treatment of the army by giving land captured from the enemy to the frontier soldiers, the *limitanei*, to cultivate as long as their sons entered the army. The statement comes from the *Historia Augusta*; it is unlikely to be true, for the whole life of Severus Alexander in the *Historia Augusta* is fictional. Professor A. H. M. Jones has recently suggested that the passage is not a reflection of the current practice in the early fourth century, but 'a veiled recommendation on policy to the emperor', who was almost certainly Constantine I. In the third and fourth centuries there is no evidence for soldiers holding land while they were serving – in fact there is some evidence to the contrary – though veterans were apparently entitled to an allotment or a cash bonus when they retired. It is not until the fifth century, after the end of Roman Britain, that there is a reference to serving soldiers cultivating land.

Native and Civil Settlements in the Third Century

The third century saw the continued expansion of the native settlements in the border counties and no doubt elsewhere in the north of England. The discovery of third-century Roman material at native sites north of Hadrian's Wall, or as stray finds, demonstrates continuing contact between Roman and native, though of course the finds are mute on the nature of this contact. We may presume, however, that it was peaceful. An inscription erected at Walldürn in Germania Superior in 232 may imply recruitment from this area in the early third century and this has been linked with a Caledonian chieftain, Lossio Veda, being at Colchester during the reign of Severus Alexander (222–35). Lossio Veda dedicated a bronze tablet to the Victory of the emperor, and to Mars and a native war god, and this has been taken as support for a military reason for his presence. However, the Caledonian could have been at Colchester for any one of several reasons while the Walldürn inscription in referring to *Brittones dediticii Alexandriani* implies that the Britons were not volunteers but conscripted men, possibly joining the army as a result of the campaigns of Severus and Caracalla.

38 Housesteads civil settlement. Scale 1 in. = 520 ft (1:6240)

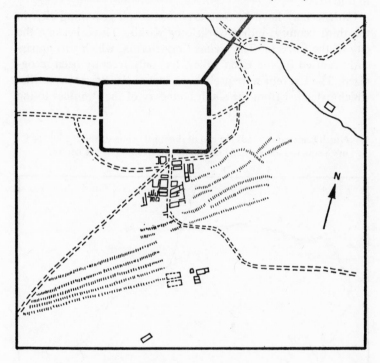

The villages or *vici* outside the forts also flourished in the third century. That at Housesteads moved north from its earlier centre on Chapel Hill a quarter of a mile south of the fort, encroached on the Vallum and eventually surrounded the fort on its three southern sides. At nearby Chesterholm the settlement extended to 10 acres, three times the size of the fort. The villages at both these sites gained some degree of self-government in these years if not before, for the *vicus* outside the fort at Carriden on

205

the Antonine Wall was self-governing in the mid second century. At Corbridge, an army base from the first century, a town of some 30 acres surrounded by a rampart grew up round the legionary base depot on the site of the old fort. Carlisle, probably founded at the same time as Corbridge, occupied 70 acres and was also enclosed by walls. Here the town survived the end of Roman Britain and there is a description of St Cuthbert's visit to it in 685.

Carlisle may have become a *civitas*, a self-governing city, in the third century; either Carlisle or Kirkby Thore became the city of the Carvetii. The *civitas Carvetiorum*, which was apparently centred on the Eden valley, has only recently been recognized. The Carvetii were probably a sept of the Brigantes, a tribe which extended from the south boundary of the Pennines to the

39 North England towards the end of the third century (about 290). The open square indicates that occupation at this time is not certain

rivers Tyne and Solway. The main part of the tribe was formed into the *civitas Brigantum*, whose seat of government was Isurium Brigantum, modern Aldborough. Another sept of the tribe was the Setantii in Lancashire and the Textoverdi of South Tynedale may have been a third. These septs, together with other outlying parts of the tribe, were apparently administered by the military. The establishment of a new *civitas* in the third century – it was in existence by 260 or shortly afterwards – points to a relaxing of the army's hold on the Pennines.

This is demonstrated in another, equally practical, way. Some time in the late third century the units garrisoning several hinter-land forts were withdrawn. Units are attested at Lanchester in the 240s and at Lancaster 20 years later so the withdrawals presum-ably took place after that, perhaps over a period of years. Not every fort was abandoned; Bainbridge, Ribchester, Moresby and possibly also Ravenglass and Watercrook were certainly in occu-pation in the fourth century according to the *Notitia Dignitatum*, while archaeological evidence suggests that other sites such as Ilkley, Low Borrow Bridge, Ambleside, Papcastle and probably Elslack were also still held. But many forts in County Durham, Yorkshire, Lancashire and Westmorland no longer contained a garrison. This both emphasizes that the units were now not required to support the troops on Hadrian's Wall and in the out-post forts, and that the Pennines were peaceful. Their removal also implies that they were needed elsewhere, not necessarily in the province.

The Later Third Century

If the later third century saw the abandonment of many hinter-land forts and the growth of civil government in north England the peaceful conditions had other, in many ways less beneficial, effects on the army. Discipline must have suffered with no enemy to fight, though we know nothing of this. The size of the units no doubt also fell below their theoretical strength, and the remodelling of barracks in the Wall forts in the early fourth century for a smaller number of men certainly supports this. But the effect went beyond this, for after all the building activity at the beginning of the third century some forts fell into disrepair towards its end. From his excavations at Halton Chesters and Rudchester Mr J. P. Gillam has concluded that many of the buildings in these forts lay in ruins in the later years of the third century and for much of the fourth. The third-century buildings had fallen down and become covered with earth before those of the next structural phase were erected. At South Shields many of the granaries built at the beginning of the century and adapted as barracks after the end of the campaigns and the abandonment of Carpow were demolished while later, probably in the early fourth century, a couple of tile kilns were built in another granary. The soot and wastes from the kiln – for only one was completed – were dumped to the north on the demolished granaries. There is the possibility, however, that these buildings were excluded from the fort at this time by a wall reducing the size of the station. A tailing-off in the pottery sequence in the later third and early fourth centuries points to a running-down of this military establishment. The fort was not entirely abandoned, for modifications were made to the headquarters building in the fourth century, while the *Notitia Dignitatum* demonstrates the presence of the *numerus barcariorum Tigrisiensium* about 400. Nor were Halton Chesters and Rudchester abandoned entirely and then later reoccupied: at Halton Chesters the unit in residence at the beginning of the third century was still there at the end of the fourth. The unit could have shrunk to very low numbers. It is not unknown for commanding officers to allow this to happen in the third and fourth centuries and draw dead men's pay and allowances. Some of the *numeri* recorded at Wall forts earlier in the third century, however, may have been withdrawn. Certainly only the *numerus Maurorum Aurelianorum* stationed at Burgh-by-Sands is mentioned in the fourth century, though that may be due to the inadequacies of our sources.

The situation now discovered archaeologically has long been attested epigraphically; an inscription erected at Birdoswald in the decade commencing in 296 states baldly that the commandant's house, which had fallen down and become covered with earth, was rebuilt and the headquarters building and bath-house repaired. This extensive rebuilding suggests that the unit was in a bad way, possibly without a permanent commanding officer for some time. If this was the case the other fort buildings must have suffered accordingly, and no doubt the size of the unit had fallen too. This presumably only reflected the slack time on the northern frontier but there is an additional factor. The third century witnessed a change in the sort of men who commanded army units. The commanders of auxiliary units were unlikely to be members of the municipal aristocracies as in the two previous centuries, but were more probably soldiers risen from the ranks. Indeed the rebuilding or repair of the three buildings at Birdoswald was carried out under the supervision not of a tribune but of a centurion acting as commander of the unit. This new type of commanding officer did not have the large household of his predecessor and therefore did not require a large building. Very possibly at Birdoswald he did not reside in the commandant's house at all and the building was allowed to fall into ruin. This was only part of the story, however, for two other major buildings in the fort needed repair at the end of the third century.

The latest coin in the third-century levels at Birdoswald is one of Elagabalus, 218–22. At milecastle 48, a mile or so to the east, the latest is of Claudius Gothicus, 269, while at Bewcastle the coin series ends with several of the Tetrici, 270–73. This may suggest abandonment, or at least reduced occupation, of these sites in the years immediately following 270. This neglect also extended to the curtain wall itself. Some years ago the curtain wall just west of Birdoswald was found to have been rebuilt from its foundations and to contain late third-century pottery. This suggests that the Wall lay in ruins and also that the fort of Birdoswald stood detached from the Wall for a time.

Constantius in Britain

The occasion for the repair work at Birdoswald and other sites on the Wall is usually taken to be the visit of the Caesar Constantius Chlorus in 296. From 286 or 287 Britain was under the rule of the usurper Carausius and his successor Allectus. A campaign launched by the central government to regain the island resulted in a victory in 296 near Silchester for Asclepiodotus, Constantius' praetorian prefect. If the Wall units formed part of the army of Allectus – as they probably did – they are unlikely to have taken part in the fighting, for Allectus was unable

209

to deploy his whole force and the brunt of the fighting was borne by his barbarian mercenaries.

It is usually assumed that the Picts took the opportunity of the absence of its garrison, which we have seen is not certain, to attack and destroy Hadrian's Wall. Signs of burning and destruction have been noted at several sites on the Wall, forts, milecastles and turrets, but no attack is recorded in the ancient sources. The burning and masonry debris could have several causes. Some sites may have been allowed to fall into decay towards the end of the third century while the burning may simply be the build-up of fires and hearths inside the turret or milecastle during many years of occupation. There is moreover no pattern to the 'destruction' deposits; for example, in the Birdoswald area masonry debris has been found below the fourth-century floors at certain sites – 48, 48a and 49b – but not at others – 48b and 52. More likely Constantius visited the northern defences himself and ordered a complete overhaul. The wide-ranging reforms which had affected the continental army, but not Britain's, was another reason to remodel accommodation. Constantius' visit may have had no connection with hostile action by the Picts, as a contemporary Panegyric implies he did not wage war on them until his second visit to Britain in 306. Shortly after his victory, like Severus a hundred years before, Constantius died at York and the imperial career of his more famous son, Constantine, began.

Inscriptions inform us that two of the forts to which Constantius turned his attention were Birdoswald and Housesteads. At Birdoswald the ruined commandant's house was completely rebuilt and the headquarters building and the bath-house repaired. Archaeological research has demonstrated that other buildings in the fort were also reconstructed. The former store-house and barrack-block lying immediately north of the *via principalis* in the east half of the *praetentura* were demolished and replaced by a building of a completely different plan. Only part of the building has been examined but the excavated section seems to have been a suite for a junior officer with a cook-house attached. In the south part of the fort the rebuilding did not follow the earlier alignment, and moreover the new barrack-blocks were very different. This new type of barrack building has

40 Housesteads barrack-block XIV. a. in the second century; b. as
rebuilt in the early fourth century. Scale 1 in. = 48 ft (1:576)

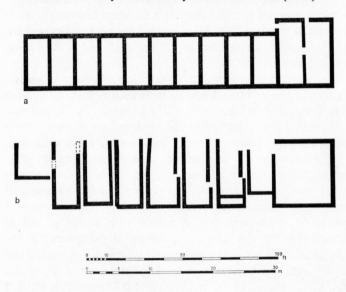

been more fully explored at another fort which saw reconstruction at this time, Housesteads. One of the barrack-blocks there
was carefully and thoroughly excavated some years ago and its
history traced through four building phases. In the early fourth
century the 160-foot-long barrack-block was demolished and
replaced by a series of chalets. Ten *contubernia* of the normal
pattern gave way to six separate barrack units measuring 34 by
12 feet internally. The individual rooms were rather longer than
their predecessors so only the equivalent of one *contubernium*
was lost in the rearrangement. The restyling of the barrack-block
suggests a corresponding change in organization of the century.
Major modifications to the army were made in the later third
century and the early fourth but their effect on unit strength and
unit organization is only imperfectly understood. The overall
size of auxiliary units may have been lowered, possibly by maintaining the number of centuries but by reducing the strength of
each. This would account for the fewer rooms yet general impression of more space. Certainly the centurion gained more

211

accommodation at this time. His 'flat' was increased in area by a half, which may have allowed him to have his wife and family in camp, a privilege previously denied him. The new style of barracks has been recognized at other forts besides Housesteads and Birdoswald: Great Chesters on the Wall and at Risingham and High Rochester.

At some sites the restoration at this time was more extensive. The fort at Chesterholm seems to have been rebuilt. A hundred years before it had been rebuilt to face south, but it was now turned round and faced north. The headquarters building, which was completely reconstructed, followed broadly the same lines as its second-century predecessor, thus emphasizing the continuity of life on the Wall; not only did the same units remain in the same forts for two hundred years and more but many of the buildings remained substantially the same. The provision of hypocausts in the rooms used by the administrative staff at Chesterholm may be part of an overall improvement in the facilities of the Wall forts. At two other forts, South Shields and Carrawburgh, hypocausts seem to have been inserted about this time. The courtyard in the new *principia* at Chesterholm was not left open as in earlier years but divided up into storehouses, and later in the fourth century the *basilica* at South Shields was treated in the same way. At Housesteads the division of the verandah of the headquarters building courtyard into a series of rooms is also usually dated to the early fourth century, but, as at Carrawburgh, the modifications probably date a century earlier. The precise reason for creating these small rooms in the *principia* is uncertain; they may have served as extra rooms for the clerks, or as storehouses for arms, equipment or possibly for the large number of documents which the garrison must have accumulated (see Fig. 41).

Some of the smaller structures on the Wall may have been repaired at this time. At a number of the milecastles and turrets on either side of the river Irthing modifications, which are usually dated to about 300, have been noted. New floors laid over masonry debris suggest repair to the superstructure while at one milecastle, 50, the accommodation was modified. At two other milecastles in this area more unusual changes took place. The normal round-arched south gateways of milecastles 50 and 52 were replaced, apparently by monolithic masonry doorposts which would presumably have carried a flat arch. New post-holes were cut through masonry of the earlier gate so that the new passage was only slightly smaller than its predecessor, and presumably still passable for wheeled traffic – unlike the north gate of milecastle 52 – while a new stone threshold cutting through the earlier road surfaces was let into the floor. The first dated appearance of this type of gate in the empire is in the Aurelian Walls at Rome constructed about 275. The remodelling of these two gateways on Hadrian's Wall must be later than 275, and possibly was part of Constantius' restoration of the frontier.

Other milecastles and turrets continued in use into the fourth century though they have produced no evidence for structural modifications. At turret 7b and milecastle 9 at the east end of the Wall fourth-century pottery has been found; at the west end of the Wall one sherd of a fourth-century cooking pot was discovered in milecastle 79, though this may be evidence for transient rather than permanent occupation. In the central sector of the Wall, however, several milecastles and turrets continued in use: milecastles 37, 38, 40, 48, 50, 51, 52 and 54 and turrets 44b, 48a, 48b and 49b, though the evidence is not always very clear. Slight structural modifications simply noted in the excavation reports as later than the early third century may also date to this time, though they could have taken place in the preceding century. The picture is of continuing occupation of a relatively small number of milecastles and turrets held for the sake of convenience, not as an integrated system of observation towers and control points. No milecastle or turret can be proved to have been abandoned as a result of reappraisal at the beginning of the fourth century. The structures which were repaired a hundred years before but did not survive into the fourth century were probably abandoned piecemeal during the intervening years, or allowed to run down in the same way as some of the forts.

Two forts on the Wall exhibit no trace of reconstruction during these years, Halton Chesters and Rudchester. The military establishments of both forts seem to have been run down in the later third century, but there was no rebuilding at the end of that century. It was not until much later in the fourth century that the forts saw a resurgence of military activity. Halton and

Rudchester may have been ignored for so long because they were well protected by the screen of outpost forts and patrols. This may simply have been carrying the policy of the abandonment of the hinterland forts in the late third century one step further. The difference between the permitted decay of forts like Halton and Rudchester and the abandonment of forts in the hinterland is that the units in the hinterland forts must have been moved elsewhere to perform a more useful function. Only this would disturb the force of inertia.

If some sites on the Wall were left to rot Constantius was not inactive further north. At Risingham and High Rochester at least part of the barrack accommodation was rebuilt in the new style. At High Rochester the rebuilding apparently included the complete restoration of the headquarters. At both sites, however, the work included the repair and remodelling of the defences: the fine west gate still visible at High Rochester was built then.

The hand of Constantius also extended to the hinterland of Hadrian's Wall. New forts at Piercebridge, Newton Kyme and possibly Elslack seem to have been built now. These were placed at strategic points and contained large garrisons – Piercebridge is 11 acres – which could strike swiftly and in strength at any force which had penetrated, or outflanked, the forward defences. They contain none of the improvements in defensive architecture of the contemporary Saxon Shore forts, thick, high walls, well-defended entrances and broad ditches, nor were these features introduced on the Wall itself, at this time or later. However, a fort of Saxon Shore type was built at Lancaster in the early fourth century, as part of a series of new or rebuilt stations along the west coast of England and Wales – the largest was built at Cardiff – designed to protect the west coast from the marauding Scots from Ireland. The legionary fortress at York received a river front incorporating the bastions characteristic of the Saxon Shore type, but it was not continued round the whole perimeter. It seems ornamental rather than functional, befitting the dignity of the *dux*. There is no reason to date the rebuilding to Constantius; it appears to be later than 335.

The credit for some of this work, habitually assigned to Constantius, should possibly be given to his son Constantine, who took the title of Britannicus in 315, for reasons unknown. There is no evidence for a Pictish invasion of north Britain in 297 and the campaign of Constantius against the Picts took place shortly before his death in 306. The Romans were no longer in a position to undertake an old-fashioned war of aggrandizement; the Picts must have given some cause for the Roman reaction. The new forts in the Pennines and on the west coast at this time were part of this same reaction to protect the provinces of Britain from the seaborne invasions of the Picts and the Scots. But there is often no clear evidence whether the building was undertaken by Constantius or by Constantine.

The Early Fourth Century

Another measure taken either now or later in the fourth century for the defence of north England was the reoccupation of many hinterland forts. The units which now garrisoned these forts were not of the old auxiliary type which had left forty and more years before, but new fourth-century creations. Chester-le-Street was now garrisoned by the *numerus vigilum*, Binchester (if that was the Morbio of the *Notitia*) by the *equites cataphractarii*, Brough-under-Stainmore by a *numerus directorum* and other forts by a *numerus Solensium*, a *numerus Pacensium* and a *numerus supervenientium Petueriensium*. South Shields was now garrisoned by the *numerus barcariorum Tigrisiensium*. The stationing of the Tigris bargemen at the mouth of the Tyne was possibly to aid navigation on the river. One of these new units, the *equites Crispiani*, was named after Constantine's eldest son, Crispus, Caesar from 317 to 326, while an older unit was renamed the *ala I Herculea* in honour of the emperor Maximian, Diocletian's colleague (286–305). The new units could have been assigned to their stations any time after they were raised but the retention of the title honouring Crispus, whose name was erased from many public inscriptions after his execution in 326, suggests that the *equites Crispiani* at least were in existence before that date and retained their title through neglect.

Whatever the date of the reoccupation of the Pennine forts, and it could have been any time between 296 and 369, the purpose was clear, to give protection against the new enemies of Rome, not against a local threat such as the Brigantes, who now

215

appeared to be peaceful members of the empire. Nor were the units to defend their immediate locality from attack. They were clearly organized with an eye to communication. Many of the units lay beside the roads leading north, Dere Street and the Stainmore route which led both to the west end of the Wall and to Cumbria. At some time in the fourth century the Cumberland Coast defences were strengthened by the occupation of Burrow Walls, possibly other forts and some of the milefortlets (12 and 20 have both produced a small amount of ceramic evidence, while milefortlet 5 continued in occupation). The new disposition was directed against invasion not from across the Solway but from Ireland. These units were support troops for Hadrian's Wall, taking up again the duties of the old hinterland forts, and also guarded against the Wall being by-passed by sea. These units may have formed a *de facto* field army although they were *vexillationes* and *auxilia*, not true field army units; they lacked the special recruiting and privileges of the field army, and they were stationed in widely spaced forts, not billeted together in towns. Constantine created this distinction between field armies (*comitatenses*) and frontier troops (*limitanei*), which marks an important step in the long process of the fossilization of the army on the frontiers of the Empire. It was the only way to restore the mobility lost by too-close identification of units with the forts on the frontier lines and by local recruiting. The *limitanei* guarded the frontiers of the Empire while the field army would be brought into action in the event of invasion – or civil war. Two hundred years before, this field army would have been formed from the auxiliary units garrisoning the Wall and hinterland forts. Now these units had a more limited function, more akin to that of the soldiers of the small forts and watch-towers of the old Stanegate line or the milecastles and turrets of the original Hadrian's Wall than the old auxiliary units; a new field army had to be created to replace them. Although the soldiers of the field army enjoyed a higher status than the frontier troops there was no radical difference between them; the *limitanei*, as we have seen, were not a peasant militia cultivating their lands in return for military service. The soldiers of the field army and the frontier army were recruited from the same area and the same type of person. It was possible for units of *limitanei* to be upgraded into regiments of the field army as was legion II Augusta, and right through into the fifth century they remained organized fighting troops, though their efficiency sadly declined.

The *limitanei* were commanded by a new imperial official, the *dux* (duke). This officer, who took over the military duties of the old provincial governor, was an invention of Diocletian, but under him *duces* were only appointed to certain frontiers of the Empire. Now Constantine extended the institution to virtually all the military provinces. A hundred years later the *Notitia Dignitatum* records that the *dux Britanniarum* commanded the units on Hadrian's Wall and in the Pennine forts. The detachment of the field army stationed in Britain at that time was under the command of the *comes Britanniarum*, while the Saxon Shore forts came under the authority of the *comes litoris Saxonici*. The rank of *comes* (count) was a creation of Constantine, who may have introduced the count of the Saxon Shore to Britain. The *comes Britanniarum* was not a permanent post until after 368. These new officials were responsible to the *magister peditum* (master of the infantry) and the *magister equitum* (master of the cavalry), the joint commanders of the central field army, by the 360s and possibly from their inception. The *duces* and the *comites* – and the *magistri* – were selected from the prefects and tribunes commanding the auxiliary regiments; they had military backgrounds, never having wielded civil authority. They were usually uneducated, and often barbarians rather than Romans. Barbarians, or free Germans, were used increasingly in the army, and in command, from the time of Diocletian. A king of the Alamanni, Crocus, commanding a contingent of his tribe in Britain, played an important part in the elevation of Constantine to Augustus at York in 306. The two army leaders, Fullofaudes and Nectaridus, caught up in the debacle of 367, clearly were barbarians. The provinces of Britain were governed by *praesides*, who having lost all military duties to the *duces* and *comites* were now purely civil officials. These men were often lawyers by profession, certainly educated, unlike the *duces*.

Britain had been divided into two provinces by Severus after the defeat of Albinus in 197, essentially to restrict the activities and power of the governor of the island, to prevent the establishment of an independent power-base across the Channel by dividing the three-legion province, eventually into a two-legion southern command and a northern province containing one legion and most of the auxiliary troops. Two other three-legion provinces were so treated: Pannonia Superior and Syria. Britain, geographically isolated, was obviously susceptible to the rise of independent usurpers; indeed it is surprising that there were not more in the 370 years of Roman Britain. A century after the division of Britain by Severus the two provinces were themselves divided by Constantine. Britannia Superior, the province of southern England and Wales, was divided into Maxima Caesariensis with its capital at London and Britannia Prima, governed probably from Cirencester. The two provinces carved out of Britannia Inferior were Flavia Caesariensis, containing the territory of the old tribes of the Iceni and the Coritani, and Britannia Secunda, roughly corresponding to the lands of the Brigantes and the Parisi, north England. York, home of VI Victrix and capital of Britannia Inferior, became the seat of the *praeses* of Britannia Secunda, the civilian governor of the north, and probably also of the *dux*, the military commander of Hadrian's Wall. The four provinces of Britain were organized into a diocese headed by a *vicarius* with his headquarters at London. The *vicarius* was the deputy of the praetorian prefect of Gaul based at Trier. Not only therefore was the authority enjoyed by the governors of Britain in the first and second centuries now fragmented into five or more separate commands, civilian and military, but the *vicarius* and the praetorian prefect were now interposed between the *praeses* and the emperor, while the *magistri militum* intervened between the *dux* and the emperor. The old governor of Roman Britain had reported direct to the emperor. The division of the provinces and the separation of civilian and military commands was for administrative convenience and to relieve the burden of work on the senior officials of the empire.

Diocletian was the author of another reform which had an effect on the troops of Hadrian's Wall. After many years of declining recruiting figures, and increasing state control, he institutionalized the long-standing traditions of the army by making military service hereditary and compulsory. Henceforth the veterans living in the *vici* who by habit had entered their fathers' units now were compelled to by law. The law was not strongly enforced, but in any case it cannot have had much effect on the young men of the north of England – there was little else with similar pay and prospects to attract the men of the *vici* and farmsteads of the north, especially when warfare was apparently so unusual in the north.

The first half of the fourth century certainly saw a continued expansion in the civil settlements. At this time the *vicus* at Chesterholm underwent extensive rebuilding, but lack of evidence prevents any discussion of the development of other *vici* in the fourth century. It does seem probable that the early fourth century saw the insertion of a new gate through the Wall, at Housesteads. The gate lies just to the north-east of the fort beside the Knag Burn. It consists of a single passage gateway flanked by guard-chambers with gates to front and rear. This would allow a party to enter the gate-passage to be searched and pay their dues before admittance to the province. Dr J. C. Mann has suggested that the gate may have been to allow beasts and vehicles easier movement through the Wall when the continuing rise of the threshold of the gate made the ramp out of the north gate of the fort too steep. Whatever the reason it made life a little easier for the people of Housesteads whether they lived in the fort or the *vicus*.

The Picts

At the same time a shadow was being cast across the peace of the northern frontier by the rise of a new nation, the Picts, who were to give the Roman army much trouble in the later fourth century. This nation resulted from a unification of the many tribes north of the Forth and Clyde isthmus mentioned by Ptolemy. The four or more tribes of the central Highlands, Strathmore and the north-east by the time of Severus had become two, the Caledonians and the Maeatae. The Picts are first mentioned in a Panegyric referring to the events of 297 addressed to Constantius Chlorus. They are clearly a fusion of the Caledonians and the Maeatae, perhaps incomplete, for there is mention in 310 of the Caledones and other Picts while the Verona List of 313 lists the Picts and the Caledonians separately.

This is the last reference to the Caledonians, at least in ancient sources, and thereafter all the people north of the Forth are known as the Picts, though they remained divided into different groups such as the Dicalydones and the Verturiones which Ammianus Marcellinus recorded in 367, the former obviously retaining the old tribal name in their new title.

Nine years after the first mention of the Picts in 297, Constantius Chlorus was in the field campaigning against them and, according to a contemporary writer, reached the end of the island. This was no doubt exaggerated but it does suggest serious activity on the part of the emperor. The Picts may have attacked Hadrian's Wall at the beginning of the century. The burning of a wattle-and-daub barrack-block at High Rochester and signs of destruction at Risingham may have been the work of the Picts, though this is not yet proved. The isolated outpost forts were peculiarly susceptible to attack. Certainly they seem to have had a rather more chequered history in the fourth century than the forts on the Wall.

Forty years after Constantius' war against the Picts such a serious situation developed in Britain that his grandson, the emperor Constans, had to visit the island in the middle of winter. The trouble which broke out late in 342 seems to have involved the northern frontier, for it was connected with the *areani*, the frontier scouts. It is possible that the outpost forts of Bewcastle, Risingham and High Rochester were destroyed at this time, though the evidence for this noted during the excavation of these sites may have resulted from repairs to strengthen them against the Picts. High Rochester may have been abandoned at this time, or a few years later when the Picts led another invasion of the province.

In 360 the Scots, who were still in Ireland, and the Picts, ignoring agreements made with Rome, laid waste the territory near the frontier. The general Lupicinus with four regiments of the field army was dispatched to Britain and although nothing is recorded in the contemporary sources he presumably succeeded in restoring the situation. But not for long, for in 364 the peace of the province was again disturbed by the Picts, Scots, Saxons and Attacotti, while in 367 they struck in earnest. The 'barbarian conspiracy' of this year saw the combined attack of Picts, Scots,

Attacotti, Franks and Saxons, against the diocese of Britain.
Nectaridus, count of the Saxon Shore, was killed and Fullofaudes,
the *dux Britanniarum*, was ambushed and surrounded. The
areani, the scouts who were supposed to give advance warning of
any impending invasion, had not informed the Romans of the
movements of the Picts, but led by bribes had betrayed to the
Picts the military dispositions of the Romans! In the catastrophe
army discipline broke down and soldiers deserted their units
while others were possibly on indefinite leave, a privilege often
sold by senior officers in the fourth century. The emperor
Valentinian, himself campaigning against the Alamanni, in the
spring of the following year 368, sent one of his senior commanders to Britain, count Theodosius, with four regiments from
his field army.

Theodosius and the Rebuilding of the Late Fourth Century

It took Theodosius many months to restore order in the diocese
and strengthen the frontier defences. His attention no doubt
turned to Hadrian's Wall; he is described as restoring the cities
and strongholds which had been founded to secure a long period
of peace, but had suffered repeated misfortunes, and protecting
the frontiers by sentinels and outposts, but it is not easy to see
precisely what he did. In the first place there is little evidence
that the Wall actually suffered from the Picts. The construction
of a series of observation posts along the Yorkshire coast,
possibly extending as far north as the Tyne, seemingly on the
orders of Theodosius suggests that the Picts attacked by sea.
In 367 they may have ignored Hadrian's Wall and simply
sailed round it. This may have been how Fullofaudes was caught
in a trap. It would also account for the lack of evidence for
the destruction of Hadrian's Wall at this time – in fact the
Wall was probably the safest place in the province. Nevertheless the presence of a senior official once again led to repairs to
the Wall forts. At Birdoswald, Housesteads and Chesterholm
various renovations and modifications are generally dated to this
time.

The work at the first two sites included the rebuilding or repair
of barrack-blocks. At Birdoswald the rebuilding of the complex

221

immediately north of the *via principalis* was securely dated in 1929 by a coin of Valentinian I, 364–75. One building was half-timbered, resting on walls bonded with clay, while inscriptions of Severus and Diocletian were reused as paving flags. One room of the building was used as a cook-house, another as a living-room or dormitory, while next door was a small building with a raised floor, possibly a ventilated store-house. In the south part of the fort a building was now built on a new alignment across the earlier *via quintana*. At Chesterholm a new building was constructed overlying the clay rampart backing on the east wall of the fort. A coin of Constans dated to 342–8 in the core of a wall of this building provides a *terminus post quem* for its erection, which may have been at the time of Theodosius. Most modifications to forts are not as well dated as this and are usually assigned to the nearest or the next 'Wall period'. In fact, of course, the buildings within forts were no doubt repaired and modified at any stage in their history.

Another modification at Chesterholm probably carried out at this time was the addition of another hypocaust and two latrines to the offices of the headquarters building. It is possible that these rooms were now actually used as living quarters. At Housesteads a large room had been created by the conversion of the two southern administrative rooms into one, probably earlier in the fourth century; it also apparently became living quarters from the evidence of the considerable quantity of cinders in the later floor levels, but perhaps after the end of Roman Britain. The northern of the administrative rooms in this building was turned into a weapons store in the late fourth century – when the fort was abandoned more than 800 arrow heads were left there still tied together in bundles. The *basilica* of the headquarters building at South Shields now if not before gained a new function also as a store-room, in this case probably for food. More significant perhaps was the rebuilding at Halton Chesters and Rudchester. These two forts, which had largely lain abandoned for going on for a hundred years, now underwent complete restoration. New buildings were constructed over the considerable depth of rubbish accumulated in the years of neglect. But the new buildings were not like the old. They followed different alignments and were of a different method of construction. They were largely of

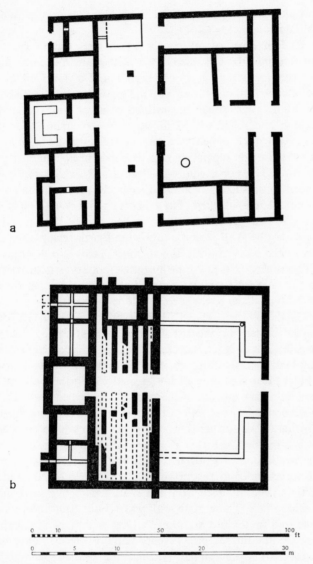

a

b

0   10   50   100 ft

0   5   10   20   30 m

41   Two headquarters buildings in the late fourth century.
a. Chesterholm; b. South Shields. At Chesterholm store-rooms surround
the courtyard, while hypocausts have been inserted into the two outer
rear rooms. Hypocausts have been inserted into several of the rear rooms
at South Shields and the *basilica* converted into a store.
Scale 1 in. = 36 ft (1:432)

timber and the uprights were set in sockets cut in large, indeed megalithic, stones.

A small number of milecastles and turrets show continuing occupation into the last thirty years of the fourth century. Late-fourth century pottery has only been found at four milecastles (9, 37, 48 and 54), one turret (7b) and possibly also the Pike Hill observation tower; single unstratified coins of Valens found at turret 44b and milecastle 52 do not prove occupation for they could have been dropped by a passing soldier or civilian. Structural evidence for repairs at this time has been found at even fewer sites. The north gate of milecastle 52, whose south gate had been so drastically rebuilt earlier in the century, was apparently completely blocked. No coins or pottery date this last modification to the milecastle so it has simply been dated by reference to the Wall periods: this is the fourth repair or modification to the gateway therefore it 'must' belong to Wall period IV, Theodosian. No late-fourth-century pottery was discovered when the milecastle was excavated, but two cooking pot rims of Huntcliff type dated to the second half of the fourth century were found at the adjacent Pike Hill observation tower. If this tower continued in use into the last years of the century so might the milecastle. One turret in this area, 51b, was now reoccupied after having lain abandoned for close on two centuries. The doorway was blocked up and a small hut erected within the walls of the turret using stone dug out of the ruins of the earlier structure. On the Cumberland Coast milefortlet 5 (Cardurnock) continued in occupation, while further down the coast it may have been now, if not before, that the fort of Burrow Walls was occupied.

The restoration of Hadrian's Wall by Count Theodosius may also have extended to the curtain. The fort at Birdoswald had for some time been divorced from the Wall, completely surrounded by a wide ditch. The curtain wall was rebuilt from the foundations to join up the fort and the Wall again perhaps at this time, though Constantius Chlorus seventy years before may have been responsible. The epigraphic evidence for other repairs to the curtain cannot be assigned to a specific period. The inscriptions record work on Hadrian's Wall undertaken by the *civitates* of the province. Two stones mention the *civitas Dumnoniorum*, two the neighbouring *civitas Durotrigum Lendiniensium*, one the

civitas Catuvellaunorum and one an unknown *civitas Bricic.*
These inscriptions are undated but they have usually been
assigned to one of the fourth-century restorations of Hadrian's
Wall. Dr J. C. Mann has pointed out that when this work was
undertaken by the southern *civitates* they are likely to have been
under the same civil authority as the Wall. This was true in the
second century; after Severus, or Caracalla at the latest, the
civitates were in a different province and unlikely to have played
any part in the defence or repair of the Wall. However in the
fourth century all the provinces of the island were in the same
diocese, under the overriding authority of the *vicarius*, and in
time of grave crisis help may have been secured from other
provinces of the island.

The strengthening of fort defences is usually considered to date
to these years. Rough repairs to the fort walls of Chesterholm
and Birdoswald, for example, have been assigned to the Theodosian period on no other evidence than that they are 'late' and
display clumsy workmanship. No formal archaeological evidence
has been forthcoming and the repairs could date to any time in
the fourth century, or before, or later. At Birdoswald, however,
the rampart backing was certainly strengthened in at least one
place in the later fourth century. Many of the walls blocking the
fort gateways have also been assigned to the late fourth century,
again on very slight evidence. Most of the blocking took place
fairly soon after the forts were built, for the thresholds of these
gates show no sign of repair. In fact there was probably an overprovision of gates in the Wall forts and some were kept closed
from the very beginning. As the gate timbers rotted they were
replaced not by new gates but by stone walls. Later other gates
were blocked up at various times when they were no longer
required. Only a very few instances of blocking can be dated, in
each case to the late second or early third century. The blocking
of the south gate of Carrawburgh, however, may belong to a later
period, for coins of Tetricus II, 270–74, were found lying on the
road surface outside the gate, suggesting that it was still open.
When the gate was built up a new, wide and shallow ditch was
dug, replacing the two or three earlier smaller ditches, and running across in front of the gate. Excavation in Germany has
demonstrated that this new type of ditch first appears in the late

third century. The broad and shallow ditch at Carrawburgh presumably belongs to the late third century, or perhaps more probably the fourth century.

The strengthening of Hadrian's Wall, in particular its eastern forts, at this time can be associated with Theodosius' action further north. He disbanded the *areani*. The remaining outpost forts were probably abandoned at the same time, though it is possible that Risingham continued in occupation for a few years – the pottery is not decisive on that point. The removal of the shield provided by the *areani* will have caused the Wall garrisons to be stiffened; abandoning Risingham should have led to the repair of the forts to its rear, which did happen. Perhaps the hinterland forts were re-occupied then rather than earlier.

It has been suggested that the *vici* outside the forts on the Wall were now abandoned but few have been extensively excavated.

42   North England towards the end of the fourth century (about 370). The open square indicates that occupation at this time is uncertain

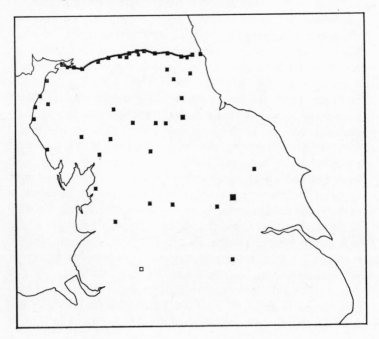

Certainly one site, Chesterholm, has recently furnished proof of a civil settlement continuing later than 367, and similar evidence may yet be found at other sites. The supposed abandonment of the *vici* after 367 has been linked with the movement into the forts of the civilians from these settlements. The evidence for civilians inside the forts is, however, very slight. At Chesters a number of infant burials were found within one of the interval towers, but these could date to any time after 367 and not necessarily to the years before 410. Late-fourth-century pottery in the granaries and trinkets – bracelets and beads – in the barrack-blocks at Housesteads also may date to any time after 367; they may not even prove that civilians lived in the fort. The pottery vessels may have been containers for corn or other food, while the trinkets may have been souvenirs collected by the soldiers or have resulted from the unauthorized presence of women in the barrack rooms. If civilians moved into the forts this happened after the end of Roman civil government in Britain, not in the 370s. We have already seen that it was not until the fifth century, after 410, that anything approaching a peasant militia came into being, and even then the men were primarily soldiers not cultivators. There is no evidence either that Theodosius introduced German barbarian troops to the Wall as has sometimes been supposed. He may, however, have left German soldiers in Britain, for in 372 Fraomar came over to take command of Alamannic soldiers stationed in the diocese, but by that time German soldiers, indeed units, had had a long connection with the island.

The abandonment of the outpost forts has been linked with another development of the fourth century, the creation of buffer states in the Lowlands of Scotland. The first kings of the four dynasties of these lands bear Roman names. On the Clyde the Damnonii gave way to the kingdom of Strathclyde, whose earliest kings of the dynasty of Coel Hen are called Cluim and Cinhil – Clemens and Quintilius in Latin. In the south-west the first ruler of Galloway is named Annwn (Antonius), while over the northern part of the Votadini, the area later known as the Manau of Goddodin, apparently reigned Catellius Decianus. The first three rulers of the house of Cunedda ruling over the Votadini are Tacit, Patern Pesrut and Aetern. The Roman origin of these names is obvious and the epithet *pesrut* (red cloak), may imply that this king was invested by the Romans with some kind of authority. The genealogies of these dynasties suggest that the first rulers flourished in the 370s and 380s, and the Roman names, especially *pesrut*, have led to the suggestion that the first kings were established as *praefecti gentium* appointed by the Romans to govern the tribes when they withdrew from the Lowlands. This receives some support in that three of the rulers appear to have been brought in from outside.

It would indeed make sense for the Romans to protect their interests by strengthening the traditionally friendly tribes of the Votadini, the Novantae, and possibly the Damnonii, and creating buffer states against the Picts lying further north, a device used elsewhere in the Empire at this time as before. Some years later Aetern's son Cunedda was to perform a more signal service for the Romans by migrating with a large part of his tribe to north Wales, where he founded the kingdom of Gwynedd as a bulwark against the Irish. Coroticus, the grandson of Clemens, was called a Roman by St Patrick in the middle of the fifth century, as if he perpetuated the power and influence of the imperial government north of Hadrian's Wall.

Doubt has recently been cast on this neat explanation. The Roman names of these kings may simply show they had become Christians, their conversion being accompanied by the adoption of new names, Romanized in honour of their new religion. Moreover in contrast to earlier years there is a complete lack of Roman pottery and other finds in the area north of the Wall. Late-Roman pottery is found abundantly on any site on Hadrian's Wall occupied at this time. If the tribes north of the Wall were philo-Roman surely some late-fourth-century pottery would have been found on their territory. The complete dearth of such finds strongly suggests that far from being pro-Roman these tribes were rabidly anti-Roman. A number of late-fourth-century coins, including one of Honorius, have been found at Traprain Law, the capital of the Votadini until the mid fifth century. However, these do not prove trade with the Romans; they could have come to Traprain Law in the same way as the hoard of early-fifth-century treasure, which originated on the continent and was probably loot.

Count Theodosius while restoring the situation completed the fragmentation of the island's administration started by Severus early in the third century when he created a fifth province, Valentia. Dr J. C. Mann has suggested that the new province lay in the north of England and consisted of part of Britannia Secunda. He further pointed out that Valentia is one of the only two provinces of Britain to be governed by a senior *praeses*, a *consularis*. This should suggest that his province included York, the old capital of Britannia Inferior. One could argue that Valentia contained the greater part of the duke's command, including Hadrian's Wall, leaving only the separate group of three units at the end of the *Notitia* list in what was left of Britannia Secunda. Thus it was the north of England where control had been lost completely for a while and there that Theodosius with judicious flattery created a new province of Valentia out of a pre-existing one. The military units of the north of England, of the provinces of Britannia Secunda and Valentia, were still commanded by the *dux Britanniarum*, whose title, duke of the Britains, demonstrates that his authority extended over a plurality of provinces.

The Last Years of Roman Britain

These measures did not lead to peace on the frontier. In 382 Magnus Maximus conducted a campaign against the Picts and Scots before he led his abortive expedition to the continent to claim the purple. In the later 390s Stilicho, the real ruler of the empire under the emperor Honorius, directed, presumably from Italy, a war against the Picts, Scots and Saxons, but a few years later these peoples were still causing trouble. None of these raids, or invasions, by the Picts and Scots have been recognized archaeologically, nor have the Roman campaigns, but they cannot have made life easy on the Wall. Nor can the various troop withdrawals of the late fourth and early fifth centuries have helped. In 383 the usurper Magnus Maximus led an army to the continent. In 401, after the campaign against the Picts and Scots, Stilicho withdrew more troops for the defence of Italy and in 407 Constantine III led the last British army to the continent to assert his claim to the Empire and to rescue Gaul from the invading barbarians. Although the troops withdrawn were mainly from the field army no doubt they included soldiers from the units on and behind the Wall. The undoubted low standard of the Wall troops at this time and their local affiliations however probably ensured that few soldiers were removed to join the continental expeditions. It is certainly clear that the Wall was not abandoned as a result of any of these possible withdrawals, though it used to be considered that Magnus Maximus milked the Wall of all its garrison for his ill-fated expedition in 383.

Several pieces of evidence demonstrate continuing occupation on Hadrian's Wall after 383. Pottery, unfortunately, does not. Pottery of the late fourth century has been found in abundance on Hadrian's Wall, but it is not possible to differentiate pottery manufactured in 400 from that made in 370. Coins later than 383 have been found at several sites on the Wall (Chesters, Chesterholm, Birdoswald, near Heddon, Walltown and in Coventina's Well, Carrawburgh) and near the Wall (South Shields, Corbridge, Carlisle and Maryport). Coins of the house of Theodosius are rare as site finds in Britain, and rarer in the north than the south, so the scarcity of coins of this dynasty on and near the Wall is not surprising. The last coins found on the Wall are two of Arcadius, 395–408, roughly contemporary with the *Notitia Dignitatum*, that enigmatic Roman army list. The Wall units listed under the heading of *item per lineam valli* are very similar to those of the early decades of the third century, though exceptions demonstrate that this section of the *Notitia* is as up to date as the rest of the document. Supporting evidence that the Wall was not abandoned prior to 410 also comes from an unusual source, the fifth-century tombstone at Chesterholm recording the death of Brigomaglos, which attests occupation of the site if not by the army at least by civilians. Presumably in these years the fires were lit on the floor of the *aedes* of the Chesterholm headquarters building, while the presence of civilians within the forts – if indeed this ever happened – no doubt also dates to the years after 410.

Most of the other evidence for the continuing occupation of sites on the line of Hadrian's Wall in the fifth century also comes from civilian rather than military contexts. Coins continued to be thrown into Coventina's Well at Carrawburgh right up to the end of the fourth century and the thousands of coins from the votive deposit include one of Honorius. A hoard of coins found in the fort itself contained worn issues of Valentinian and Valens, which may suggest that it was buried in the fifth century. At Corbridge nine coins of Arcadius and Honorius have been found, the most from any site in the vicinity of the Wall. Corbridge too has produced Saxon artefacts, unusual for sites on the Wall or in its neighbourhood. Only one place in this area, however, can be shown to have continued in occupation for any length of time, Carlisle. This town was still very much alive when St Cuthbert visited it, and was shown its sights, in 685. At the other end of the Wall there was also some kind of life at South Shields in the seventh century, for this was the birthplace of king Oswy and was renamed Caer Urfe. And, of course, the homesteads and settlements lived on. The round stone-built huts which are characteristic of the farmsteads of the Northumbrian plain during the Roman period, and their predecessors, the round timber huts, survived into the Middle Ages.

The End of Roman Britain

When Roman Britain ended in 410 all that happened was that the central government ceased paying the salaries of the civil service and the army. In the mid fifth century the *cohors IX Batavorum*, which had been stationed at Passau in Noricum Ripense for 400 years, sent soldiers to Rome to collect the money due to it when the last pay chests did not arrive; the soldiers were murdered on the way by barbarians. This is how the troops who survived barbarian onslaughts realized that Rome's rule was over – the pay did not arrive. The soldiers stationed on Hadrian's Wall were not withdrawn. They no doubt stayed where they were, for they were local recruits, probably from the civil settlement outside the fort or a nearby farm, and many of the soldiers had families in the houses beyond the fort walls. Some more adventurous soldiers may have joined the bands of brigands which were ever a prey on settled life, others the mercenary armies which became such a feature of fifth-century life. The more home-loving, or simply the lazy, stayed where they had always lived. Not only would the pay have dried up but also supplies. Food, pottery, armour, weapons were no longer delivered to the forts of the Wall. Some of these could be, and were, made in the fort or in the *vicus*, and others, pottery for example, were replaced by other commodities. There is little evidence for Saxons – and none for Picts or Scots – on Hadrian's Wall and we must accept that the soldiers of the Wall returned to the soil from which they had sprung.

Eight

Conclusion

The preceding chapters have put forward a particular view of the Wall. The idea of a frontier clearly marked by a running barrier was the concept of Hadrian, a concept which marked an important change in the Roman outlook, the final abandonment of the automatic expansion which would one day bring all the world under Rome's predestined sway. Although there was expansion from time to time after Hadrian, as before his reign there had been caution, his rule marks a turning-point. The artificial barriers which supplemented the rivers and the deserts so convenient for border control, though not necessarily effective military obstacles, strengthened the tendency of the Roman armies, who had won their victories through mobility, to settle down on frontier lines and do police work. Local recruiting, early adopted for administrative convenience, strengthened local links till movement of whole units, as opposed to detachments, became virtually impossible.

Hadrian's Wall ranks not as the first but as the most substantial and elaborate of these frontier barriers. It marked the abandonment of the first natural Roman ambition of eventual total conquest of Britain. From Mons Graupius, when Agricola in his own eyes stood on the threshold of total victory, to the inception of Hadrian's Wall no satisfactory alternative had been found. Yet the price of total conquest, the restoration of the army of Britain to a strength of four legions and vigorous support by the emperor, had been too high. Trajan seems to have accepted this. Now Hadrian dictated the final solution, the physical separation of barbarians from Romans, to push the barbarians into virtually a different island, leaving the Romans in an artificial island of their own – what Tacitus had said a Forth-Clyde line might do.

The advance under Pius, possibly to win easy military prestige, involved abandoning Hadrian's Wall but the need for a barrier remained. In the end Hadrian's Wall was finally chosen, but not till an emperor, Septimius Severus, had tried in person total conquest once more, only to find like Edward I after him that he could not enforce his will on his son from the grave. If Domitian had not been hard pressed on the Danube, if Severus had not died, Scotland might have been conquered, and Ireland too. The success of the solution as applied after Severus is itself an enigma, for it seems only to have incorporated elements already invented in the 160s.

The fluctuation between Hadrian's Wall and the Antonine is not merely a fascinating exercise in reconstructing history. It also enables us to follow the development of a system of frontier control and of military defence, and see how the two, originally distinct, came to be merged, partly because the fighting troops were available on the spot, partly because military problems lost their urgency in the third century; the pressure on the troops to become immersed in frontier control became irresistible. Local recruitment tied unit, fort and fort settlement ever more closely, creating an immobilized army on the frontier, degenerating under continuing peaceful conditions till Constantius used stern measures to return it to full military efficiency, but only as the frontier-troops of the fourth century.

The men stationed in the forts of the Wall and their dependants, who included not only their immediate families, but the majority of the people in the *vici*, had a life similar to that in and around forts Empire-wide. This fact deserves emphasis. Though the province did not lack individuality, the similarities far outweigh the differences, and life on the Wall was the ordinary life of the Roman frontiers.

The Wall then was an artificial frontier, the finest Roman artificial frontier in its elaboration and in the impressiveness of its remains. Its history and development mirrored that of the Roman frontier system in general, and though it shared the weaknesses of that system it had some success, for the barbarians from the north never made a lasting settlement within its range.

This study, even within its self-imposed limits, has thrown up questions which are still without answers. First, too little is known of the antecedents of the Wall, particularly its immediate predecessor in Britain, the Stanegate system. The very existence of the system as it is generally described has yet to be demonstrated. On the details of the building of the Wall, it would be useful to know which is the XX Valeria Victrix type of milecastle, turret and curtain, which the VI Victrix type. When was the rest of the turf wall, beyond the section converted to narrow gauge under Hadrian, rebuilt in stone? In the later second century we need an agreed chronology, or at least an agreed order if dates cannot be agreed, for the two occupations of Hadrian's Wall and the two occupations of the Antonine Wall. Linked with these is the question of the antecedents of the successful third-century system.

Our knowledge of Roman forts, paradoxically, is poor. No complete fort plan is available for the four types of auxiliary unit which contained cavalry. No stable has been completely excavated. Many buildings in forts are of uncertain purpose, and the precise reconstruction even of such familiar buildings as granaries is unclear. Some common statements rest on little evidence, such as the assignment of rooms in the rear range of headquarters buildings to the *cornicularius* and *signiferi* respectively. Similar doubts arise regarding the troops. What was the pay of the auxiliary compared with that of the legionary? How soon were soldiers recruited locally in Britain, and were they all volunteers? Who are the Germans who turn up at a number of forts? How much free time did the soldiers have? The questions are endless.

In the later centuries our ignorance deepens. How widespread were the conditions of decay in the third century known archaeologically at Halton Chester and Rudchester, and epigraphically at Birdoswald? What was the real strength of the units on the Wall in the fourth century? How did the lay-out and nature of the buildings in their forts change? When were the forts behind the Wall reoccupied by the new units listed in the *Notitia*? What happened north of the Wall after 367?

There is still much to know about the civil settlements, their size, lay-out and composition. How quickly and how systematically did their development proceed? What was their history after 369, and indeed after 410? Most pressing of all, perhaps, is the history of the real people of the land, who lived with the Wall in their midst, who seemed little-affected by Rome materially but nevertheless enjoyed or endured the *pax Romana*, with peace, communications, and markets as never before.

There is thus no shortage of questions about the Wall. Answers must come through steady and methodical work in the field and in the study, careful investigation and careful evaluation of results. For the authors the Wall retains its fascination, and they hope that their readers will feel this too, like the sixteenth-century antiquarian William Camden: 'Verily I have seene the tract of it over the high pitches and steepe descents of hilles, wonderfully rising and falling.'

Appendix One

Roman Emperors and Governors of Britain

This list is intended simply to elucidate references in the main text. The list of governors is based on that in A. R. Birley, 'The Roman governors of Britain', *Epigraphische Studien*, 4 (1967), 163–202, with the following exceptions: the unknown of RIB 995* is rejected, as not certainly Hadrianic; –dius is rejected as a Hadrianic governor, following the doubts expressed by R. P. Wright regarding RIB 1997 and 1998 being from the same stone; a later date than the 180s is preferred for Antius Crescens, following A. R. Birley's alternative placing; the second Ulpius Marcellus is rejected, see p. 130; a number of governors who cannot be closely dated are omitted; the view is accepted here that the northern frontier remained under the control of a consular governor under Severus. The list of governors of Britannia inferior is taken down to Nonius Philippus (A.D. 262). The list of emperors has been cut down to the bare minimum of 'legitimate' emperors in the third century, and in the fourth has been cut down even further. Where Britain is under the control of another than the 'legitimate' emperor or one only of Constantine's sons this is indicated.

It should be noted that after Agricola neither the starting nor finishing dates of any governor are known with certainty, though in the case of Statius Priscus dates for his preceding and succeeding activities tightly confine the possible length of his governorship.

* RIB numbers refer to the catalogue in R. G. Collingwood and R. P. Wright, *The Roman Inscriptions of Britain*, Oxford, 1965.

Date	Emperor	Date	Governor of Britain
31 B.C.	Augustus		
A.D. 14	Tiberius		
37	Gaius (Caligula)		
41	Claudius	43	A. Plautius *succeeded by*
		47	P. Ostorius Scapula *succeeded by*
		51/2	A. Didius Gallus *succeeded by*
54	Nero		
		57/8	Q. Veranius *succeeded by*
		58/9	C. Suetonius Paulinus *succeeded by*
		61	P. Petronius Turpilianus *succeeded by*
		63	M. Trebellius Maximus *succeeded by*
68	Galba		
69	Otho		
	Vitellius	69	M. Vettius Bolanus *succeeded by*
	Vespasian		
		71	Q. Petilius Cerialis *succeeded by*
		73/4	Sex. Iulius Frontinus *succeeded by*
		78	Cn. Iulius Agricola *succeeded by*
79	Titus		
81	Domitian		
		84/5	*Unknown*
96	Nerva		Sallustius Lucullus
		97/8	P. Metilius Nepos *succeeded by*
98	Trajan	98	T. Avidius Quietus
		103	L. Neratius Marcellus
			M. Appius (*or* Atilius) Bradua

Appendix 1: Roman Emperors and Governors of Britain

Date	Emperor	Date	Governor of Britain
A.D. 117	Hadrian		
		–122	Q. Pompeius Falco *succeeded by*
		122–4+	A. Platorius Nepos
		127/33	Sex. Iulius Severus
		135	P. Mummius Sisenna
138	Antoninus Pius		
		139–42	Q. Lollius Urbicus
		146	Cn. Papirius Aelianus
		158	Cn. Iulius Verus
		?159/60	—anus
161	Marcus Aurelius *and* Lucius Verus	161/2	M. Statius Priscus
		163	Sex. Calpurnius Agricola
169	Marcus Aurelius *alone*	between 169	Q. Antistius Adventus
176	Marcus Aurelius *with* Commodus	and 180	(Caerellius Priscus)
180	Commodus *alone*	c. 180/82	*Unknown*
		184	Ulpius Marcellus
		185/190	P. Helvius Pertinax
192	Commodus *assassinated*	192–7	D. Clodius Albinus
193	Pertinax		
	Didius Iulianus		
	Pescennius Niger		
	Septimius Severus		
195	Albinus Caesar		
196	Caracalla Caesar		
197	Albinus *defeated and killed*	197	Virius Lupus
198	Caracalla Augustus		M. Antius Crescens iuridicus vice legati (?)
		205	C. Valerius Pudens
		205/7	L. Alfenus Senecio

Date	Emperor	Date	Governor of Britain
A.D. 209	Geta Augustus		
211	Caracalla *and* Geta *on death of* Severus		
212	Caracalla *alone*		BRITANNIA INFERIOR
		213	C. Iulius Marcus
		216	(M. Antonius Gor(?)) dianus
217	Macrinus		
218	Elagabalus		
		219	Modius Iulius
		220	Ti. Claudius Paulinus
		221–2	Marius Valerianus
222	Severus Alexander		
		223	Claudius Xenophon
		225	Maximus
			Claudius Apellinus
			Calvisius Rufus
			Valerius Crescens Fulvianus
235	Maximinus		
		237	(T(?))uccianus
238	Gordian I *and* Gordian II		
	Gordian III		Maecilius Fuscus
			Egnatius Lucilianus
		242	Nonius Philippus
244	Philip I		
249	Decius Traianus		
250–	Decius II		
251	Gallus *and* Volusianus		
253	Valerian *and* Gallienus		
			GALLIC EMPIRE
		258	Postumus

Appendix 1: Roman Emperors and Governors of Britain

Date	Emperor	Date	Governor of Britain
A.D. 259	Gallienus *alone*		
268	Claudius II	268	Victorinus
270	Aurelian	270	Tetricus
273	*recovers Gallic Empire*		
275	Tacitus		
276	Probus		
282	Carus		
283	Numerian *and* Carinus		
284–305	Diocletian		
286–305	Maximian		'BRITISH' EMPERORS
		287–93	Carausius
293–306	Constantius Chlorus Caesar (*Augustus* 305)	293–6	Allectus
293–311	Galerius Caesar (*Augustus* 305)		
306–37	Constantine I		EMPEROR CONTROLLING BRITAIN
317–40	Constantine II	337–40	Constantine II
333–50	Constans	340–50	Constans
324–61	Constantius II	350–61	Constantius II
		(350–3	Magnentius)
355–63	Julian Caesar (*Augustus* 360)		
363–4	Jovian		
364–75	Valentinian I		
367–83	Gratian		
375–92	Valentinian II	383–8	Magnus Maximus
379–95	Theodosius	392–4	Eugenius
395–408	Arcadius *East*		
395–423	Honorius *West*	407–11	Constantine III

Appendix Two

The Regiments of Hadrian's Wall

The evidence presented here is for the forts on the Wall itself, the outpost forts, and those on the Cumberland coast. In many cases the assignment of a unit's period of garrison to the time of a particular emperor is on grounds of inherent probability rather than on the basis of a dated inscription. Cases where the evidence is unambiguous are identified by an asterisk. In the third century, where most dated inscriptions occur and when the units seem to have taken up permanent positions, the earliest attested date for the unit's presence is given.

BY FORTS

Wallsend

Under Hadrian: cohors quingenaria equitata (*?*)
Under Marcus Aurelius: cohors II Nerviorum civium Romanorum (*?*)
Third century: cohors IV Lingonum equitata
Notitia: cohors IV Lingonum*

The cohors II Nerviorum could have been the Hadrianic garrison, although it was not *equitata*. The inscriptions of cohors IV Lingonum from the fort (RIB 1299–1301) are not dated, but are certainly late and are probably third century.

Newcastle

Under Hadrian: no evidence
Under Marcus Aurelius: no evidence
Third century: no evidence
Notitia: cohors prima Cornoviorum*

It is impossible to say if cohors I Thracum (RIB 1323), attested on a building record, was in garrison at Newcastle.

Appendix 2: The Regiments of Hadrian's Wall

Benwell

Under Hadrian: ala quingenaria (*?*)
Under Marcus Aurelius: cohors I Vangionum milliaria equitata
Under Commodus (*Ulpius Marcellus governor*): ala
Third century: ala I Asturum (205–8)*
Notitia: ala I Asturum*

The inscriptions by legionary centurions (RIB 1327 and 1330) do not necessarily indicate the presence of a full legionary detachment under Antoninus Pius.

Rudchester

Under Hadrian: cohors quingenaria equitata (*?*)
Under Marcus Aurelius: no evidence
Third century: no evidence, fort run down from 270s till 370s
Notitia: cohors prima Frixagorum (*presumably* Frisiavonum

Halton Chesters

Under Hadrian: cohors quingenaria equitata (*?*)
Under Marcus Aurelius: no evidence
Third century: ala Sabiniana
Notitia: ala Sabiniana*

The fort was run down from the 270s till the 370s, but the unit apparently survived in name at least. There is an inscription of it from the fort (RIB 1433) which is apparently third century.

Chesters

Under Hadrian: cohors milliaria equitata (*??*)
Under Pius: auxiliary regiment (*146*)*
Under Marcus Aurelius: no evidence
Under Commodus (*Ulpius Marcellus governor*): ala II Asturum*
Third century: ala II Asturum (*205–8*)*
Notitia: ala II Asturum*

The inscriptions under Pius of II Augusta are building inscriptions (RIB 1460–61) and do not prove that a detachment of the legion was in garrison. On the other hand the diploma of 146 found at the fort suggests strongly that there was an auxiliary regiment in garrison then. The tombstone to the daughter of a commanding officer of cohors I Vangionum (RIB 1482) is not easily explained as a death on a visit to the fort, and the wife's *nomen* Aurelia suggests a date not earlier than 161. The cohors I Delmatarum is also recorded at the fort, and must have been in garrison at some time in the second century.

Carrawburgh

Under Hadrian: cohors quingenaria equitata (*?*)
Under Marcus Aurelius: no evidence
Third century: cohors I Batavorum equitata (*213–17*)*
Notitia: cohors I Batavorum equitata*

There are a large number of units attested here, cohorts I
Aquitanorum, I Cugernorum, I Frisiavonum, II Nerviorum and I
Tungrorum. It is possible that some were not in garrison, but merely
honouring the local goddess Coventina. There is no evidence that RIB
1545 is earlier than RIB 1544, here used to give the earliest certain
date that I Batavorum was at Carrawburgh.

Housesteads

Under Hadrian: cohors milliaria peditata
Under Marcus Aurelius: no evidence
Third century: cohors I Tungrorum milliaria, numerus Hnaudifridi,
cuneus Frisiorum Ver. (Severus Alexander)*
Notitia: cohors I Tungrorum*

The inscriptions of cohors I Tungrorum and the numerus
Hnaudifridi are undated, but a third-century date seems probable. A
sculpture of an archer from Housesteads has been dated to the
second century, with uncertain implications. The inscription referring
to *mil(ites) leg. II Aug. agentes in praesidio* (RIB 1583) is generally
taken with RIB 1582 to refer to a garrisoning of Housesteads by
soldiers of that legion, though there is no evidence when this was.

Chesterholm

*Under Hadrian: presumably evacuated when the forts were built on the
Wall*
Under Marcus Aurelius: cohors II Nerviorum civium
Romanorum (*??*)
Third century: cohors IV Gallorum equitata (*213*)*
Notitia: cohors IV Gallorum*

The inscription of cohors II Nerviorum is discounted in RIB 1693 as
evidence for the garrison of Chesterholm, but it is no better and no
worse than other evidence, and the alternative explanation in RIB is
unsatisfactory.

Great Chesters

Under Hadrian: cohors VI Nerviorum
Under Marcus Aurelius: cohors – Raetorum (*166–9*)*

Third century: cohors II Asturum (*225*),* Raeti gaesati (*?*)
Notitia: cohors I Asturum (*presumably error for II Asturum*)*

Carvoran

Under Hadrian: cohors I Hamiorum (*136–8*)*
Under Marcus Aurelius: cohors I Hamiorum (*governor Calpurnius Agricola*)*
Third century: cohors II Delmatarum equitata
Notitia: cohors II Delmatarum*

The inscription of cohors II Delmatarum (RIB 1795) is undated, but a third century date is probable.

Birdoswald

Under Hadrian: cohors I Tungrorum milliaria (*?*)
Under Marcus Aurelius: no evidence
Third century: cohors I Aelia Dacorum milliaria (*205–8*),* venatores Bannienses
Notitia: cohors I Aelia Dacorum*

The evidence for the Hadrianic garrison is a tile stamp (*Ephemeris Epigraphica* IX 1279). For the venatores Bannienses, whose inscription is undated, but for whom a third-century date is probable, see p. 258. The question whether the cohors I Thracum civium Romanorum also mentioned on RIB 1909 was simply helping with the building rather than based on the fort cannot at present be answered. For the problem regarding the *Notitia* entry see p. 273ff.

Castlesteads

Under Hadrian: cohors IV Gallorum equitata (*?*)
Under Marcus Aurelius: no evidence
Third century: cohors II Tungrorum equitata c. l. (*241*)*
Notitia: no entry (omitted in error, see p. 275)

Stanwix

Under Hadrian: ala Petriana (*?*)
Under Marcus Aurelius: no evidence
Third century: ala Augusta Petriana bis torquata civium Romanorum
Notitia: ala Petriana*

The rejection of Petriana as the name of the fort leaves open the question of the second-century garrisons, though the apparent size of the fort would suggest it was built for a milliary *ala*, and the ala Petriana is the only such unit known in Britain.

Hadrian's Wall

Burgh-by-Sands

Under Hadrian: cohors quingenaria equitata/milliaria peditata (?)
Under Marcus Aurelius: no evidence
Third century: cohors I Nervana Germanorum milliaria equitata (?),
numerus Maurorum Aurelianorum *(253–8)**, cuneus Frisionum
Aballavensium *(241)* (?)
Notitia: numerus Maurorum Aurelianorum*

The *numerus* was under the charge of a tribune of a cohort in 253–8,
and cohors I Nervana would fit best at this time (see below p. 250).
Although the references to the *cuneus* come from Papcastle (RIB
882–3) the inscriptions seem to refer to a transfer of some one to
the unit called cuneus Frisionum Aballavensium (the cavalry unit of
Frisiones of Burgh) from an unnamed unit, presumably from the one
in garrison at Papcastle to the unit at Burgh. It seems difficult and
unnecessary to assume that the *cuneus* had been moved to Papcastle,
and it is a well-attested Roman practice to set up inscriptions
recording promotion on transfer at the post one is leaving. A *cohors
milliaria peditata* is unlikely under Hadrian, as there are only two
attested in the province, and there was presumably at the time one at
Housesteads and one at Birdoswald.

Drumburgh

The history of this fort is uncertain; no unit is attested there by an
inscription, and the *Notitia* entry for Congavata normally associated
with it may in fact refer to another fort, see p. 275.

Bowness

Under Hadrian: cohors milliaria equitata (?)
Under Marcus Aurelius: no evidence
Third century: cohors milliaria *(251–3)**
Notitia: no entry

There are too many forts with evidence for milliary cohorts in the
third century for the seven milliary cohorts attested in this country
unless there was transfer of units during the third century or the
splitting up of units. The latter is more likely – most of the forts
are too small to hold full-size milliary units.

Beckfoot

Under Hadrian: cohors quingenaria peditata
The only unit attested at any time is the cohors II Pannoniorum.

Appendix 2: The Regiments of Hadrian's Wall

Maryport

Under Hadrian: cohors I Hispanorum equitata, *upgraded to* milliaria *during Hadrian's reign**
Under Pius: cohors I Delmatarum equitata
Under Marcus Aurelius: cohors I Baetasiorum civium Romanorum
Third century: cohors milliaria (*?*)

The suggestion of a milliary unit as a third-century garrison rests on the dedication by a *tribunus cohortis*, RIB 812, which has a feature, a *signum*, commonly thought not to appear before the third century. For the difficulties of too many forts for the number of milliary units known in the third century see p. 246.

Burrow Walls

No unit is recorded in connection with this fort, which seems to have been built for a *cohors quingenaria peditata*. Mr J. P. Gillam has suggested that it was first built in the fourth century.

Moresby

Under Hadrian: cohors II Lingonum equitata (*??*)
Cohors II Thracum equitata is also attested.

South Shields

Under Hadrian: ala Sabiniana (*?*)
Under Marcus Aurelius: cohors
Third century: cohors V Gallorum (*222*)*
Notitia: numerus barcariorum Tigrisiensium*
The tombstone of a freedman of a trooper of the ala I Asturum (RIB 1064) still presents problems.

Bewcastle

Under Hadrian: cohors I Dacorum milliaria peditata
Under Marcus Aurelius: no evidence
Third century: cohors milliaria (*?*)

The inscriptions of two tribunes dedicating to Cocidius (RIB 988–9) suggest a milliary cohort was stationed here in the third century; for the difficulties see p. 246.

Netherby

Under Hadrian: no evidence
Under Marcus Aurelius: no evidence

Third century: cohors I Aelia Hispanorum equitata (*214–16*)*
Notitia: cohors I Aelia Hispanorum (*?*)

The suggestion that the third-century garrison was still at Netherby at the time of the *Notitia* list is dealt with on p. 275. The inscription of the third or early fourth century referring to a dedication to Cocidius by a commander of cohors I Nervana (RIB 966) may not belong to this fort.

Birrens

Under Hadrian: no evidence
Under Pius: cohors II Tungrorum milliaria equitata c. l. (*158*)*
Under Marcus Aurelius: no evidence
Third century: fort abandoned

Cohors I Nervana Germanorum milliaria equitata, attested at this fort, may have been in garrison either under Hadrian or early in the reign of Pius.

Risingham

Under Hadrian: not yet built
Under Pius: no evidence
Under Marcus Aurelius: cohors IV Gallorum equitata*
Third century: cohors I Vangionum milliaria equitata (*205–8*)*, vexillatio Raetorum gaesatorum (*213*)*, exploratores Habitancenses (*213*)*

The dedication to the numina Augustorum (RIB 1227) by cohors IV Gallorum must be to joint emperors, and only Marcus and Verus or Marcus and Commodus can come into consideration on the known history of the cohort and the fort.

High Rochester

Under Hadrian: not occupied
Under Pius: cohors I Lingonum equitata*
Under Marcus Aurelius: cohors I Da— (*?*)
Third century: cohors I fida Vardullorum civium Romanorum milliaria equitata (*213*)*, exploratores Bremenienses (*238–41*)*

RIB 1289, referring to an Aurelius of coh. I Da—, ought to be after 161, and it is unlikely that the unit was based at High Rochester in the third century in addition to or as replacement for those recorded

Appendix 2: The Regiments of Hadrian's Wall

BY UNITS

These are arranged under *alae* and *cohortes*, subdivided into milliary
and quingenary. The period covered is from Hadrian to the end of
the Roman period. Their mention on diplomas is recorded as
evidence for their presence in Britain, the undated Walcot diploma
being omitted. The milliary units appear to have been kept in the
Wall zone throughout the period, though direct evidence for the ala
Petriana is slight. The quingenary units on the other hand seem rarely
to have been in the zone both in the second and third centuries.
Again this is clearer for the cohorts than the *alae*. There was clearly
a massive reshuffle of units within the province in the late second or
early third century. The letters A and B distinguish respectively those
units which were in the area up to *c*. 180 and those which were in the
area in the third century, possibly from as early as 184 or
thereabouts.

ALAE

Of the fifteen cavalry regiments securely attested in Britain only four
are certainly attested on the Wall.

ala Augusta Gallorum Petriana milliaria civium Romanorum (ala milliaria)

Originally raised: Gaul
Diplomas: 98, 122, 124, 135
Under Hadrian: Stanwix (*presumably*)
Under Marcus Aurelius: Stanwix (*possibly*)
Third century: Stanwix (*presumably*)
Notitia: Stanwix* (*entry bungled, see p. 275*)

A number of forts have been suggested for this unit, but none has
been demonstrated conclusively to have housed it, apart from
Stanwix, and in the first century Corbridge, when the unit was still
quingenary (RIB 1172).

ala I Hispanorum Asturum (ala quingenaria) (B)

Originally raised: Asturia (*north-west Spain*)
Diplomas: 98, 122, 124, 135, 146
Third century: Benwell (*perhaps under Commodus, see under Benwell*)
Notitia: Benwell

The problem of RIB 1064 is referred to above under South Shields.

ala II Asturum (ala quingenaria) (B)

Originally raised: Asturia (*north-west Spain*)
Diploma: 122
Under Commodus: Chesters (*under Ulpius Marcellus*)*
Third century: Chesters*
Notitia: Chesters*

RIB 586 may attest its presence at Ribchester.

ala I Pannoniorum Sabiniana (ala quingenaria)

Originally raised: Pannonia (*approximately modern Hungary*)
Diplomas: 122, 146
Under Hadrian: South Shields (*?*)
Third century: Halton Chesters
Notitia: Halton Chesters*

COHORTES

There are only seven *cohortes milliariae* attested in Britain, and it is important to note that they tend to be all stationed in the Wall area throughout the period whenever the Wall is occupied, compensating for the absence of the distant legions.

I Aelia Dacorum (cohors milliaria)

Originally raised: Dacia (*approximately modern Romania*) in the early second century A.D.
Diploma: 146
Under Hadrian: Bewcastle (*?*)
Third century: Birdoswald (*205–8*)*
Notitia: Birdoswald*

For the problem regarding the *Notitia* entry see p. 274f.

I Nervana Germanorum equitata (cohors milliaria)

Originally raised: Germania (*the Rhineland*)
Diploma: 122

It was at Birrens, probably before 158, either under Hadrian or under Pius during the first Antonine period in Scotland. In the third century it seems to have been at Burgh. An inscription at Netherby seems to be a stray dedication to Cocidius from Bewcastle, which need not imply that the unit was in garrison at Bewcastle or Netherby.

Appendix 2: The Regiments of Hadrian's Wall

I Aelia Hispanorum equitata (cohors milliaria)

Originally raised: Spain (*as a quingenary cohort*)
Diplomas: 98, 103, 105, 122, 124, 146
Under Hadrian: Maryport (*there doubled in size*)
Third century: Netherby (*214–16*)*
Notitia: Axelodunum (Netherby)*

For the problem regarding the *Notitia* entry see p. 275.

I Tungrorum (cohors milliaria)

Originally raised: Gallia Belgica (*modern Belgium*)
Diplomas: 103 (*noted as already milliary*), 122, 124
Under Hadrian: Birdoswald (*?*)
Under Pius: Castlecary*
Third century: Housesteads
Notitia: Housesteads*

A detachment of the cohort was for a period which included the years 122 and 124 in Noricum (modern Austria). It seems to have returned by the time of the Castlecary inscription. An inscription from Cramond (RIB 2135), now lost, cannot be closely dated.

II Tungrorum equitata c. l. (cohors milliaria)

Originally raised: Gallia Belgica (*modern Belgium*)
Diplomas: –
Under Pius (second period?)*:* Birrens (*158*)*
Under Marcus Aurelius: Birrens (*?*)
Third century: Castlesteads (*241*)*
Notitia: omitted (*in error* (*?*), *see p. 275*)

This unit also seems to have been half-strength for a time, the detachment in this case being at Eining (Bavaria) in 147 and 153. The expansion *c(ivium) L(atinorum)* is unjustifiable.

I Vangionum equitata (cohors milliaria)

Originally raised: Germania superior (*the upper Rhineland*)
Diplomas: 103, 122, 124, 135
Third century: Risingham (*205–8*)*

It was at Benwell, where it would best fit in some time between Hadrian and the governorship of Ulpius Marcellus, but an inscription from Chesters recording the death of a commanding officer's daughter cannot well be earlier than 161.

251

I fida Vardullorum equitata (cohors milliaria)

Originally raised: north Spain
Diplomas: 98, 105, 122, 124, 135, 146, 159
Under Pius: Castlecary
Under Marcus Aurelius: Corbridge(?) (*161–3*); Lanchester (*175–6*)*
Third century: High Rochester (*213*)*

Much hinges on the restoration of this unit on RIB 1128 from
Corbridge. If for instance I or preferably II Tungrorum were to be
restored the Vardulli need only make the one move, from Castlecary
to Lanchester. The dedication to the mother-goddesses by a
detachment of this cohort from outside milecastle 19 (RIB 1421)
cannot be closely dated. The inscription at Jedburgh (RIB 2118 – a
carry from Cappuck?) seems to imply that the unit or part of it was
on outpost duty.

About half of the almost fifty *cohortes quingenariae* attested in
Britain found themselves on the Wall at one time or another, in
contrast with only one quarter of the *alae*. Over thirty of the fifty
were equitatae, and about half of these saw service in the Wall zone.

I Aquitanorum equitata (cohors quingenaria) (A)

Originally raised: south-west France
Diplomas: 122, 124
Under Hadrian: Carrawburgh (*130–33 ? ?*)*
Under Pius (second period): Brough-on-Noe, Derbyshire (*c. 158*)*

The reading of RIB 1550 remains uncertain as between the governors
Sex. Iulius Severus and Cn. Iulius Verus; it is already attested under
the latter governor at Brough-on-Noe.

II Asturum equitata (cohors quingenaria) (B)

Originally raised: Asturia (*north-west Spain*)
Diplomas: 105, 122, 124
Third century: Great Chesters (*225*)*
Notitia: Great Chesters (*?*)

For the probability that the *Notitia* entry I Asturum is an error for II
Asturum see p. 274.

I Baetasiorum civium Romanorum (cohors quingenaria) (A)

Originally raised: Germania inferior (*Holland*)
Diplomas: 103, 122, 124, 135

Appendix 2: The Regiments of Hadrian's Wall

Under Pius (first period): Bar Hill (*attested under Pius*)*
Under Pius (second period): Old Kilpatrick
Under Marcus Aurelius: Maryport
Notitia: Reculver, Kent*

I Aelia classica (cohors quingenaria) (B)

Originally raised: unknown
Diploma: 146
Notitia: Tunnocelum (*Moresby?*)

I Cornoviorum (cohors quingenaria) (B)

Originally raised: Welsh Marches (*only unit known on the Wall originally raised in Britain*)
Notitia: Newcastle*

I Ulpia Traiana Cugernorum civium Romanorum (cohors quingenaria)

Originally raised: Germania inferior (*north Germany*)
Diplomas: 103, 122, 124

There is an altar of a soldier of this unit at Carrawburgh, which is later than 161.

I Da—

See the next entry.

I Delmatarum equitata (cohors quingenaria)

Originally raised: Jugoslavia
Diplomas: 122, 124, 135
Under Pius: Maryport
Under Marcus Aurelius: High Rochester (*?*)

An inscription from Chesters is difficult to fit in; perhaps the redistribution of garrisons in the second Antonine period meant a move for this cohort. Perhaps the High Rochester inscription (RIB 1289) should be understood as I Dacorum, as Delmatarum is commoner than Dalmatarum, in which case it must be assumed either that the Aelia of I Aelia Dacorum was omitted or that there was another I Dacorum in Britain.

II Delmatarum equitata (cohors quingenaria) (B)

Originally raised: Jugoslavia
Diplomas: 105, 122, 135

Third century: Carvoran
Notitia: Carvoran*

The inscription (RIB 1795) referring to the cohort at Carvoran is not dated, but the Hamians were at Carvoran under Hadrian and under Marcus Aurelius, so the third-century suggestion seems reasonable.

I Frisiavonum (cohors quingenaria) (B)

Originally raised: Scheldt area
Diplomas: 105, 122, 124
Notitia: Rudchester

An undated altar to Coventina at Carrawburgh by an *optio* of this cohort (RIB 1523) might just be an expression of devotion by a soldier not garrisoned at the fort.

IV Gallorum equitata (cohors quingenaria) (A/B)

Originally raised: Gaul
Diplomas: 122, 146
Under Pius: Castlehill, Antonine Wall
Under Marcus Aurelius: Risingham*
Third century: Chesterholm *(213)**
Notitia: Chesterholm*

The two altars from Castlesteads, RIB 1979 and 1980, prove a period in garrison there, perhaps rather the second period under Pius than under Hadrian. The unit was at Templeborough (Yorks.) in the first century, and stamped tiles have also been found at Castleford (Yorks.).

V Gallorum equitata (cohors quingenaria) (B)

Originally raised: Gaul
Diplomas: 122, 135
Third century: South Shields *(222)**

The unit was at one time stationed at Cramond (RIB 2134).

I Hamiorum sagittariorum (cohors quingenaria) (A)

Raised: Syria
Diplomas: 122, 124, 135
Under Hadrian: Carvoran*
Under Pius (second period): Bar Hill
Under Marcus Aurelius: Carvoran*

Appendix 2: The Regiments of Hadrian's Wall

The return to Carvoran is the only case known of a unit which returned to its original fort on the Wall, apart from the probable but special case of the ala Petriana, which only one fort on the Wall, Stanwix, could accommodate.

I Lingonum equitata (cohors quingenaria)

Originally raised: Germania superior (*around Langres, eastern France*)
Diplomas: 105, 122
Under Pius (first period): High Rochester*
Third century: Lanchester (*238–44*)*

This strictly is not a Wall unit at all, for it was at High Rochester when that fort was not part of the Wall complex.

II Lingonum equitata (cohors quingenaria)

Originally raised: Germania superior (*around Langres, eastern France*)
Diplomas: 98, 122, 134
Under Marcus Aurelius: Ilkley
Notitia: Congavata*

There is no necessity to identify Congavata as Drumburgh, cf. p. 275. II Lingonum is also attested at Moresby.

IV Lingonum equitata (cohors quingenaria) (B)

Originally raised: Germania superior (*around Langres, eastern France*)
Diplomas: 103, 122, 146
Third century: Wallsend
Notitia: Wallsend*

II Nerviorum civium Romanorum (cohors quingenaria) (A)

Originally raised: Gallia Belgica (*in area of modern Belgium*)
Diplomas: 98, 122, 124, 146
Third century: Whitley Castle (*213*)*

This unit is recorded at Wallsend, Carrawburgh (a detachment) and possibly at Chesterholm (an altar found reused two miles from the fort). All of these forts have known third-century garrisons.

VI Nerviorum (cohors quingenaria) (A)

Originally raised: Gallia Belgica (*in area of modern Belgium*)
Diplomas: 122, 124, 135, 146
Under Pius (first period): Rough Castle*
Third century: Bainbridge (*205*)*

It is attested at Great Chesters, where it could have been under Hadrian, but hardly later.

I Pannoniorum equitata (cohors quingenaria)

Originally raised: Pannonia (*modern Hungary*)

This regiment is included here because of RIB 1667, a tombstone of a soldier, apparently of this unit, from Milecastle 42 which might have come from Great Chesters. Perhaps the soldier was in II Pannoniorum; the stone is broken.

II Pannoniorum equitata (cohors quingenaria)

Originally raised: Pannonia (*modern Hungary*)
Diplomas: 105, 124

Attested at Beckfoot. A lead seal from Chesterholm does not prove the unit's presence, as such seals were presumably fixed on goods in transit, cf. the evidence from Brough-under-Stainmore.

? Raetorum (cohors quingenaria)

Originally raised: Raetia (*parts of Switzerland and Germany*)
Under Marcus Aurelius: Great Chesters (*166–9*)*

I Thracum civium (cohors quingenaria)

Originally raised: Thrace (*southern Bulgaria and European Turkey*)

This regiment was helping with building at Birdoswald in the early third century (RIB 1909). It may be distinct from the I Thracum equitata recorded on the 122 diploma, which was at Bowes in the early third century, and if so it may possibly have been based at Birdoswald as an extra unit in the third century.

II Thracum equitata (cohors quingenaria)

Originally raised: Thrace (*southern Bulgaria and European Turkey*)
Diplomas: 103, 122
Under Pius (second period): Mumrills
Notitia: Gabrosentum*

NUMERI

A number of irregular units may conveniently be grouped under this heading. They need not necessarily have anything in common in their organization apart from the fact that they are not *alae* or *cohortes*.

Appendix 2: The Regiments of Hadrian's Wall

numerus barcariorum Tigrisiensium

Notitia: South Shields*

This unit is apparently distinct from the *numerus barcariorum* attested at Lancaster, see now *Britannia*, 4 (1973), 206–9 and cf. B. Dobson and D. J. Breeze *Army of Hadrian's Wall*, Newcastle-upon-Tyne, 1972, 47. The name means 'lightermen'; their precise function is unknown.

exploratores Bremenienses

Third century: High Rochester (*238–44*)*

The name means 'scouts'; a similar force existed at Risingham, and presumably at Netherby, which is called Castra Exploratorum ('camp of the scouts') in the Antonine Itinerary, see p. 142.

exploratores Habitancenses

Third century: Risingham (*213*)*

See discussion under the previous entry.

cuneus Frisionum Aballavensium

Originally raised: Frisia (*Holland*)

Although mentioned on inscriptions at Papcastle in 241 the unit clearly belongs to Burgh (Aballava) and the inscriptions need not imply its presence at Papcastle, see above p. 246. A *cuneus* was a regiment of irregular cavalry.

cuneus Frisiorum Ver.

Originally raised: Frisia (*Holland*)
Third century: Housesteads

A *cuneus* was a regiment of irregular cavalry.

numerus Hnaudifridi

Originally raised: Germany, *possibly from outside the Empire*
Third century: Housesteads

The inscription (RIB 1576) referring to this unit is undated, but the Alaisiagae honoured on it were goddesses brought to the fort by one of the units in the third century.

numerus Maurorum Aurelianorum

Originally raised: North Africa

257

Third century: Burgh *(253–8)**
Notitia: Burgh

As its earliest attestation is earlier than the emperor Aurelian the name must be derived from one of the earlier emperors, starting with Marcus Aurelius himself, who were known officially as Marcus Aurelius.

vexillatio gaesatorum Raetorum

Originally raised: Raetia *(Switzerland and parts of Germany)*
Third century: Great Chesters

This is probably a distinct unit from the following one, as there is no reference to a *tribunus cohortis* in overall command.

Raeti gaesati

Originally raised: Raetia *(Switzerland and parts of Germany)*
Third century: Risingham *(213)**

See discussion under previous entry. The altar to IOM at Jedburgh (RIB 2117 – a carry from Cappuck?) presumably refers to an outposting from Risingham, as a tribune, who can only be a tribune of the milliary cohort stationed at the latter fort, is mentioned as being in overall command.

venatores Bannienses

Third century: Birdoswald

The third-century date is suggested in conformity with the appearance of the other irregular units on the Wall. It seems clear that this is a unit rather than a collection of the men in the cohort who held the post of *venator* ('hunter'); the form of the title – a place-name added to a descriptive term – is common to a number of irregular units, and Dr J. C. Mann has furnished us with a parallel from the *Notitia*, *sagittarii venatores* (*Occ.* V 45). The term 'hunters' is not inappropriate for an army unit, but no more implies that the men concerned spent their time hunting animals than the term *vigiles* for the unit at Chester-le-Street implies that they were firemen.

Appendix Three

The Gods Worshipped on the Wall

The gods worshipped on Hadrian's Wall did not differ greatly from those worshipped by soldiers all over the Empire, and hardly at all from those worshipped in the rest of the military zone in Britain. Such differences as there were arose mainly in the cults peculiar to provinces or areas within provinces. On the Wall the native cults of Coventina, Antenociticus, Belatucadrus, Cocidius and Vitiris give a local flavour to a blend of beliefs that could otherwise be easily paralleled from anywhere else in the Empire. There is the occasional varied response to an Empire-wide cult from province to province; thus in Britain unofficial emperor-worship found expression in the cult of the *numina Augusti*, while in other provinces similar feelings found expression in dedications *pro domu divina*. A god might even be imported by a unit, as Mars Thincsus was apparently at Housesteads. But there were no gods of the Wall as such.

Here the dedications from the forts on the line of the Wall, the outpost forts and those of the Cumberland coast are examined. The evidence comes from inscriptions, the easiest to interpret; some account is taken of other evidence, which though important is often difficult to use because the god honoured is uncertain. The inscriptions and some other material from Corbridge, Carlisle and South Shields are also included; presumably because Corbridge had legionary connections and all three places had larger civilian populations, some gods are represented at these sites which are not known from the forts on the Wall. With these provisos we have here the attitudes of a typical cross-section of the auxiliaries of the army in Britain, and not very different from such a cross-section anywhere in the Empire.

The Official Religions

The official military calendar is best attested by the *Feriale Duranum*, a fascinating document showing the religious festivals observed by a

259

unit of the Roman army, the *cohors XX Palmyrenorum*, at Dura-Europos in the third century.

The most obvious symbol of official religious activity is the great series of altars to Jupiter Best and Greatest, represented at practically every fort and in particularly large numbers at Birdoswald and Maryport. At Maryport they were discovered in great pits, where they had been buried at intervals. It seems that one was dedicated annually; they stood beside the parade-ground, until periodically cleared away. The Maryport altars, mainly from the second century, show variation in phrasing between different garrisons. Where a prefect was commander for more than a year he seems to have dedicated only his first altar on behalf of the cohort; in succeeding years he dedicated each time in his own name. Maenius Agrippa at Maryport dedicated his 'personal' altars to 'IOM* et numen Augusti'. Interestingly enough the only altar that varies from 'IOM' to 'IOM et numen Augusti' at Birdoswald is the only example of a second altar by the same prefect that has survived there. At Housesteads the regular dedication by the cohors I Tungrorum was to 'IOM et numina Augustorum'. Of the other two gods of the Capitoline Triad who presided over the destinies of Rome Juno is only honoured once, not in an official capacity, as the dedicator is a woman. If a statue at Corbridge is correctly identified the legionaries stationed there included Juno in official ceremonies. Minerva, the third member, apparently has a temple at High Rochester, with three dedications, two of them by tribunes. The cohort at Birrens honoured her while the dedication to Brigantia there portrays her with the attributes of Minerva Victrix. This last-named dedication was by an *architectus*, whose patron goddess would be Minerva. Elsewhere she is honoured by individuals, including another *architectus*. The Corbridge legionaries may have honoured her also, again in the guise of Minerva Victrix. However the Birrens dedications may be regarded simply as evidence for a local cult; auxiliaries as opposed to legionaries worshipped only IOM of the Capitoline triad.

Other gods and goddesses are honoured by whole units, and such worship may have had at least a semi-official character. Local gods – such as Antenociticus at Benwell, Cocidius at Birdoswald, the Matres at Housesteads, and Silvanus at Moresby – were honoured, and the soldiers' gods – Hercules at Housesteads and Burgh, Mars at Chesterholm and Birdoswald, and a god brought in by a unit, Mars Thincsus, at Housesteads. At Maryport *cohors I Baetasiorum* has left two altars, presumably from the parade ground, to Mars Militaris, as well as one

* IOM was the standard abbreviation for '*Iuppiter Optimus Maximusque*', 'Jupiter Best and Greatest'.

to Jupiter, and two to Victoria Augusta. Dedications by commanding officers do not necessarily have any official character, but they may betray a unit's special reverence for a god when three commanders dedicate to the same deity, such as Hercules at Risingham. Coventina at Carrawburgh is a special case. Dedications to Mithras come into a different category, as Mithraism was an international religion well-represented in the army at commanding officer level.

Jupiter Best and Greatest, with some support from Mars and Victory, dominated the parade ground, and represented the traditions of Rome. The goddess Roma herself has only one doubtful semi-official dedication, though there was clearly a temple to her at Corbridge and she also appears on linked dedications from Maryport, discussed below. In the religious calendar the gods and festivals of Rome are overshadowed by the birthdays and accession days and victories of the god-emperors. Direct emperor-worship was however foreign to Roman sentiment. Dedications therefore are not to the emperor, but for his safety and well-being, *pro salute*, to his Victory or his Virtue (manliness rather than moral character) and his Discipline. There was an unofficial but widely spread cult of his *numen*, a difficult concept which represents his supernatural guiding spirit, his superhuman power and wisdom. It is only twice worshipped on its own in the group under study, by the cohort at Risingham and by an unknown dedicator at Halton. Normally it or they were revered (the concept could be plural, even for a single emperor) together with other gods, the official worship of Jupiter, Mars, and the standards, the classical god Mercury, the local god Antenociticus, the god of the unit Mars Thincsus, the eastern god Dolichenus, the regional god Maponus, and Celtic gods such as Mars Ocelus and the Matres. Most but not all dedications were by prefects and cohorts. In other provinces the worship of the *numina Augusti/Augustorum* was replaced by dedications on behalf of the imperial family, *pro domu divina*. In this group the only example of the latter type of dedication is at Chesterholm, where the *vicus*-dwellers in fact linked it with *numen*-worship.

The third element in the official religious worship was the gods of the army itself, particularly the standards which represented in sacred form loyalty to the unit and to one's comrades. The cult of the *signa* is represented at Birdoswald, coupled with the *numen*, and at High Rochester, where it is linked with the *genius* or guardian spirit both of the cohort and of the *exploratores* stationed there.

These then were the gods of the headquarters shrine and the parade-ground, or at least gods who might be honoured in their own temples by the unit as a whole. Outside these lay a whole wealth of deities;

apart from the deities already referred to and such popular local gods as Belatucadrus and the Veteres, few could command large groups of worshippers. Even fewer were honoured in elaborate shrines, for which the offerings of the faithful had to pay.

A number of gods were concerned with the fort itself or its environs. At Chesterholm there is evidence for the worship of the spirit presiding over the commander's house, the *praetorium*. Three formal inscriptions were set up, in each case by the prefect of the cohort, and in two cases linked with Jupiter Best and Greatest. In the bathhouse Fortuna, protectress of man in his naked helpless state against the evil eye, reigned supreme, sometimes described as Augusta or Conservatrix (Preserver). Fortuna Redux (Fortune the Homebringer) is worshipped on three occasions, all by tribunes, and on two of them at Maryport is linked with Roma Aeterna. One of these is further linked with the Genius Loci, the spirit that presided over the place, Maryport, and Bonum Fatum, good luck. A free rendering of the thought behind this might be: 'May the gods of this place be good to me, and Fortune bring me a quick posting home.' The commanding officer was perhaps the one man in the fort who had a home away from it to go to.

The cavalry had special goddesses, the *matres campestres*, who were linked with the *genius* of the *ala* in a dedication by the prefect at Benwell, and the horse goddess Epona, who was the subject of a dedication at Carvoran.

The Gods of Greece and Rome

The gods of Greece and Rome without official altars did not fare well on the whole. They did occasionally receive sacrifices during the official round of festivals, it is true, but this did not ensure them regular worship. Identification with local gods may account for a number of dedications. Thus Mercury is quite well-represented, in the towns possibly because of his commercial connections as god of travel and trade, but in the forts because of similarities to native gods. Caesar fastened on Mercury as the god most like the gods of Gaul. Neptune comes out quite well on dedications, perhaps because his associations were with flowing water, rivers as well as seas. Silvanus was a woodland god, worshipped under his own name and in identification with native gods. The two dedications to Asclepius, the god of medicine, one in Greek, one from South Shields, may have been dedicated by people with professional loyalties to the doctors' god. Vulcan the smith god is honoured by the *vicus*-dwellers at Chesterholm, and at Maryport by a prefect. Apollo, unfortunate in that his identification is with a rare native god, Maponus, is not well-represented, and neither is Diana. Venus does not appear on inscriptions, nor does her associate Cupid, although there is perhaps a crude representation of her on a large sculpture from High Rochester. Here the number of pipe-clay figurines found of Venus give a more balanced picture. The private religion of an individual might well be represented by figurines, and not find expression in words on stone at all.

The Native Gods

The native gods rather overshadow those of Greece and Rome once the official ceremonies are over, apart from the soldiers' gods Mars and Hercules. Antenociticus at Benwell had his own temple and was revered by the unit, and Coventina at Carrawburgh, whatever her origin, native or imported, was honoured at every military and social level. Three other gods stand out for the number of their dedications, Belatucadrus, Cocidius, and the god or gods known to his worshippers as Vetris, Vitiris, Veteres, Votris, Hviteres, Hviteris and Hvitris. Belatucadrus is sometimes identified with Mars, and is mainly a god of the west; his inscriptions range from Carvoran to Netherby, with an outlying dedication at Carrawburgh. His worshippers have almost as much difficulty with spelling his name as the worshippers of Vetris, and like them are relatively unimportant socially. They do not put their names on their small altars, or they give one name rather than the three of the Roman citizen. An *optio* is the only soldier of any rank attested for Belatucadrus, an *imaginifer* for the Vetris god. Dedications to the Vetris god stretch along the Wall from Benwell to Carvoran, which has no less than sixteen dedications, and stop there, apart from an outlier at Netherby. He is not identified with any Roman god, but is linked with Mogons at Netherby. Mogons is honoured at Risingham by a *beneficiarius consularis*, at High Rochester by a decurion, and at Chesterholm. The third native god honoured on a large scale is Cocidius. His dedications begin at Housesteads and extend along the Wall to the area of Stanwix, and north to Risingham, Netherby and Bewcastle, where his dedications occur on silver plaques found in the headquarters building. It has been suggested that Bewcastle was Fanum Cocidi, the shrine of Cocidius, which according to the Ravenna Cosmography was in the general area (see p. 272). Cocidius is identified with Silvanus at Housesteads and associated with him at Risingham, but at Bewcastle and in the Castlesteads-Stanwix area Cocidius is identified with Mars. Cocidius is definitely of superior social status in comparison with Belatucadrus. He was honoured by the cohort at Birdoswald, by commanding officers at Housesteads, Chesterholm, Netherby and Bewcastle, and by soldiers of all three legions of Britain in the area between Birdoswald and Stanwix.

Maponus is also possibly a god of some social standing, but dedications to him are rare on the Wall and elsewhere. There is only one inscription in stone, which has no exact provenance, set up by four Germans; otherwise there are at Corbridge inscriptions by a prefect of the camp, a tribune and a legionary centurion. However the discovery of a silver *lunula* from Chesterholm dedicated to Maponus extends the

43   Gods of the Wall. Distribution of the find-spots of altars to:
a. Belatucadrus; b. Cocidius; c. Mogons; d. the Veteres

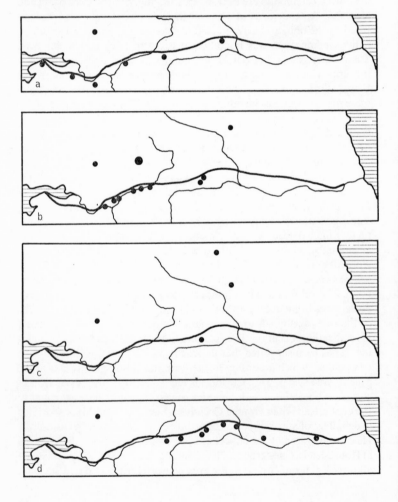

recorded area of the cult, but without knowledge of the dedicator, clearly a man of some wealth, firm conclusions can hardly be suggested. The same is true of the figure allegedly of Maponus associated with a serpent at Birrens.

The territorial deity is presumably Brigantia, but the few scattered dedications give no coherent pattern, though presumably the places where they were erected, South Shields, Corbridge and Birrens, fell in her territory.

A god clearly introduced from overseas is Mars Thincsus, brought to Housesteads by the cuneus Frisiorum or the numerus Hnaudifridi from Germania. Ricagambeda and Viradecthis were honoured by men from different districts in Germania serving in the *cohors II Tungrorum* at Birrens. The Hamians at Carvoran, continuing to recruit from their Syrian homeland, worshipped Dea Syria, who was identified with Jupiter, Hammia and alone on the Wall IOM Heliopolitanus, the local deity of Heliopolis in Syria. Of more general appeal but also apparently first introduced from overseas was the cult of the mother goddesses, represented as a powerful triad. They have already been encountered as the protectresses of the cavalry parade-ground at Benwell. They also appear as goddesses of the overseas homeland (*tramarinae patriae*), common to all (*communes*), of all people (*omnium gentium*), of the household (*domesticae*), German, or just my mother goddesses (*suae*). They also identified with the Fates (Parcae). Units, offices and individuals honour them and their dedications are fairly evenly distributed. Apart from the special case of Coventina they are the most popular goddesses, not surprisingly perhaps.

The antecedents of a number of these gods are uncertain. Many gods who appear once or twice only on dedications are just names: Harimella, Iu, tres Lamiae (the three witches), Latis (twice), Matunus, Ratis (twice), Sattada, Setlocenia and Sucabus.

In this context reference may be made to the well-established cult of the severed human head. For the Celt all the virtue of a slain enemy dwelt in his head, and heads of noted warriors might be treated as family heirlooms. The efforts made to secure and retain these trophies are reflected in a number of scenes from Trajan's Column. This passed naturally into their religious activity, and a number of stone heads have been found and identified as cult objects – so many that the question of authenticity arises. They are nameless, although attempts have been made to identify some of them.

Before turning to those gods from the East who established themselves all over the Roman world a word may be said on the process by which different gods with similar attributes were identified as one and the same. Thus Maponus was identified with Apollo. Belatucadrus was identified with Mars. Brigantia at one stage was identified with Caelestis, and on another occasion given the attributes of Minerva Victrix. The Matres were identified with the Parcae. The two non-Roman gods, Vitiris and Mogons, are identified with each other. Most strikingly of all Cocidius was identified in one area with Mars, in another with Silvanus. This last example shows the problems that might arise over identification. The Graeco-Roman gods had become specialized, dealing with some aspect of human activities, though they often retained other aspects than those we immediately associate with them. The Celtic gods were less specialized, differing in territory rather than in characteristics, so any identification with a specialist god would be an inadequate representation of the Celtic god's sphere of activity. Cocidius sometimes seemed like Mars, sometimes like Silvanus, sometimes completely different from either. It is not surprising that Mars is a frequent identification, for the warrior aspect of the tribal god is bound to be very pronounced. A number of identifications of him with Celtic gods from other areas turn up in the towns, Mars Alator at South Shields, Mars Barrex and Mars Ocelus at Carlisle, reflecting the larger and more cosmopolitan civilian population in these places.

The identification of Jupiter with the local supreme deity was a natural one. It has already been seen in the case of I O M Heliopolitanus. In the case of Jupiter of Doliche, a town in Syria, however, the worship of the god identified with Jupiter oversprang any local boundaries. He had his own group of associated subordinate deities, Sun, Moon and Heavenly Twins, and is honoured in Britain at four Wall forts, three outpost forts and at Corbridge, where fragments of a temple survive. Corbridge seems to have harboured a community receptive to Eastern influences, for Astarte and Heracles of Tyre, Phoenician deities, are honoured there. Both inscriptions are in Greek, the latter by a priestess, and here perhaps some one from the East was brought in to serve the temple, for Greek although common in the eastern empire would have been in Britain restricted to traders and other travellers from the east, and to the well-educated. Also at Corbridge the Magna Mater, Cybele, centre of an Oriental and orgiastic cult, was worshipped.

Mithras

The cult that has attracted most modern attention is that of Mithras. He had his special temples (*mithraea*) at Rudchester, Carrawburgh and Housesteads, and dedications at Castlesteads and High Rochester may suggest that there are temples to be found there also. As E. Birley noted, at no Wall site are both Mithras and Dolichenus recorded. Mithraism was a Roman adaptation of an ancient religion of the East, centring on the struggle between light and darkness, good and evil. A subordinate figure in the original concept, Mithras came to be the one most invoked. Born from the rock, he pursued, caught, brought back to his cave and killed the bull, thereby releasing creative power for mankind. This bull-slaying, the act of redemption, generally formed the central scene in every *mithraeum*. *Mithraea* often recalled the cave in their form. The best-preserved one on the Wall, at Carrawburgh, was basically a nave with benches on either side, with a sanctuary at one end and at the other a narthex, an ante-room for those not yet initiated. It was dimly lit by clerestory lighting. After a farewell feast Mithras had returned to heaven to be men's guide and aide, and his votaries after initiation shared ritual meals, progressing from grade to grade by ordeals. The cult appealed to the army, officers in particular, for Mithras was the Unconquered, but it was exclusively male and did not demand uncondi-tional and exclusive allegiance, two grave weaknesses. It bulks large in our thought, for it attracted the special hatred of Christians, largely because of what were thought to be blasphemous imitations of the Christian gospel and its rites. However it never came near to being universal. The worshippers recorded on the Wall are senior officers, mainly commanders of auxiliary units, and the history of the Carraw-burgh *mithraeum* suggests that it was often difficult to find sufficient initiates in the fort to keep services going.

Other Temples

Mithraea are very specialized temples. Other temples tend to be either classical, rectangular on a raised platform, or Roman–Celtic, small square, polygonal or circular shrines surrounded by porticoes. Neither type was intended for congregational worship; people made individual vows. On feast days ceremonies could be held in the open air. There are no big temples on the Wall; there were too many competing cults. Temples are not always easy to recognize on excavation, and inscrip-tions do not necessarily demonstrate their presence, unless they appear in large numbers. There was at least one temple at Wallsend (RIB 1305) but the god is not known, and perhaps the figure of Mercury came from that or another temple. It is uncertain whether the two inscriptions of VI Victrix (RIB 1319, 1320) came from a shrine on the Tyne bridge. The temple of Antenociticus at Benwell is known, a simple apsidal building. The Campestres also had a temple there, as the dedication refers to its restoration. A *mithraeum* is known at Rudchester, and a temple to the Matres existed somewhere near Milecastle 19. Carrawburgh had its *mithraeum*, the shrine of Coventina, built in the Roman–Celtic style, a

44 Temples on the Wall. a. Carrawburgh Mithraeum; b. Antenociticus, Benwell; c. Coventina's Well, Carrawburgh; d. Corbridge Temple I. Scale 1 in. = 36 ft (1:432)

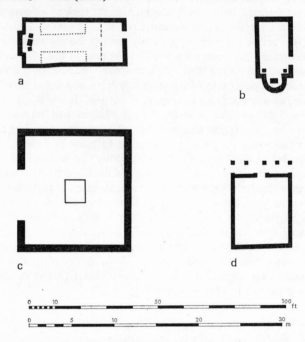

shrine to the Nymphs, and perhaps another temple. At Housesteads there was a *mithraeum*, and a temple to Mars Thincsus which has been provisionally identified. At Carvoran a temple appears to have been built to a god 'M . . '. At Castlesteads a temple was restored to the Matres, and apparently a temple was dedicated to the same deities at Bowness. There seems a strong case for a temple to Mercury at Birrens, where there was a guild of worshippers, and the inscriptions all come from the same building. A temple to an unknown god was restored by the cohort at Netherby. A fragmentary inscription at Netherby probably implies the existence of another temple. Three altars to Minerva in a building outside the fort at High Rochester point to a temple there, as does the existence of a guild of worshippers, and an inscription implies the construction of a *mithraeum* there. At South Shields there was a temple to an unknown goddess. A shrine is mentioned at Carlisle. At Corbridge there is a well-known group of temples, but not all are definitely temples, and none can be assigned to a particular deity. Sculptural fragments suggest a temple to Dolichenus and another to Dea Roma. All this shows the urgent need for a complete plan of the environs of a Wall fort, showing the temples. A minimum of three or four outside every fort ought to be allowed for.

Other Religious Objects

No attempt is made here to enter into a discussion in detail of the assemblage of religious objects other than dedications. Among famous objects may be mentioned the sculpture of the Genii Cucullati at Housesteads, a triad of cowled Celtic deities, the pots from Corbridge which display a Celtic smith god (not Dolichenus), the pottery mould also from Corbridge which shows apparently the god Tanaris with his wheel and the silver lanx. The decoration of the lanx connects it with the Greek mystery religions of the East, but it is an imported object belonging to some rich individual, and does not imply any important influence of these religions in the area. On the other hand it adds to the evidence of Eastern religions at Corbridge.

The Strength of Paganism

Before turning to Christianity one more element remains to be emphasized. Paganism on the whole was not strong on theology or organization. It was strong in its ability to respond to the needs of all men. Intellectuals might need philosophical systems or mystics the mystery religions, and they got them; ordinary people were just afraid, superstitious, anxious to protect themselves against malign powers. There is therefore a goodly element of magic, amulets and charms, in the lives of the people studied here. One very clear example of this is the appearance of phallic symbols, representing fertility and good fortune, and therefore potent against the evil eye, on structures and as finds. They appear at Chesters on the lowest course of the bath-house basement, on the bridge abutment, and in the headquarters courtyard, and on the curtain wall rebuilt in stone east of Birdoswald. They remind us forcibly of the element of straightforward fear.

Christianity

What about Christianity? There is scarcely one piece of material evidence from the Wall that has not been disputed. There are two reasons for this shortage of evidence. First of all, Christianity at this period did not leave much in the way of material relics. Inscriptions of the fourth century are rare in Britain, and the formulae on the tombstones that survive may have been used by Christians but not exclusively. Christian churches of this period are not always easy to recognize. The chi–rho sign is perhaps the only indisputable evidence, but it tells us little about the date and nothing about the number of Christians involved.

The second point is that when Constantine was converted and gave the Christian church peace from persecution in 312, Christians were a minority in the Empire. Indeed Professor A. H. M. Jones reckoned them a tiny minority, and predominantly in the urban lower class. Although Constantine banned sacrifices and confiscated temple lands and treasures, sacrifice was tolerated from 361 to 391, and at other times the law against it was laxly enforced. It is no surprise then that Coventina's well, for instance, continued to receive offerings. Not till the early fifth century were pagans excluded from governmental positions, and although the army must have had its official calendar modified to suit Christian beliefs, as the military oath was, the army remained a stronghold of paganism. The pagans had the advantage that unlike Christians, who had jibbed in the past over observing pagan rites, they made no difficulty over observing official Christian rites; there were few pagan martyrs. But the strength of paganism lay in its deep roots in the age-old practices of peasants, and for the educated in the traditions, literature and glory of Rome. It is therefore unlikely that Christianity on any scale came to the Wall before 312, and thereafter its main channel was probably as the official military religion. The official gods were displaced and perhaps other gods of Greece and Rome who had no strong local roots. The local gods no doubt held on as did Coventina. The temples of Mithras may have come in for harsh treatment, though if so not on any general legal basis. The first recorded official act against a *mithraeum* was the destruction of one in Rome in 377; individual temples could be destroyed on petition. Thus the most positive evidence for Christianity on the Wall may be acts of destruction, at Rudchester and Carrawburgh.

This is not the whole story; there is evidence that the Celtic kingdoms, both those that grew up in the Lowlands, Strathclyde and Manau Gododdin, and those that succeeded Roman Britain in northern England, were Christian in the fifth century. Patrick, a third-generation Christian, may have come from north-west England in the early fifth century, and Bede retains the tradition that Ninian was bishop at Whithorn early in the fifth century and apostolized the southern Picts. It is possible that Christianity made substantial progress in the north during the last decades of Roman Britain and therefore began to affect seriously the beliefs of the men on the Wall. But the evidence is still to be found.

Appendix Four

The Roman Names of the Forts on Hadrian's Wall

The sources for the Roman names of the forts on the Wall, the outpost forts and those on the Cumberland coast are as follows:

The Rudge Cup and Amiens Skillet. These are a small bowl and skillet (small vessel with a long handle) respectively, with a running border around their rims representing the Wall, and carrying the names of the Wall forts in the western sector. Presumably there were matching vessels completing the series. The absolute date suggested for the Rudge Cup on the basis of its decoration is c. 150, but a date when the Wall was standing empty seems improbable, and the evidence does not rule out the reign of Hadrian, a more probable date.

The Antonine Itinerary. This is apparently a collection of some 225 routes used for particular journeys. The longest route has been associated with a journey taken by the emperor Caracalla, but this does not necessarily date the others. There is a discussion of the date of the route which includes Blatobulgium (Birrens) and Castra Exploratorum (Netherby) above (p. 142).

The Notitia Dignitatum. An official document which gives among other things a list of army units under the command of the generals of the Empire. The date of the British section has been much discussed. Here the view is taken that this part of the document dates to the very end of the Roman period in Britain, c. 410. The section includes a sub-section entitled 'also, along the line of the wall' and the certain identifications show garrisons which are the same as those known in the late second and early third century.

The Ravenna Cosmography. A compilation of the late seventh century of the countries, towns and rivers of the known world. The British section seems to be based on reading off names from roadbooks or maps.

	Rudge Cup Amiens Skillet	Ravenna	Notitia Dignitatum	Other
South Shields			Arbeia	
Wallsend		Serduno	Segeduno	
Newcastle			Ponte Aeli[o]	
Benwell		Condecor	Conderco	
Rudchester		Vindovala	Vindobala	
Halton Chesters		Onno	Hunno	
Chesters		Celunno	Cilurno	
Carrawburgh		Brocoliti	Procolitia	
Housesteads		Velurcion	Borcovicio	Ver-*
Chesterholm		Vindolande	Vindolana	Vindolandess -es*
Great Chesters	Esica	Esica	Aesica	
Carvoran		Magnis	Magnis	
Birdoswald	Banna	Banna		Bannienses*
Castlesteads	Camboglans	Gabaglanda	[C]amboglanna	
Stanwix	Uxellodum	Uxelludamo	Petrianis	
Burgh-by-Sands	Aballava	Avalava	Aballaba	
Drumburgh				
Bowness	Mais	Maia		
Beckfoot (??)		Bribra		
Maryport (?)		Alauna		
Burrow Walls (??)		Gabrocentio	Gabrosenti	
Moresby (??)		Iuliocenon	Tunnocelo	
Birrens				Blatobulgium†
Netherby			Axeloduno (?)	Castra exploratum†
Bewcastle (?)		Fanococidi		
Risingham				Habitanci*
High Rochester				Brem–* Bremenium†

* From an inscription.
† From the Antonine Itinerary.

Appendix 4: The Roman Names of the Forts on Hadrian's Wall

There is no debate about the names of the forts on the Wall reading east to west from Wallsend to Great Chesters. The difficulty lies in fitting names to the known forts west of Great Chesters, as the sources disagree among themselves. No satisfactory solution has yet been offered. The suggestions here, which are not original, differ from the present conventional solution for reasons which will be explained.

The Rudge Cup and the Amiens Skillet

A start may be made with the Rudge Cup and Amiens Skillet. These differ only in that the latter has an extra name, that of Aesica, Great Chesters. As has been noted, all the forts from Great Chesters eastwards have agreed names, so the cup and skillet must cover the forts to the west. They give the same five names in the same order:

A MAIS ABALLAVA UXELLODUM CAMBOGLANS BANNA

Seven forts are known between Bowness and Great Chesters inclusive: Bowness, Drumburgh, Stanwix, Castlesteads, Birdoswald, Carvoran and Great Chesters. The formula is A MAIS i.e. starting from Maiae, so it seems reasonable to conclude that the starting-point is Bowness and the direction west to east, a conclusion confirmed by the addition of Esica (Great Chesters) on the end on the Amiens Skillet. The next fort to Bowness, Drumburgh, is very small, and may be discounted, particularly as there is strong evidence that Burgh-by-Sands is Aballava. It would seem logical to continue westwards and identify Stanwix as Uxellodum, Castlesteads as Camboglans, and Birdoswald as Banna. Opportunely an inscription from Birdoswald refers to a unit called the *venatores Bannienses*; normally this would be sufficient to establish that Birdoswald was Banna. The omission of Carvoran on the Amiens Skillet may be explained by its location south of the Wall line, beyond the Vallum; Castlesteads though south of the Wall line is included by the Vallum and was one of the primary forts. Sir Ian Richmond long ago pointed out that the Ravenna list also omitted Magnae (Carvoran), and concluded that the cup and skillet were based on itineraries. This is not necessarily so; no road linked the Wall forts till the Military Way was built well after the latest date proposed for the cup, and if the cup and skillet were to refer to the Wall, as their decoration suggests, there need be no direct reference to an itinerary. The correspondence may show only that Carvoran was not felt to belong to the Wall by the designers of the cup and skillet, and that Carvoran was classed as part of the Stanegate itinerary by the compilers of Ravenna.

Hadrian's Wall

The Notitia Dignitatum

The difficulty in accepting these identifications lies in reconciling them
with the *Notitia* list. This follows the line of forts westwards from
Wallsend, giving wherever it can be checked the third-century garrison
still in place, except at Great Chesters, where I Asturum replaces II
Asturum, but this surely is a scribal error. The relevant section following
Great Chesters reads:

tribunus cohortis secundae Dalmatarum, Magnis
tribunus cohortis primae Aeliae Dacorum, Amboglanna
praefectus alae Petrianae, Petrianis
praefectus numeri Maurorum Aurelianorum, Aballaba
tribunus cohortis secundae Lingonum, Congavata
tribunus cohortis primae Hispanorum, Axeloduno
tribunus cohortis secundae Thracum, Gabrosenti
tribunus cohortis primae Aeliae classicae, Tunnocelo
tribunus cohortis primae Morinorum, Glannibanta
tribunus cohortis tertiae Nerviorum, Alione

If the list of identifications proposed for the Rudge Cup and Amiens
Skillet is compared with this:

Banna	*Birdoswald*
Camboglanna	*Castlesteads*
Uxellodunum	*Stanwix*
Aballava	*Burgh*
Maiae	*Bowness*

it will be noted that neither Banna nor Maiae appear in the *Notitia*
list; Axelodunum if the same as Uxellodunum is not placed between
Aballava and Camboglanna; Birdoswald, the home of cohors I Aelia
Dacorum on incontrovertible inscriptional evidence, is called Cambog-
lanna; Stanwix, the home of the ala Petriana, is called Petriana. One
solution is to suppose that Banna on the Rudge Cup and Amiens
Skillet is Bewcastle, an outpost fort evacuated by the time that the
Notitia was compiled. This however supposes that the omission of
Stanwix results from the list being taken from an itinerary, on which
Stanwix was replaced by Carlisle. However this is hardly satisfactory;
the cup and skillet represent the Wall, not a road, and to include one
and only one outpost fort instead of a major Wall fort would seem a
remarkable error. Moreover this explanation is only acceptable on the
assumption that the one inscription mentioning Banna, of the *venatores
Bannienses* at Birdoswald, was set up there by troops garrisoned at
Bewcastle or carried there from that fort. The alternative view that
Banna is Carvoran has the same difficulties, and involves the further
assumption that Magnis in the *Notitia* is a corruption of Banna.

Appendix 4: The Roman Names of the Forts on Hadrian's Wall

A way out of these difficulties has been put forward by Mr M. Hassall. He suggests that on the *Notitia* list the name of the unit, Petriana, is accidentally repeated as the name of the fort (the name is unsupported by any other evidence), which should have been Uxellodunum, and that the name Banna and the unit in garrison at Camboglanna have been omitted. Mr Hassall suggested further that Congavata is a corruption of *torquata* and Axelodunum a corruption of Uxellodunum, inserted in the wrong place. These do not necessarily follow; here is the list with the first modifications proposed by Mr Hassall:

tribunus cohortis secundae Dalmatarum, Magnis [*Carvoran*]
tribunus cohortis primae Aeliae Dacorum, *Banna* [*Birdoswald*]
tribunus cohortis secundae Tungrorum, Camboglanna [*Castlesteads*]
praefectus alae Petrianae, *Uxelloduno* [*Stanwix*]
praefectus numeri Maurorum Aurelianorum, Aballava [*Burgh*]
tribunus cohortis secundae Lingonum, Congavata
tribunus cohortis primae Hispanorum, Axeloduno

There is no evidence that Congavata is Drumburgh, as the Wall forts in order seem to finish with Aballava. Maiae (Bowness) is omitted, as are Bribra and Alauna, mentioned in the Ravenna Cosmography and generally identified with the next two forts down the Cumberland coast, Beckfoot and Maryport respectively. It would appear that after Aballava the *Notitia* simply lists the forts held in the north-west. In that case the entry for Axeloduno, giving the garrison known to have been at Netherby in the third century, may refer to Netherby. There is no evidence that the fort was evacuated by this time, and the only other name known for the fort is Castra Exploratorum, a somewhat artificial Latin name as opposed to the Latinized Celtic place-names common in the region. Is it possible that this name had been dropped in favour of an older Celtic one of Axelodunum when the *exploratores* disappeared. They had been replaced by or renamed as the *areani* by 340–1, and in 368 the *areani* themselves were disbanded.

The modifications may seem outrageous but they are preferable to assuming the omission of Stanwix on the Rudge Cup and Amiens Skillet; the inclusion of Bewcastle and no other outpost fort on them; the setting-up of a stone by a unit stationed at Bewcastle at Birdoswald or that stone's transport there; the name of Stanwix to be the otherwise unattested Petriana – every other fort name on the Wall is attested twice with the significant exception of Congavata; the movement of the garrison of Netherby to Castlesteads to replace the third-century garrison there; and the displacement of its entry in the *Notitia* list, not simply the omission of the name Uxelloduno.

The Ravenna Cosmography

The evidence of the Ravenna Cosmography must now be examined. It is important to keep to the order of the relevant sections, as if a site has already appeared in the lists it is passed over in silence:

Ravenna	Antonine Itinerary	Notitia	Modern name
Alicuna			
Camuloduno			
Caluvio	Galacum		Burrow-in-Lonsdale (?)
Galluvio	Galava		Ambleside
Mediobogdo		.	Hardknott
Cantiventi	Clanoventa	Glannibanta	Ravenglass
Iuliocenon		Tunnocelo	
Gabrocentiuo		Gabrosenti	
Alauna			
Bribra			
Maio			
Derventione			
Bravoniaco	Brovonacis		Kirkby Thore

If Maio is Maia the four forts lying between it and Clanoventa (Ravenglass) in the Ravenna list may be Cumberland Coast forts, and two of those names appear in the *Notitia*. However it is most unusual for a name to appear twice in the Ravenna list, and the possibility cannot be excluded that Maio represents another fort. There should really be a fort between Beckfoot and Bowness, for the gap between them is 14⅔ miles, two-fifths of the total distance from Bowness to Moresby. The list continues as shown on the next page.

The road to Carlisle is now followed through Brough-under-Stainmore, Old Penrith and Carlisle, then the writer moves his finger up the Maiden Way from Kirkby Thore, already mentioned so not repeated, to the fort near the junction with the Stanegate, Carvoran. He then lists the fort immediately to the west, Camboglanna, and the fort immedi-

Appendix 4: The Roman Names of the Forts on Hadrian's Wall

Ravenna	Itinerary	Notitia	Modern name
Valteris	Verteris	Verteris	Brough-under-Stainmore
Bereda	Voreda		Old Penrith
Lagubalium	Luguvallo		Carlisle
Magnis		Magnis	Carvoran
Gabaglanda		Amboglanna	Castlesteads (?)
Vindolande		Vindolana	Chesterholm

ately to the east, Chesterholm. On the interpretation adopted here Camboglanna would be Castlesteads. As that fort probably preceded Hadrian's Wall, though it was carefully incorporated into it by the Vallum, it may well have had a road link with the Stanegate. The conventional identification with Birdoswald has to find a road link, and explain why the writer did not then naturally follow up the road which ran from Birdoswald to Bewcastle, Banna on the conventional interpretation. Instead he moves to the line of the Wall:

Ravenna	Rudge Cup, Amiens Skillet	Notitia	Modern name
Serduno		Segeduno Ponte Aelio	Wallsend Newcastle
Condecor		Conderco	Benwell
Vindovala		Vindobala	Rudchester
Onno		Hunno	Halton Chesters
Celunno		Cilurno	Chesters
Brocoliti		Procolitia	Carrawburgh
Velurcion		Borcovicio	Housesteads
Esica	Aesica	Aesica Magnis	Great Chesters Carvoran
Banna	Banna Camboglans	Camboglanna	Birdoswald (?) Castlesteads (?)
Uxelludamo	Uxellodum	Petrianis	Stanwix
Avalava	Aballava	Aballaba	Burgh-by-Sands
Maia	Mais		Bowness

Newcastle is omitted by Ravenna, curiously, but then we know little of its history. The next omission is of Magnis, already mentioned in Ravenna, and not apparently regarded as belonging to the Wall on the Amiens Skillet. Camboglanna is also omitted by the Ravenna but not by the Rudge Cup and Amiens Skillet, so they are not working from the same source. Ravenna omitted it because it had been mentioned already. The omission of Banna from the *Notitia* is startling; Banna cannot be identical with Magnis for in Ravenna both names appear. There follow the entries for the fort Uxellodunum; clearly Stanwix must either be omitted altogether from Ravenna, the Rudge Cup and the Amiens Skillet or be Uxellodunum. The argument that an itinerary would only mention Carlisle and omit Stanwix is invalid. The list in Ravenna is following either the Wall or the Military Way; in either case the list must have come to Stanwix, and there is no warrant to suppose Stanwix was subsumed in Carlisle. The Rudge Cup and Amiens Skillet had nothing but the Wall to follow.

Summary

Ravenna, the cup and the skillet agree that there were three forts between Aesica = Great Chesters and Aballava = Burgh-by-Sands. It seems to solve more problems to assume that Banna = Birdoswald, confirmed by an inscription, Camboglanna = Castlesteads and Uxellodunum = Stanwix. This interpretation seems better to explain the Rudge Cup and Amiens Skillet, take proper account of the inscription of the *venatores Bannienses*, and is at least as easy to reconcile with the Ravenna Cosmography as the traditional explanation that Banna = Bewcastle or Carvoran, Camboglanna = Birdoswald and Uxellodunum = Castlesteads. It supposes, following Mr M. Hassall, a bad blunder in the *Notitia* list as we have it, but on any interpretation so far offered there is a blunder; the point at issue is its nature and magnitude.

Appendix Five

The Evidence on the Ground

This list is not exhaustive, but it contains the best places to see the visible evidence relating to the building and history of Hadrian's Wall.

General

Stone curtain: Thorny Doors (41a–b: highest standing stretch), Walltown, Willowford–Birdoswald

Turf wall: 49b–51
  Section: Appletree
Ditch: Chesters–Sewingshields, Willowford–Appletree
  End of ditch at crags: Sewingshields (34)
  Uncompleted ditch: Limestone Corner (30)
Turrets: 7b (Denton), 48a (Willowford east), 52a (Banks east)
Milecastles: 37 (Housesteads), 48 (Poltross Burn)
Forts
  General: Housesteads, Chesters
  Defences: Carrawburgh (fort platform)
  Walls: Housesteads
  Ditches: Great Chesters, Carrawburgh
  Gates: Chesters east and west (iron collars for door pivots), Housesteads west (bar holes), Birdoswald east
  Wall towers: Chesters, Birdoswald
  Headquarters buildings: Chesters, Housesteads, Chesterholm
  Strong rooms: Chesters, Great Chesters, South Shields (note window sill)
  Commandant's house: Housesteads
  Granaries: Housesteads, South Shields
  Hospital: Housesteads
  Barracks: Chesters, South Shields
  Latrine: Housesteads
  Water tanks: Housesteads
  Aqueduct: Great Chesters, South Shields
  Bath-houses: Chesters, Chesterholm
Bridges: Chesters, Willowford
Vallum: Cawfields, Limestone Corner
Crossing: Benwell

Hadrian's Wall

The Building of the Wall

Milecastles
  Legion II: 37 (Housesteads), 42 (Cawfields)
  Legion VI: 48 (Poltross Burn)
  Legion XX: 39 (Castle Nick) (both gates later modified)
Turrets
  Legion VI: 48a and b (Willowford)
  Legion XX: 7b (Denton), 26b (Brunton)
Curtain
  Broad wall standard A: 7b (Denton), Heddon (11b–12)
  Broad wall standard B: Willowford (48a–Bridge) (the broad wall standard B
    has the later narrow wall standard A on top)
  Narrow wall standard A: Shield-on-the-Wall (41a)
  Narrow wall standard C: Walltown (45a–b), Birdoswald sector (49–49a)
Narrow wall turret
  legion uncertain: 44b (Mucklebank)
Points of Reduction from broad wall to narrow wall
  Curtain: Planetrees (26a)
  Milecastles: 42 (Cawfields), 48 (Poltross Burn)
  Turrets: 26b (Brunton), 29a (Blackcarts), 48a and b (Willowford)
  Narrow wall on broad wall: 48–Willowford Bridge, Chesters Bridge
  Narrow wall on broad foundation: Shield-on-the-Wall (41a)
Relationship between forts and curtain
  Turret demolished and replaced by fort: Housesteads (36b)
  Narrow wall and fort walls bonding: Chesters, Housesteads north-west
    corner, Great Chesters
  Narrow wall abutting fort wall: Housesteads north-east corner, Birdoswald
Turf wall
  Turrets: 51a (Piper Syke), 51b (Lea Hill), 52a (Banks east)
  Realignment of wall: Birdoswald north-west corner
  Intermediate gauge: Walton (55b)
  New stone milecastle: 49 (Harrow Scar)
  New stone turret: 49b (Birdoswald)

History of the Wall

Turrets
  Raising of threshold: 33b (Coesike)
  Blocking of recess: 33b (Coesike), 35a (Sewingshields Crag), 41b (Caw
    Gap)
Milecastles
  Narrowing of gates: 37 (Housesteads), 48 (Poltross Burn), 49 (Harrow
    Scar)
  Rebuilding of gate: 39 (Castle Nick)
  Rebuilding of accommodation: 48 (Poltross Burn)
Gate through wall: Knag Burn (Housesteads)

Appendix 5: The Evidence on the Ground

Forts

    Severan supply base: South Shields

    Blocking of gates: Great Chesters west gate, Birdoswald east gate, Housesteads east gate, Chesters south gate

    Headquarters buildings: Housesteads (remodelling of rear rooms, partitioning of verandah), Chesterholm (store-rooms in courtyard, hypocaust in rear rooms), South Shields (hypocausts in rear rooms)

    Commandant's House: Chesters

    Barracks: Housesteads and Great Chesters (rebuilt in early fourth century)

    Vici: Chesterholm (houses, shops, *mansio*), Housesteads (houses and shops), Carrawburgh (temples of Mithras and Coventina), Benwell (temple of Antenociticus)

Museums

Main collections: Newcastle-upon-Tyne (Museum of Antiquities), Carlisle (Tullie House), South Shields (Roman Remains Park), Chesters, Housesteads, Chesterholm

1 Bertha
2 Strageath
3 Ardoch
4 Carpow
5 Camelon
6 Lurg Moor
7 Outerwards
8 Bothwellhaugh
9 Loudon Hill
10 Castledykes
11 Lyne
12 Crawford
13 Durisdeer
14 Barburgh Mill
15 Carzield
16 Glenlochar
17 Ward Law
18 Redshaw Burn
19 Milton
20 Fairholm
21 Birrens fort and Burnswark fortlet
22 Raeburnfoot
23 Broomholm
24 Netherby
25 Bewcastle
26 Cramond
27 Inveresk
28 Oxton
29 Newstead
30 Cappuck
31 Chew Green
32 High Rochester
33 Risingham
34 Beckfoot
35 Maryport
36 Burrow Walls
37 Moresby
38 Papcastle
39 Caermote
40 Old Carlisle
41 Carlisle
42 Wreay

43 Old Penrith
44 Brougham
45 Kirkby Thore
46 Brampton
47 Whitley Castle
48 Corbridge
49 Washing Well
50 Chester-le-Street
51 Ebchester
52 Lanchester
53 Binchester
54 Piercebridge
55 Brough-under-Stainmore
56 Bowes
57 Greta Bridge
58 Low Borrow Bridge
59 Ambleside
60 Hardknott
61 Ravenglass
62 Watercrook
63 Brough-by-Bainbridge
64 Burrow-in-Lonsdale
65 Lancaster
66 Kirkham
67 Ribchester
68 Long Preston
69 Elslack
70 Ilkley
71 Aldborough
72 Malton
73 York
74 Newton Kyme
75 Castleford
76 Slack
77 Castleshaw
78 Melandra
79 Manchester
80 Wigan
81 Chester
82 Brough-on-Noe
83 Templeborough
84 Doncaster
85 Brough-on-Humber

Select Bibliography

List of Abbreviations

AA$^{2-5}$	*Archaeologia Aeliana*, series 2–5
CIL	*Corpus Inscriptionum Latinarum*
Handbook	J. C. Bruce, *Handbook to the Roman Wall* (12th edn by I. A. Richmond), Newcastle-upon-Tyne, 1966
ILS	H. Dessau, *Inscriptiones Latinae Selectae*, Berlin, 1893–1916
JRS	*Journal of Roman Studies*
Mann	J. C. Mann (ed.), *The Northern Frontier in Britain from Hadrian to Honorius: Literary and Epigraphic Sources*, Newcastle-upon-Tyne, n.d. [1971]
PSAS	*Proceedings of the Society of Antiquaries of Scotland*
TAASDN	*Transactions of the Architectural and Archaeological Society of Durham and Northumberland*
TCWAAS	*Transactions of the Cumberland and Westmorland Antiquarian and Archaeological Society*
TSSAHS	*Transactions of the South Shields Archaeological and Historical Society*

GENERAL WORKS

A. R. Birley, 'The Roman governors of Britain', *Epigraphische Studien*, 4 (1967), 163–202.

A. R. Birley, *The Ninth Pilgrimage of Hadrian's Wall, 7–12 September 1969*, Kendal, 1969.

E. Birley, *Research on Hadrian's Wall*, Kendal, 1961.

D. J. Breeze and B. Dobson, 'Hadrian's Wall: some problems', *Britannia*, 3 (1972), 182–208.

J. C. Bruce, *Handbook to the Roman Wall* (12th edn by I. A. Richmond), Newcastle-upon-Tyne, 1966.

R. G. Collingwood and I. A. Richmond, *The Archaeology of Roman Britain*, London, 1969.

C. M. Daniels, 'Problems of the Roman northern frontier', *Scottish Archaeological Forum*, 2 (1970), 91–101.

284

Select Bibliography

S. S. Frere, *Britannia* (2nd edn), London, 1974.

J. P. Gillam, 'The Frontier after Hadrian – a history of the problem', *AA*[5], 2 (1974), 1–15.

J. P. Gillam and J. C. Mann, 'The northern British frontier from Antoninus Pius to Caracalla', *AA*[4], 48 (1970), 1–44.

B. R. Hartley, 'Some problems of the military occupation of the north of England', *Northern History*, 1 (1966), 7–20.

B. R. Hartley, 'Roman York and the northern military command', *Soldier and Civilian in Roman Yorkshire* (ed. R. M. Butler), Leicester, 1971, 55–69.

B. R. Hartley, 'The Roman occupation of Scotland: the evidence of samian ware', *Britannia*, 3 (1972), 1–55.

M. G. Jarrett and J. C. Mann, 'Britain from Agricola to Gallienus', *Bonner Jahrbücher*, 170 (1970), 178–210.

J. C. Mann (ed.), *The Northern Frontier in Britain from Hadrian to Honorius: Literary and Epigraphic Sources*, Newcastle-upon-Tyne, n.d. [1971].

J. C. Mann, 'The northern frontier after A.D. 369', *Glasgow Archaeological Journal*, 3 (1974), 34–42.

Ordnance Survey, *Map of Hadrian's Wall* (2nd edn, 1972).

I. A. Richmond (ed.), *Roman and Native in Roman Britain*, Edinburgh, 1958.

CHAPTER 1   THE CONCEPT OF A FRONTIER

Roman imperialism in general (pp. 5ff.)

A. R. Birley, 'Roman Frontiers and Roman frontier policy: some reflections on Roman imperialism', *TAASDN*, n.s., 3 (1974), 13–25.

P. A. Brunt, Review of H. D. Meyer, *Die Aussenpolitik des Augustus und die Augusteische Dichtung*, *JRS*, 53 (1963), 170–76.

J. C. Mann, 'The frontiers of the Roman Principate', *Aufstieg und Niedergang der römischen Welt II Principat 1* (ed. H. Temporini), Berlin, 1974, 508–33; the quotation is from 509.

G. Webster, *The Roman Imperial Army*, London, 1969, chapter 2, 'The frontier systems'.

C. M. Wells, *The German Policy of Augustus*, Oxford, 1972, especially chapter 1, 'Augustus in the tradition of Roman imperialism'.

Julius Caesar in Britain (p. 10f.)

C. E. Stevens, 'Britain and the Lex Pompeia Licinia', *Latomus*, 12 (1953), 14–21.

J. Sabben-Clare, *Caesar and Roman Politics 60–50 B.C.*, Oxford, 1971; on the return in 54 B.C. and the possibility that Caesar heard of Julia's death in Britain see 119 and cf. 121.

Britain from Caesar to Claudius (p. 11)

C. E. Stevens, 'Britain between the invasions', *Aspects of Archaeology in Britain and Beyond* (ed. W. F. Grimes), London, 1951, 332–44.

Select Bibliography

Britain from Claudius to the Flavians (p. 13)

G. Webster, 'The military situations in Britain between A.D. 43 and 71', *Britannia*, 1 (1970), 179–97, especially figs 1 (180), 2 (185) and 3 (194), none of which are of linear dispositions.

Britain under Agricola (p. 14f.)

R. M. Ogilvie and I. A. Richmond (ed.), *Cornelii Taciti de Vita Agricolae*, Oxford, 1967.

Britain after Agricola (pp. 15ff.)

B. R. Hartley, 'The Roman occupation of Scotland: the evidence of samian ware', *Britannia*, 3 (1972), 4–15.

E. Birley, 'Britain after Agricola and the end of the Ninth Legion', *Roman Britain and the Roman Army*, Kendal, 1953, 20–30.

Domitian in Germany (p. 18f.)

H. Schönberger, 'The Roman frontier in Germany: an archaeological survey', *JRS*, 59 (1969), 144–97, especially 155–64. The quotation is from 160.

Tencteri and Hermunduri (p. 19)

Tacitus, *Histories*, 4, 64 (Tencteri); *Germania*, 41 (Hermunduri).

The Stanegate System (pp. 20ff.)

E. Birley, *Research on Hadrian's Wall*, Kendal, 1961, 132–50 is the most detailed description; for comments cf.

C. M. Daniels, *Scottish Archaeological Forum*, 2 (1970), 94 f.

Trajan in Germany (pp. 19f., 25)

H. Schönberger, 'The Roman frontier in Germany: an archaeological survey', *JRS*, 59 (1967), 164–7.

Legionary fortresses (p. 25f.)

RIB 330, 464, 665.

CHAPTER 2   THE BUILDING OF HADRIAN'S WALL

Hadrian (p. 28)

Scriptores Historiae Augustae, Hadrian.
Cassius Dio, 69.
ILS, 308.

Britain in 117 (pp. 28f.)

Scriptores Historiae Augustae, Hadrian, 5 (Mann 1).
Cornelius Fronto, p. 218 Naber (Loeb ed., ii 22, Mann 2).
H. Mattingly and E. A. Sydenham, *The Roman Imperial Coinage*, 577a (Mann 3).
E. Birley, 'The fate of the Ninth Legion', *Soldier and Civilian in Roman Yorkshire* (ed. R. M. Butler), Leicester, 1971, 71–80.
W. Eck, 'Zum Ende der *legio IX Hispana*', *Chiron*, 2 (1972), 459–62.

Hadrian in Britain (p. 29)

Scriptores Historiae Augustae, Hadrian, 10–11 (Mann 4–5).

Description of the Wall (pp. 29ff.)

See the articles listed in *Handbook*, and E. Birley, *Research on Hadrian's Wall*, Kendal, 1961. In addition note: D. Charlesworth, 'A re-examination of two turrets on Hadrian's Wall', *AA*[5], 1 (1973), 97–110.

V. A. Maxfield and R. Miket, 'The excavation of turret 33b (Coesike)', *AA*[4], 50 (1972), 145–78.

C. C. Woodfield, 'Six turrets on Hadrian's Wall', *AA*[4], 43 (1965), 87–200.

The Turf Wall (pp. 32f.)

F. G. Simpson and I. A. Richmond, 'The turf Wall of Hadrian, 1895–1935', *TCWAAS*[2], 35 (1935), 1–18.

D. Charlesworth, 'Hadrian's Wall, turret 51A (Piper Sike)', *TCWAAS*[2], 73 (1973), 67–78.

The Top of the Wall (pp. 36, 39)

R. L. Bellhouse, 'Roman sites on the Cumberland coast, 1967–68', *TCWAAS*[2], 68 (1969), 79–93.

J. D. Cowan and I. A. Richmond, 'The Rudge Cup', *AA*[4], 12 (1935), 310–42.

J. Heurgon, 'The Amiens Patera', *JRS*, 41 (1952), 22–4.

D. Charlesworth, 'Recent work on Hadrian's Wall, Cawfields', *AA*[4], 46 (1968), 73–4.

The Rhine and the Danube Frontiers (p. 37f.)

Tacitus, *Histories*, 4, 64; *Germania*, 41.

The Purpose of Hadrian's Wall (pp. 37ff.)

E. Birley, 'Hadrianic frontier policy', *Carnuntina*, 3 (1956), 25–33.

R. G. Collingwood, 'The purpose of the Roman Wall', *Vasculum*, 8 (1921).

D. J. Breeze and B. Dobson, 'Hadrian's Wall: some problems', *Britannia*, 3 (1972), 182–93.

The Use of Troops in Detachments (p. 40)

D. J. Breeze, 'The Roman fortlet at Barburgh Hill, Dumfriesshire', *Britannia*, 5 (1974), 145–7.

C. Bradford Welles, R. O. Fink and J. F. Gilliam, *The Excavations at Dura-Europos, Final Report V part I: The Parchments and Papyri*, New Haven, 1959, 100, 101.

Pliny, *Letters*, 10, 20.

Finds from milecastles and turrets (p. 40)

E. Birley, *Research on Hadrian's Wall*, Kendal, 1961, 271.

J. R. Dockerill, 'Pottery from the milecastles and turrets on Hadrian's Wall' (unpublished M.A. thesis), University of Durham, 1969, 394.

The Cumberland Coast (p. 40f.)

See R. L. Bellhouse's articles in *TCWAAS*[2] over the last twenty years, especially:

Select Bibliography

'Roman sites on the Cumberland coast, 1967–68', *TCWAAS²*, 69 (1969), 54–101.

'Roman sites on the Cumberland coast, 1968–69', *TCWAAS²*, 70 (1970), 9–47.

The South Bank of the Tyne (p. 42)

E. Birley, *Research on Hadrian's Wall*, Kendal, 1961, 157–9.

The Outpost Forts (p. 43)

RIB, 974, 995.

Transactions of the Dumfries and Galloway Natural History and Archaeological Society, 38 (1959–60), 143 f.

RIB, 2091.

F. G. Simpson, I. A. Richmond and J. K. St Joseph, 'The turf-wall milecastle at High House', *TCWAAS²*, 35 (1935), 220–9.

The New Forts on the Wall (pp. 43ff.)

D. J. Breeze and B. Dobson, 'Fort types on Hadrian's Wall', *AA⁴*, 47 (1969), 15–32.

B. Swinbank and J. E. H. Spaul, 'The spacing of the forts on Hadrian's Wall', *AA⁴*, 29 (1951), 221–38.

D. J. Breeze and B. Dobson, 'Hadrian's Wall: some problems', *Britannia*, 3 (1972), 190.

The Vallum (pp. 49ff.)

B. Heywood, 'The Vallum – its problems restated', *Britain and Rome* (ed. M. G. Jarrett and B. Dobson), Kendal, 1966, 85–94.

F. G. Simpson and I. A. Richmond, 'The Vallum at milecastles 51, Wall Bowers, and 50 TW, High House', *TCWAAS²*, 37 (1937), 157–77.

D. J. Breeze and B. Dobson, 'Hadrian's Wall: some problems', *Britannia*, 3 (1972), 191.

Sally-ports (p. 51f.)

Handbook, 26.

Frontinus, *Strategemata*, 2, 6.

Vegetius, *de re militari*, 3, 21.

The Building of Hadrian's Wall (pp. 53ff.)

C. E. Stevens, *The Building of Hadrian's Wall*, Kendal, 1966.

J. Hooley and D. J. Breeze, 'The building of Hadrian's Wall: a reconsideration', *AA⁴*, 46 (1968), 97–114.

D. J. Breeze and B. Dobson, 'Hadrian's Wall: some problems', *Britannia*, 3 (1972), 182–208.

B. Dobson and D. J. Breeze, *The Building of Hadrian's Wall* (3rd edn), Newcastle-upon-Tyne, 1973.

R. L. Bellhouse, 'Roman sites on the Cumberland coast 1967–68', *TCWAAS²*, 69 (1969), 93–101.

V. A. Maxfield and R. Miket, 'The excavation of turret 33b (Coesike)', *AA⁴*, 50 (1972), 158.

288

Select Bibliography

Hadrian's Other Frontiers (p. 54)

E. Birley, 'Hadrianic Frontier Policy', *Carnuntina*, 3 (1956), 25–33.
H. Schönberger, 'The Roman frontier in Germany: an archaeological survey',
   JRS, 59 (1969), 144–97.
D. Baatz, *Der Römische Limes*, Berlin, 1973.
J. Baradez, *Fossatum Africae*, Paris, 1949.

The Cost of Hadrian's Wall (pp. 72ff.)

Robert Rawlinson's figures are quoted in:
   J. C. Bruce, *The Roman Wall*, Newcastle-upon-Tyne, 1851, 94–5.
Hunter Davies, *A Walk Along the Wall*, London, 1974, 286 f.

CHAPTER 3   THE ANTONINE WALL

The Move North (pp. 79ff.)

Pausanias, *Description of Greece*, 8, 43 (= Mann 40).
Scriptores Historiae Augustae, Antoninus Pius, 5 (= Mann 39).
A. R. Birley, 'Roman frontiers and Roman frontier policy: some reflections on
   Roman Imperialism', *TAASDN*, n.s., 3 (1974), 17 f.
B. Swinbank, 'The activities of Lollius Urbicus as evidenced by inscriptions',
   TAASDN, 10 pt 4 (1953), 382–403.

The Abandonment of Hadrian's Wall (p. 82)

Cockmount Hill: *JRS*, 30 (1940), 132.
RIB 1460.
RIB 1330.
J. Leach and J. J. Wilkes, 'Excavations in the Roman fort at Housesteads,
   1961', *AA*[4], 40 (1962), 83–96.
M. G. Jarrett, 'The garrison of Maryport and the Roman army in Britain',
   Britain and Rome (ed. M. G. Jarrett and B. Dobson), Kendal, 1966, 34.
M. G. Jarrett and J. C. Mann, 'Britain from Agricola to Gallienus', *Bonner
   Jahrbücher*, 170 (1970), 191.

The Occupation of Scotland (pp. 83ff.)

G. Jobey, 'Notes on some population problems in the area between the two
   Roman Walls, I', *AA*[5], 2 (1974), 17–26.
K. A. Steer, 'John Horsley and the Antonine Wall', *AA*[4], 43 (1964), 1–21.
D. Baatz, *Kastell Hesselbach* (*Limesforschungen* 12), Berlin, 1973.
S. N. Miller (ed.), *The Roman Occupation of South-western Scotland*, Glasgow,
   1952.
D. J. Breeze, 'The Roman fortlet at Barburgh Mill, Dumfriesshire', *Britannia*,
   5 (1974), 130–62.
G. S. Maxwell, 'The Excavation of the Roman fort at Crawford, Lanarkshire',
   PSAS, 104 (1971–2), 147–200.

The Antonine Wall (pp. 85ff.)

G. S. Macdonald, *The Roman Wall in Scotland* (2nd edn), Oxford, 1934.

Select Bibliography

A. S. Robertson, *The Antonine Wall*, Glasgow, 1973.

I. A. Richmond, 'The Antonine frontier in Scotland', *JRS*, 26 (1936), 190–94.

K. A. Steer, 'The Antonine Wall 1934–1959', *JRS*, 50 (1960), 84–93.

K. A. Steer and E. A. Cormack, 'A new distance slab from the Antonine Wall', *PSAS*, 101 (1968–9), 127–9.

Temporary Camps (p. 88f.)

R. W. Feachem, 'Six Roman camps near the Antonine Wall', *PSAS*, 89 (1955–1956), 329–39.

G. S. Maxwell, 'The building of the Antonine Wall', *Actes du IXᵉ Congrès international d'études sur les frontières Romaines*, Bucharest, 1974, 327–32.

K. A. Steer, 'The nature and purpose of the expansions on the Antonine Wall', *PSAS*, 90 (1956–7), 161–9.

The Forts on the Wall (pp. 89ff.)

A. S. Robertson, *An Antonine Fort, Golden Hill, Duntocher*, Glasgow, 1957.

D. J. Breeze, *The Roman Fort at Bearsden, 1973 Excavations. An Interim Report*, Edinburgh, 1974.

D. J. Breeze, *The Antonine Wall*, Edinburgh, 1974, for plans of Rough Castle and Castlecary.

Fife (p. 96)

G. S. Maxwell, 'Excavations at Drumcarrow, Fife: an Iron Age unenclosed settlement', *PSAS*, 100 (1967–8), 100–8.

The Building of the Antonine Wall (pp. 98ff.)

G. S. Maxwell, 'The Building of the Antonine Wall', *Actes du IXᵉ Congrès international d'études sur les frontières Romaines*, Bucharest, 1974, 327–32.

D. J. Breeze and B. Dobson, 'The development of the northern frontier in Britain from Hadrian to Caracalla', *Actes du IXᵉ Congrès international d'études sur les frontières Romaines*, Bucharest, 1964, 321–6.

J. P. Gillam, 'Possible changes in plan in the course of the construction of the Antonine Wall', *Scottish Archaeological Forum*, 7 (1976).

Comparison of the Two Walls (pp. 85ff. *passim*)

D. J. Breeze and B. Dobson, 'The development of the mural frontier in Britain from Hadrian to Caracalla', *PSAS*, 102 (1969–70), 109–21.

CHAPTER 4   THE TWO WALLS

The 'Brigantian' Revolt (pp. 105ff.)

F. Haverfield, 'Discovery of Roman inscriptions etc. at Newcastle', *AA²*, 25 (1904), 142–4.

G. Jobey, in *Discovery and Excavation in Scotland*, 1970, 21.

W. Manning, 'Iron work hoards in Iron Age and Roman Britain', *Britannia*, 3 (1972), 243–6.

J. P. Gillam and J. C. Mann, 'The northern British frontier from Antoninus Pius to Caracalla', *AA⁴*, 48 (1970), 10–12.

M. Todd, 'Romano-British mintages of Antoninus Pius', *Numismatic Chronicle* (1966), 147–53.

A. S. Robertson, 'Romano-British coin hoards', in *Coins and the Archaeologist* (ed. J. Casey and R. Reece), *British Archaeological Reports*, 4 (1974), 29–31. The large number of coin hoards deposited in Britain between 140 and 170 provide corroborative evidence for the unsettled conditions prevailing in those years, but not support for the 'Brigantian revolt'.

Britain on the accession of Marcus (p. 109)

Scriptores Historiae Augustae, Marcus Aurelius, 8.

For comparison see: *Scriptores Historiae Augustae, Hadrian*, 5; *Antoninus Pius*, 5; Cassius Dio, 72, 8.

Governors of Britain (p. 109f.)

A. R. Birley, 'The Roman governors of Britain', *Epigraphische Studien*, 4 (1967), 71–7.

E. Birley, 'Senators in the emperors' service', *Proceedings of the British Academy*, 39 (1953), 197–214.

Trouble in the 170s and 180s (p. 110f.)

Scriptores Historiae Augustae, Marcus Aurelius, 22 (= Mann 78).

Cassius Dio, 71, 16 (= Mann 79).

Cassius Dio, 72, 8 (= Mann 83).

Scriptores Historiae Augustae, Pertinax, 3; Cassius Dio, 73, 4.

The Events of the 190s and 200s (p. 111f.)

Cassius Dio, 75, 5, 4; 67, 11; 76, 12, 1; 76, 13, 1; Herodian, 3, 14 (= Mann 97, 112, 113, 118, 123, 128–31, 133).

Structural evidence (pp. 112ff.)

J. P. Gillam and J. C. Mann, 'The northern British frontier from Antoninus Pius to Caracalla', *AA*[4], 48 (1970), 1–44.

M. G. Jarrett and J. C. Mann, 'Britain from Agricola to Gallienus', *Bonner Jahrbücher*, 170 (1970), 185–205.

K. A. Steer, 'John Horsley and the Antonine Wall', *AA*[4], 43 (1964), 21–40.

K. A. Steer, 'Excavations at Mumrills Roman fort', *PSAS*, 94 (1960–61), 97–9.

S. N. Miller, *The Roman Fort at Balmuildy*, Glasgow, 1922, 54 f.

D. J. Breeze, *The Roman Fort at Bearsden, 1973 Excavations: An Interim Report*, Edinburgh, 1974, 12–19.

I. A. Richmond, 'Excavations at the Roman fort of Newstead, 1947', *PSAS*, 84 (1949–50), 14.

G. S. Maxwell, 'Excavations at the Roman fort at Crawford, Lanarkshire', *PSAS*, 104 (1971–2), 147–80.

Pottery (p. 114f.)

B. R. Hartley, 'The Roman occupation of Scotland: the evidence of samian ware', *Britannia*, 3 (1972), 15–42.

J. P. Gillam, 'Sources of pottery on northern military sites', *Current Research in Romano-British Coarse Pottery* (ed. A. Detsicas), London, 1973, 55–62.

Select Bibliography

J. P. Gillam and J. C. Mann, 'The northern British frontier from Antoninus Pius to Caracalla', *AA*[4], 48 (1970), 1–44.

Numismatic evidence (p. 115f.)

A. S. Robertson, 'Roman coins found in Scotland, 1961–70', *PSAS*, 103 (1970–71), 133.

A. S. Robertson, 'A hoard of Roman silver coins from Briglands, Rumbling Bridge, Kinross-shire', *PSAS*, 90 (1956–7), 241–6.

The Second Occupation of the Antonine Wall (pp. 120ff.)

D. J. Breeze, 'The Roman fortlet at Barburgh Mill, Dumfriesshire', *Britannia*, 5 (1974), 130–62.

D. J. Breeze, *The Roman Fort at Bearsden, 1973 Excavations: An Interim Report*, Edinburgh, 1974, 12 f.

S. N. Miller, *The Roman Fort at Old Kilpatrick*, Glasgow, 1928, 58.

S. N. Miller, *The Roman Fort at Balmuildy*, Glasgow, 1922, 106–8.

Castlecary (p. 122f.)

B. R. Hartley, 'The Roman occupation of Scotland: the evidence of samian ware', *Britannia*, 3 (1972), 28, fig. 2A.

RIB 2138: M. G. Jarrett and J. C. Mann, 'Britain from Agricola to Gallienus', *Bonner Jahrbücher*, 170 (1970), 194.

The Abandonment of the Antonine Wall (pp. 122ff.)

J. P. Gillam, 'Calpurnius Agricola and the northern frontier', *TAASDN*, 10 pt 4 (1953), 359–75.

J. P. Gillam, 'The Frontier after Hadrian – a history of the problem', *AA*[5], 2 (1974), 1–12.

D. J. Breeze, 'The abandonment of the Antonine Wall: its date and implications', *Scottish Archaeological Forum*, 7 (1976).

The Rebuilding of the Turf Wall (p. 125)

I. A. Richmond and J. P. Gillam, 'Milecastle 79 (Solway)', *TCWAAS*[2], 52 (1952), 17–40.

G. Simpson, 'The close of period 1A on Hadrian's Wall and some Gaulish potters', *AA*[4], 49 (1971), 109–18.

Rebuilding in the Pennines (p. 126)

J. P. Gillam and J. C. Mann, 'The northern British frontier from Antoninus Pius to Caracalla', *AA*[4], 48 (1970), 25.

The Invasion of the Early 180s (pp. 128ff.)

D. J. Breeze and B. Dobson, 'Hadrian's Wall: some problems', *Britannia*, 3 (1972), 200–6.

RIB 2034 (= Mann 82) from Kirksteads.

RIB 1234 (= Mann 99) from Risingham.

RIB 1465 (= Mann 170) from Chesters.

Cassius Dio, 75, 5, 4 (= Mann 97)

RIB, 1463 and 1464 (= Mann 85 and 86) from Chesters record work under Ulpius Marcellus.

The Modifications to Hadrian's Wall in the 180s (pp. 130ff.)

V. A. Maxfield and R. Miket, 'The excavation of turret 33b (Coesike)', *AA*⁴, 50 (1972), 158 f.

D. J. Breeze and B. Dobson, 'Hadrian's Wall: some problems', *Britannia*, 3 (1972), 203, note 121.

The Severan Period (pp. 132ff.)

A. R. Birley, *Septimius Severus*, London, 1971.

A. R. Birley, 'Virius Lupus', *AA*⁴, 50 (1973), 179–89.

M. G. Jarrett and J. C. Mann, 'Britain from Agricola to Gallienus', *Bonner Jahrbücher*, 170 (1970), 195–205.

J. P. Gillam and J. C. Mann, 'The northern British frontier from Antoninus Pius to Caracalla', *AA*⁴, 48 (1970), 39–44.

J. K. St Joseph, 'Air Reconnaissance in Britain, 1965–1968', *JRS*, 59 (1969), 114–19.

J. K. St Joseph, 'Air Reconnaissance in Britain, 1969–1972', *JRS*, 63 (1973), 230–33.

R. P. Wright, 'Carpow and Caracalla', *Britannia*, 5 (1974), 289–92.

The Third Century Reorganization (pp. 137ff.)

I. A. Richmond, 'The Romans in Redesdale', *Northumberland County History*, 15, 82–106.

K. A. Steer, 'The Severan reorganisation', *Roman and Native in North Britain* (ed. I. A. Richmond), Edinburgh, 1961, 91–111.

I. A. Richmond and O. G. S. Crawford, 'The British section of the Ravenna Cosmography', *Archaeologia*, 93 (1949), 15, 19.

The Development of the Frontier (pp. 143ff.)

D. J. Breeze and B. Dobson, 'The development of the mural frontier in Britain from Hadrian to Caracalla', *PSAS*, 102 (1969–70), 109–21.

D. J. Breeze and B. Dobson, 'The development of the northern frontier in Britain from Hadrian to Caracalla', *Actes du IXᵉ Congrès international d'études sur les frontières Romaines*, Bucharest, 1974, 321–6.

CHAPTER 5   THE ARMY OF THE WALL

B. Dobson and D. J. Breeze, *The Army of Hadrian's Wall*, Newcastle-upon-Tyne, 1973.

G. Webster, *The Roman Imperial Army*, London, 1969.

H. M. D. Parker, *The Roman Legions*, Oxford, 1928.

G. L. Cheesman, *The Auxilia of the Roman Imperial Army*, Oxford, 1914.

Recruiting of Legions (p. 148f.)

B. Dobson and J. C. Mann, 'The Roman army in Britain and Britons in the Roman army', *Britannia* 4, (1973), 191–205.

Select Bibliography

Officers of Legion (p. 149f.)

E. Birley, 'Senators in the emperors' service', *Proceedings of the British Academy*, 39 (1954), 197–214.

E. Birley, 'The equestrian officers of the Roman army', *Roman Britain and the Roman Army*, Kendal, 1953, 133–53.

E. Birley, 'The origins of legionary centurions', *Roman Britain and the Roman Army*, Kendal, 1953, 104–24.

E. Birley, 'Promotions and transfers in the Roman army II. The centurionate', *Carnuntum-Jahrbuch*, 1963/4 (1965), 21–33.

B. Dobson, 'The significance of the centurion and "primipilaris" in the Roman army and administration', *Aufstieg und Niedergang der römischen Welt II Principat 1* (ed. H. Temporini), Berlin, 1974, 393–434.

Trajan's Column (p. 151f.)

There is still no satisfactory publication of this important monument. L. Rossi, *Trajan's Column and the Dacian Wars*, London, 1971, is inadequate and badly illustrated. For a discussion of some important scenes see:

I. A. Richmond, 'Trajan's army on Trajan's Column,' *Papers of the British School at Rome*, 13 (1935), 1–40.

Roman Army Organization (pp. 153ff.)

D. J. Breeze and B. Dobson, 'Fort types on Hadrian's Wall', *AA*[4], 47 (1969), 15–32.

R. W. Davies, 'A note on a recently discovered inscription from Carrawburgh', *Epigraphische Studien*, 4 (1967), 108–11.

I. A. Richmond, 'Roman Britain and Roman military antiquities', *Proceedings of the British Academy*, 41 (1955), 297–315.

Sources for Unit Size (p. 153f.)

Hyginus, *liber de munitionibus castrorum*.

Arrian, *Tactica*, 18.

R. O. Fink, *Roman Military Records on Papyri*, New Haven, 1971.

Cohortes Equitatae (p. 153f.)

R. W. Davies, 'Cohortes equitatae', *Historia*, 20 (1971), 751–63.

Organization of First Cohort of Legion (p. 154)

D. J. Breeze, 'The organization of the legion: the first cohort and the *equites legionis*', *JRS*, 59 (1969), 50–55.

Milliary Units (pp. 154ff.)

E. Birley, '*Alae* and *cohortes milliariae*', *Corolla Memoriae Erich Swoboda Dedicata*, Graz, 1966, 54–67.

Numeri (p. 157)

H. Callies, 'Die fremden Truppen im römischen Heer des Prinzipats und die sogenannten nationalen Numeri. Beitrage zur Geschichte des römischen Heeres', *Bericht der Romisch-Germanischen Kommission 1964*, 45 (1965), 130–227.

J. C. Mann, 'A note on the numeri', *Hermes*, 82 (1954), 501–6.

Select Bibliography

The Roman Fort (pp. 157ff.)

R. G. Collingwood and I. A. Richmond, *The Archaeology of Roman Britain*, London, 1969.

G. Webster, *The Roman Imperial Army*, London, 1969, 166–220.

V. E. Nash-Williams, *The Roman Frontier in Wales* (2nd edn revised by M. G. Jarrett), Cardiff, 1969.

Headquarters Building (pp. 160ff.)

H. von Petrikovits, 'Die Spezialgebäude römischer Legionslager', *Legio VII Gemina*, Leon, 1970, 238.

Granary Capacity (p. 162)

F. Haverfield and R. G. Collingwood, 'The provisioning of Roman forts', *TCAAWS*[2], 20 (1920), 127–42.

W. Bulmer, 'The provisioning of Roman forts: a re-appraisal of ration storage', *AA*[4], 47 (1969), 7–13.

G. E. Rickman, *Roman Granaries and Store Buildings*, Cambridge, 1971.

Stables (p. 164)

D. J. Breeze and B. Dobson, 'Fort types on Hadrian's Wall', *AA*[4], 47 (1969), 15–32.

D. J. Breeze and B. Dobson, 'Fort types as a guide to garrisons: a reconsideration', *Roman Frontier Studies 1969* (ed. E. Birley, B. Dobson, M. G. Jarrett), Cardiff, 1964, 13–19.

I. A. Richmond, 'Roman Britain and Roman Military Antiquities', *Proceedings of the British Academy*, 41 (1955), 297–315.

CHAPTER 6   LIFE ON THE WALL

G. R. Watson, *The Roman Soldier*, London, 1969.

R. W. Davies, 'The daily life of the Roman soldier under the Principate', *Aufstieg und Niedergang der römischen Welt II Principat 1* (ed. H. Temporini), Berlin, 1974, 299–338.

Recruitment (p. 170)

B. Dobson and J. C. Mann, 'The Roman army in Britain and Britons in the Roman army', *Britannia*, 4 (1973), 191–205.

Training (p. 170f.)

R. W. Davies, 'Joining the Roman army', *Bonner Jahrbücher*, 169 (1969), 208–32.

R. W. Davies, 'Fronto, Hadrian and the Roman army', *Latomus* 27, part 1 (1968), 75–95.

R. W. Davies, 'The training-grounds of the Roman cavalry', *Archaeological Journal*, 125 (1968), 73–100.

R. W. Davies, 'Roman Wales and Roman military practice-camps', *Archaeologia Cambrensis*, 117 (1968), 103–20.

Select Bibliography

Hadrian's speech (p. 172)

CIL VIII 2532 = 18042 = *ILS* 2487.

Swimming of Danube (p. 172)

ILS 2558.

Pay (pp. 172ff.)

G. R. Watson, *The Roman Soldier*, London, 1969, 99 ff. M. Speidel, 'The pay of the auxilia', *JRS*, 63 (1973), 141–7, suggests five-sixths or two-thirds of legionary pay for the auxiliary infantrymen, but there are unresolved difficulties in this hypothesis, cf. G. R. Watson. 'Transfers to the *alae* from the legions', *Vestigia* 17, 540–2.

Letters from soldiers (p. 172)

There is no convenient collection, as R. O. Fink, *Roman Military Records on Papyri*, New Haven, 1971, gives only official documents. G. R. Watson, *The Roman Soldier*, London, 1969, and R. W. Davies quote them extensively, and the former gives a hand-list of military documents, including letters.

Promotion (pp. 174ff.)

D. J. Breeze, 'Pay grades and ranks below the centurionate', *JRS*, 61 (1971), 130–35.

D. J. Breeze, 'The organization of the career structure of the *immunes* and *principales* of the Roman army', *Bonner Jahrbücher*, 174 (1974), 245–92.

J. F. Gilliam, 'The appointment of auxiliary centurions', *Transactions of the American Philological Associations*, 88 (1958), 155–68.

Three decurions to a turma (p. 176)

Polybius, VI, 25, 1–2.

Documentation (pp. 176ff.)

R. O. Fink, *Roman Military Records on Papyri*, New Haven, 1971.

G. R. Watson, 'Documentation in the Roman army', *Aufstieg und Niedergang der römischen Welt II Principat* 1 (ed. H. Temporini), Berlin, 1974, 493–507.

Trajan (p. 176f.)

The desire, Pliny, *Letters*, 10, 20; the reality, R. O. Fink, *Roman Military Records on Papyri*, New Haven, 1971, no. 63.

Arms and armour (pp. 179ff.)

H. Russell Robinson, *The Armour of Imperial Rome*, London, 1975.

On mailed cavalry J. W. Eadie, 'The development of Roman mailed cavalry', *JRS*, 57 (1967), 161–73 dates its development too late.

Sports helmets (p. 181)

F. Kiechle, 'Die "Taktik" des Flavius Arrianus', *Bericht der Römisch-Germanischen Kommission 1964*, 45 (1965), 87–129.

296

Newstead horses (p. 181)

J. Curle, *A Roman Frontier Post and its People*, Glasgow, 1911, 362–71 (by J. C. Ewart).

Artillery (p. 181f.)

E. W. Marsden, *Greek and Roman Artillery, Historical Development*, Oxford, 1969, 191.

Religion (pp. 183ff.)

See notes to Appendix 3, pp. 259ff.

Survival (p. 186)

A. R. Burn, 'Hic breve vivitur', *Past and Present*, 4 (1953), 2–31.

Food (p. 186)

R. W. Davies, 'The Roman military diet', *Britannia*, 2 (1971), 122–42.

Clothing (p. 186)

E. Sander, 'Die Kleidung des römischen Soldaten', *Historia*, 12 (1963), 144–66.

Military medical service (p. 187)

R. W. Davies, 'The Roman military medical service', *Saalburger Jahrbuch*, 27 (1970), 84–104.

R. W. Davies, 'The medici of the Roman armed forces', *Epigraphische Studien*, 8 (1969), 83–99.

Missio causaria (p. 187f.)

G. R. Watson, *The Roman Soldier*, London, 1969, 123 f.

Death (p. 188f.)

Royal Commission on Historical Monuments (England), *Eboracum, Roman York*, London, 1962.

L. P. Wenham, *The Romano-British Cemetery at Trentholme Drive, York*, London, 1968.

Diplomas (p. 188f.)

G. Alföldy, 'Zur Beurteilung der Militärdiplome der Auxiliarsoldaten', *Historia*, 17 (1968), 215–27.

The civil settlements (pp. 191ff.)

P. Salway, *The Frontier People of Roman Britain*, Cambridge, 1965.

R. E. Birley, *Civilians of the Roman Frontier*, Newcastle-upon-Tyne, 1973.

The commanding officers (pp. 194ff.)

E. Birley, 'The equestrian officers of the Roman army', *Roman Britain and the Roman Army*, Kendal, 1953.

E. Birley, '*Alae* and *cohortes milliariae*', *Corolla Memoriae Erich Swoboda Dedicata*, Graz, 1966, 54–67.

Select Bibliography

The late Roman army (pp. 196ff.)

A. H. M. Jones, *The Decline of the Ancient World*, London, 1966.

The local population (pp. 199ff.)

G. Jobey, 'Homesteads and settlements of the frontier area', *Rural Settlement in Roman Britain* (ed. C. Thomas), London, 1966, 1–14, with detailed bibliography.

CHAPTER 7 THE THIRD AND FOURTH CENTURIES

Modifications to forts (p. 202f.)

M. G. Jarrett and J. C. Mann, 'Britain from Agricola to Gallienus', *Bonner Jahrbücher*, 170 (1970), 202–10.

Army reforms (p. 203f.)

E. Birley, 'Septimius Severus and the Roman army', *Epigraphische Studien*, 8 (1969), 63–82.

R. E. Smith, 'The army reforms of Septimius Severus', *Historia*, 21 (1972), 481–500.

Soldiers' wives (p. 203f.)

Scriptores Historiae Augustae, Severus Alexander, 58, 4–5.

R. Macmullen, *Soldier and Civilian in the Later Roman Empire*, Cambridge (Mass.), 1963, 13.

A. H. M. Jones, *The Later Roman Empire*, Oxford, 1964, 649 f.

R. P. Wright, 'A Roman altar from Westerwood on the Antonine Wall', *PSAS*, 100 (1967–8), 192 f.

Native and civil settlements in the third century (pp. 204ff.)

P. Salway, *The Frontier People of Roman Britain*, Cambridge, 1965, 192–7.

G. Jobey, 'Homesteads and settlements of the frontier area', *Rural Settlement in Roman Britain* (ed. C. Thomas), London, 1966, 6–13.

I. A. Richmond, *Roman Art and Archaeology*, London, 1969, 25 (Walldürn inscription).

I. A. Richmond and K. A. Steer, 'Castellum Veluniate and civilians on a Roman frontier', *PSAS*, 90 (1956–7), 1–6.

R. E. Birley, *Vindolanda*, Newcastle-upon-Tyne, 1973.

E. Birley, 'Hadrian's Wall and its neighbourhood', *Studien zu den Militär- grenzen Roms*, Berlin, 1967, 11–13 (the Carvetii).

The withdrawal of army units (p. 207)

J. C. Mann, 'The northern frontier after A.D. 369', *Glasgow Archaeological Journal*, 3 (1974), 37–40.

Notitia Dignitatum Occ. XL, 51–3.

The later third century (pp. 207ff.)

J. P. Gillam, R. M. Harrison and T. G. Newman, 'Interim Report on Excavations at the Roman Fort of Rudchester 1972', *AA⁵*, 1 (1973), 82.

298

J. P. Gillam, 'The Frontier after Hadrian – a history of the problem', *AA*[5], 2 (1974), 12–15.

D. J. Breeze, 'Excavations at South Shields, 1966 and 1967', *TSSAHS*, 2 pt 5 (1970). 42–5.

J. P. Gillam, 'Excavations at Halton Chesters, 1961', *University of Durham Gazette*, n.s., 9, no. 2.

I. A. Richmond, 'Excavations on Hadrian's Wall in the Birdoswald–Pike Hill Sector, I Birdoswald Fort'. *TCWAAS*[2], 30 (1930), 171 f.

Constantius in Britain (pp. 209ff.)

J. J. Wilkes, 'Early fourth century rebuilding in Hadrian's Wall forts', *Britain and Rome* (ed. M. G. Jarrett and B. Dobson), Kendal, 1966, 114–38.

J. J. Wilkes, 'Excavations at Housesteads fort 1960', *AA*[4], 39 (1961), 279–300.

E. Birley, I. A. Richmond and J. A. Stanfield, 'Excavations at Chesterholm–Vindolanda: Third Report', *AA*[4], 13 (1936), 221–9.

I. A. Richmond, *The Roman Fort at South Shields: A Guide*, South Shields, 1953, 7.

D. J. Breeze, 'Excavations at the Roman fort of Carrawburgh, 1967–1969', *AA*[4], 50 (1972), 96–115.

D. J. Breeze and B. Dobson, 'Hadrian's Wall: some problems', *Britannia*, 3 (1972), 200–206.

F. G. Simpson and I. A. Richmond, 'Bankshead milecastle, 52', *TCWAAS*[2], 35 (1935), 247–56.

I. A. Richmond, 'The Romans in Redesdale', *Northumberland County History* 15, 106–12.

The campaigns against the Picts (pp. 210, 214f.)

Pan. Constantio Caes. = *Pan. Lat. Vet.* VIII (V) 11, 4 (= Mann 185).

Pan. Constantino Aug. = *Pan. Lat. Vet.* VI (VII) 7, 1–2 (= Mann 188).

Anonymus Valesianus, 2, 4 (= Mann 189).

Army reforms (p. 215f.)

A. H. M. Jones, *The Later Roman Empire*, Oxford, 1964, 607–16 *passim*.

The Picts (pp. 219ff.)

F. Wainwright, 'The Picts and the problem', *The Problem of the Picts* (ed. F. Wainwright), Edinburgh, 1955, 1–53.

J. C. Mann, 'The northern frontier after A.D. 369', *Glasgow Archaeological Journal*, 3 (1974), 40–42.

Ammianus, 20, 1, 1; 28, 3, 8; 26, 4, 5; 27, 8 (= Mann 193–7).

Theodosius and the rebuilding of the late fourth century (pp. 221ff.)

For individual sites see notes to 'The later third century', p. 298f.

I. A. Richmond, 'Roman and native in the fourth century A.D. and after', *Roman and Native in North Britain* (ed. I. A. Richmond), Edinburgh, 1958, 112–30.

J. C. Mann, 'The northern frontier after A.D. 369', *Glasgow Archaeological Journal*, 3 (1974), 34–42.

Select Bibliography

H. von Petrikovits, 'Fortifications in the north-western Roman Empire from the third to the fifth century A.D.,' *JRS*, 61 (1971), 197.

RIB, 1672, 1673, 1843, 1844, 1962 (*civitates*).

Blocking of fort gates (p. 225f.)

D. J. Breeze and B. Dobson, 'Hadrian's Wall: some problems', *Britannia*, 3 (1972), 193–7.

Vici after 369 (p. 226f.)

R. E. Birley, *Civilians on the Roman Frontier*, Newcastle-upon-Tyne, 1973.

The late fourth century (pp. 226ff.)

I. A. Richmond, 'The Romans in Redesdale', *Northumberland County History* 15, 112–16.

J. C. Mann, 'The northern frontier after A.D. 369', *Glasgow Archaeological Journal*, 3 (1974), 34–42.

L. Alcock, *Arthur's Britain*, London, 1971.

J. Morris, *The Age of Arthur*, London, 1973.

J. P. C. Kent, 'Coin evidence and the evacuation of Hadrian's Wall', *TCWAAS*², 51 (1951), 4–15.

APPENDIX 1   ROMAN EMPERORS AND GOVERNORS OF BRITAIN

A. R. Birley, 'The Roman governors of Britain', *Epigraphische Studien*, 4 (1967), 163–202.

APPENDIX 2   THE REGIMENTS OF HADRIAN'S WALL

E. Birley, 'The Beaumont inscription, the Notitia Dignitatum and the garrison of Hadrian's Wall', *TCWAAS*², 39 (1939), 190–226.

M. G. Jarrett, 'The garrison of Maryport and the Roman army in Britain', *Britain and Rome* (ed. M. G. Jarrett and B. Dobson), Kendal, n.d. [1966].

APPENDIX 3   THE GODS WORSHIPPED ON THE WALL

C. M. Daniels, *Mithras and his Temples on the Wall* (2nd edn), Newcastle-upon-Tyne, 1967.

B. Dobson, 'Patterns of religious dedications in the north', *Proceedings of the Roman Impact on the North Conference*, in press.

A. von Domaszewski, 'Die Religion des romischen Heeres', *Westdeutsche Zeitschrift für Geschichte und Kunst*, 14 (1895), 1–121.

E. and J. R. Harris, *The Oriental Cults in Roman Britain*, Leiden, 1965.

M. J. T. Lewis, *Temples in Roman Britain*, Cambridge, 1966.

I. A. Richmond, 'Roman legionaries at Corbridge, their supply-base, temples and cults', *AA*⁴, 21 (1943), 127–224.

A. Ross, *Pagan Celtic Britain*, London, 1967.

Official military calendar (p. 259f.)

R. O. Fink, *Roman Military Records on Papyri*, New Haven, 1971, no. 117; the major study is R. O. Fink, A. S. Hoey and W. F. Snyder, 'The *Feriale Duranum*', *Yale Classical Studies*, 7 (1940), 1–222.

References to individual inscriptions (pp. 260–69)

These may be traced in *RIB* under the site named. Detailed references appear in B. Dobson, 'Patterns of religious dedications in the north', *Proceedings of the Roman Impact on the North Conference*, in press. Inscriptions not in *RIB* are identified.

Juno at Corbridge (p. 260)

I. A. Richmond, 'Roman legionaries at Corbridge, their supply-base, temples and cults', *AA*⁴, 21 (1943), 156–8.

Minerva at Corbridge (p. 260)

I. A. Richmond, 'Roman legionaries at Corbridge, their supply-base, temples and cults', *AA*⁴, 21 (1943), 154–6.

Roma at Corbridge (p. 261)

I. A. Richmond, 'Roman legionaries at Corbridge, their supply-base, temples and cults', *AA*⁴, 21 (1943), 173–6.

Mercury (p. 262)

Caesar, *de bello Gallico*, 6, 17.

Venus at High Rochester (p. 263)

A. Ross, *Pagan Celtic Britain*, London, 1967, 207 identifies the sculpture simply as a trio of nymph goddesses.

Vetris (p. 263)

To the examples in *RIB* add *Britannia*, 4 (1973), 329, n. 11, 12 (Chesterholm).

Mogons (p. 263)

To the examples in *RIB* add *Britannia*, 4 (1973), 329, n. 10 (Chesterholm).

Maponus (p. 264f.)

To the examples in *RIB* add *Britannia*, 2 (1971), 291, n. 12 (*lunula*, Chesterholm). Birrens figure, *JRS*, 58 (1968), 209, n. 28.

Matres (p. 265)

To the examples in *RIB* add *Britannia*, 1 (1970), 309, n. 16.

Sucabus (p. 265)

Britannia, 2 (1971), 292, n. 14.

Severed head (p. 265)

A. Ross, *Pagan Celtic Britain*, London, 1967, 61–126.
Trajans' Column, XXIV (58, 60), CXIII (303).

301

Select Bibliography

Mars Alator (p. 266)

Ephemeris Epigraphica, VII, 399.

IOM Dolichenus at Corbridge (p. 266)

I. A. Richmond, 'Roman legionaries at Corbridge, their supply-base, temples and cults', *AA*⁴, 21 (1943), 179–96.

Temples at Corbridge (p. 268f.)

I. A. Richmond, 'Roman legionaries at Corbridge, their supply-base, temples and cults', *AA*⁴, 21 (1943), 136–46. Temples IV and V did not exist, III is doubtful as a temple.

Christianity (p. 269f.)

A. H. M. Jones, *The Later Roman Empire*, Oxford, 1964, chapter 23.

G. R. Watson, 'Christianity in the Roman army in Britain', *Christianity in Britain 300–700* (ed. M. W. Barley and R. P. C. Hanson), Leicester, 1968, 51–4.

APPENDIX 4   THE ROMAN NAMES OF THE FORTS ON HADRIAN'S WALL

J. D. Cowan and I. A. Richmond, 'The Rudge Cup', *AA*⁴, 12 (1935), 310–42.

J. Heurgon, 'The Amiens Patera', *JRS*, 41 (1951), 22–4.

A. L. F. Rivet, 'The British section of the Antonine Itinerary', *Britannia*, 1 (1970), 34–82.

I. A. Richmond and O. G. S. Crawford, 'The British section of the Ravenna Cosmography', *Archaeologia*, 93 (1949), 1–50.

It was a suggestion by Mr Mark Hassall that Banna ought to be Birdoswald and Uxellodunum Stanwix that sparked off the reconsideration presented here. The suggestion that there was an omission in the *Notitia* of the name Banna and the garrison of Castlesteads is his, and the idea that Petriana is an error derived from the name of the unit. He however prefers to suppose that Axelodunum is the same as Uxellodunum, the name having become misplaced through the confusion over Petrianis.

Index

Aballava: *see* Burgh-by-Sands
actarius, 175, 176
aedes in headquarters buildings, 161, 184–5, 230, 261
Aesica: *see* Great Chesters
Aetern, king of Votadini, 227–8
Africa:
  frontier in, 29, 54
  Hadrian's visit to, 172
  recruitment from, 151–2, 181, 257
Agricola, Sex. Calpurnius, governor of Britain, 109, 110, 118, 121, 124, 239
Agricola, Cn. Iulius, governor of Britain, 13, 14–17, 20, 82, 233, 238
ala I Asturum, 130, 140, 141, 243, 247, 249
ala II Asturum, 130, 140, 141, 243, 250
ala I Herculea, 215
ala Petriana, 48, 140, 182, 196, 245, 249, 255, 274, 275
ala Sabiniana, 48, 140, 243, 247, 250
ala I Tungrorum, 94, 97
alae, 20, 151
  on Antonine Wall, 94, 95, 97, 122
  on Hadrian's Wall, 47–8, 139–141, 249
  organization, 153–6
  pay, 172–3
  recruitment and training, 171–2
  standard, 185

See also cavalry; commanding officers; decurion; *turma*
Alaisiagae, goddesses, 185, 257
Alamanni, tribe, 217, 221, 227
Alauna: *see* Maryport
Albinus, D. Clodius, governor of Britain, 111, 119, 130, 132, 217, 239
Aldborough, capital of Brigantes, 207, Fig. 45
Allectus, usurper in Britain, 209, 241
Allolee, unfinished ditch at, 31
Ambleside, fort, 126, 217, 276, Fig. 45
Amiens Skillet, 36, 39, 271–5, 277–278
Ammianus Marcellinus, historian, 220
Annwn, king of Galloway, 227
Antenociticus, god, 130, 259–61, 263, 267, 268, 281, Fig. 44, Pls. 26–7
Antonine Itinerary, 142, 257, 271, 272, 276–7
Antonine Wall, 79–147 *passim*, 234
  abandonment (*c.* A.D. 158), 112–114, 120–22
  abandonment (*c.* A.D. 163), 115–116, 122–4
  beacon platforms, 94, Fig. 20
  berm, 86, 87, Fig. 18
  building of, 85–104
  distance slabs, 88
  ditch, 86, 87, Fig. 18
  fortlets, 92, 94, 98–9, Figs. 16, 20

Index

Index

Index

Index

Index

Index

Index

Raeti gaesati: *see* vexillatio Raetorum gaesatorum
Raetia, province, 54
    units raised in, 256, 258
Ratis, god, 265
Ravenglass, fort, 207, 276, Fig. 45
Ravenna Cosmography, 138, 142, 146, 263, 271, 272, 276–8
Rawlinson, R., 72, 74
Reculver, fort, 253
Red Rock fault, 30, 33, 89
religion, 183–5, 194, 259–70
Rhine:
    as a frontier, 8, 14, 18, 19, 29, 37
    wars on, 12, 16
Ribchester, fort, 110, 126, 207, 250, Fig. 45
Ricagambeda, goddess, 265
Richmond, Sir Ian, 273
Risingham, fort, Fig. 45
    garrison, 140, 248, 251, 254, 257, 258
    history: under Marcus, 127; under Commodus, 128–9; in third century, 133, 135, 137, 140–42, 146, 203; c. A.D. 300, 212, 214; in fourth century, 220; abandonment, 226
    religious dedications at, 261, 263
    Roman name, 272
    siting of, 158
rivers as boundaries, 8, 14, 26, 29, 52, 157, 233
roads, 9, 13, 21, 54, 200
    building, 178
    in forts, 159–60
    See also Antonine Wall (military way); Hadrian's Wall (military way); Dere Street; Maiden Way; Stanegate
Robinson, H. R., 3
Roman army:
    strategy in early first century, 7–8

strategy in North Britain, 114–115, 143–7
tactics on Antonine Wall, 104, 145
tactics on Hadrian's Wall, 39–40, 49, 143
Roman citizenship, 148–9, 157, 170, 179, 189–90, 192–3, 198, 263
Roman empire:
    frontiers, 7–9, 18–19, 28, 29, 85, 233
    frontier control, 19, 23, 25, 29, 37–40, 51, 143, 233, 234
    growth of, 5, 7, 9, 16–17, 26
Roman republic, 9, 148, 151
Rome:
    city of, 5, 10–11, 19, 136, 148, 149, 188, 189, 213, 260
    dedications to, 185, 261, 262, 269
Rough Castle:
    beacon platforms, 94
    fort, 91–2, 95, 97–100, Figs. 16, 19, Pl. 10; garrison, 95, 97, 255
    wagon park, 100
Rudchester, fort, Figs. 1, 8
    garrison, 48, 140, 243, 254
    history: under Hadrian, 44, 46, 56, 68, 76; under Commodus, 118, 128; in third century, 140, 208, 235; in fourth century, 213–14, 222
    religious dedications and temples at, 266, 267, 270
    Roman name, 272, 277
Rudge Cup, 36, 39, 271–5, Pl. 9
Rumbling Bridge, hoard of coins, 116

sagittarii venatores, 258
St Albans: *see* Verulamium
St Bee's Head, 40, 42, 43, 126
St Cuthbert, 206, 231
St Joseph, J. K. S., 135
St Patrick, 228, 270
Sarmatians, tribe, 84, 110, 118
Sattada, goddess, 265

320

Index

323

Index